School Di

Continuum Discourse Series
Series Editor: Professor Ken Hyland, Director of the Centre for Applied English Studies, University of Hong Kong, Hong Kong.

Discourse is one of the most significant concepts of contemporary thinking in the humanities and social sciences as it concerns the ways language mediates and shapes our interactions with each other and with the social, political and cultural formations of our society. The *Continuum Discourse Series* aims to capture the fast-developing interest in discourse to provide students, new and experienced teachers and researchers in applied linguistics, ELT and English language with an essential bookshelf. Each book deals with a core topic in discourse studies to give an in-depth, structured and readable introduction to an aspect of the way language is used in real life.

Titles in the Continuum Discourse Series:
Academic Discourse: English In A Global Context, Ken Hyland
Discourse Analysis: An Introduction, Brian Paltridge
Historical Discourse: The Language of Time, Cause and Evaluation, Caroline Coffin
Metadiscourse: Exploring Interaction in Writing, Ken Hyland
Narrative Discourse, Julio Gimenez
Professional Discourse, Britt-Louise Gunnarsson
The Discourse of Blogs and Wikis, Greg Myers
Using Corpora in Discourse Analysis, Paul Baker
Workplace Discourse, Almut Koester

School Discourse
Learning to write across the years of schooling

Frances Christie
Beverly Derewianka

continuum

Continuum International Publishing Group

The Tower Building	80 Maiden Lane
11 York Road	Suite 704
London SE1 7NX	New York NY 10038

www.continuumbooks.com

© Frances Christie and Beverly Derewianka 2008

First published 2008
This paperback edition published 2010

British Library Cataloguing-in-Publication Data
A catalogue record for this book is available from the British Library.

ISBN: 978-0-8264-9992-9 (Hardback)
       978-1-4411-3131-7 (Paperback)

Library of Congress Cataloging-in-Publication Data
The Publisher has applied for CIP data.

Typeset by Newgen Imaging Systems Pvt Ltd, Chennai, India

For Helen, Shoshana and Sally, in recognition of their valued contributions to this book.

Contents

Acknowledgements

We owe a particular debt to our colleagues, Helen Lewis, Shoshana Dreyfus and Sally Humphrey, who had significant roles in the collection and analysis of texts used in this book, as well as the larger corpus from which these texts are drawn. We thank them for their considerable assistance and support. We also thank several people who read and made helpful comments on drafts of chapters, including Margaret Burchett, Caroline Coffin, Kay O'Halloran, Clare Painter and Katina Zammit. For assistance in helping us locate some texts used in the book we thank Susan Feez and Claire Acevedo.

Special thanks must also go to the many schools, teachers and students whose work we have scrutinized and used in writing the book. Finally, we thank the Australian Research Council, which funded a three-year research project 2005–07, enabling us to collect many of the texts used in the book.

Frances Christie
Beverly Derewianka

In Chapter 7 'Venus' © Michael Trollip; 'Bats' © Bahia Chawan; 'How do plants fertilize?' is reprinted with the kind permission of UNSW Press; 'Electromagnetic radiation from mobile phones is a health risk' © Alaric Lewis and chromosomal arrangements image (http://en.wikipedia.org/wiki/Down_syndrome#Genetics).

Notations

Throughout this book, we shall use the following set of notations when displaying texts:

A double slash //will mark clause boundaries:
We got off the bus//and we went inside the house.

Marked themes will be displayed in Bold:
__When we got off the bus__//we went in the mansion.

Embedded clauses will be displayed thus:
A poor man [[named Cody]] once roamed the beautiful green hills . . .

Embedded phrases will be displayed thus:
The seeds [in the bottle with the cap off]

Enclosed clauses will be displayed thus:
At the end of the game << after we proudly screamed out or team anthem>> we trudged our way to Richmond station . . .

Appraisal values will be displayed thus:
Affect (to do with feelings) with a row of dots below the words:
I was really excited

Appreciation (to do with valuing things and events) with double underlining:
This book is brilliant

Judgement (to do with assessments of behaviours) with a wavy line:
In the ancient times there was a minotaur [[that was very nice and kind // and lived in a cave]]

A row of dots in citing texts will indicate that some text has been removed.

The symbol ^ will indicate sequence.

Chapter 1

A Functional Approach to Writing Development

In a period of history when unprecedented attention is given to the importance of literacy, there is a surprising lack of research into the nature of writing development. Myhill (2005) for example, expresses concern at 'the dearth of systematic exploration of the linguistic characteristics of children's writing, particularly in the secondary phase'. Applebee (2002), after reviewing research on various models of writing development, concludes that development in writing is ill defined and difficult to assess. Similarly, Wray and Medwell (2006) observe that the nature of writing development is only imprecisely known, with a lack of agreement on what is meant by improvement or appropriate developmental expectations. While there is a great deal written on pedagogical strategies for fostering writing development, rarely is there a study on what development in writing actually looks like.

This book has been written as a contribution towards an understanding of the ontogenesis of writing capacity from early childhood to late adolescence. The study on which it is based is distinctive in that it adopts a systemic functional linguistic (SFL) framework (Halliday and Matthiessen, 2004) with which both to characterize the nature of language, spoken and written, and to trace developmental changes in writing from childhood to adolescence. We shall argue the particular values of the SFL model, because it is functional, in that it illuminates how meaning is realized in language, and because it provides tools for interpreting and explaining the nature of language development over time. While proposing the claims of a functional approach to the study of writing development, we nonetheless acknowledge the contributions made by a number of other researchers, some of them linguists, others using different theoretical frames. Hence, we shall briefly review some other relevant writing research before going on to provide an account of the SFL theory that informs this book.

A brief survey of previous research

The great majority of studies on writing development focus on the early years of infancy and childhood (e.g. Ferreiro and Teberosky 1982; Sulzby 1996).

The emphasis in very early studies has been on emergent literacy: concepts of print, letter-sound correspondence, alphabet knowledge, 'scribbling', word formation and invented spelling. On entry to school, we find a number of studies investigating the transition from speech to writing (e.g. Dyson and Freedman 1991; Czerniewska 1992; Kress 1994) and tracing patterns of development in samples of young children's work (e.g. Clay 1975; Bissex 1980; King and Rental 1982; Edelsky 1986; Wells 1986). Harpin (1976), mapping the written language of children aged 6–12, traced emergent control of written language through to late childhood. Perera (1984) also traced the emergence of writing capacity from childhood to the age of 12.

Much less attention has been paid to writing development from late childhood into adolescence. Britton et al.'s (1975) research into writing by 11–18-year-olds was one example, and important in its day, in that it represented an early attempt to identify different uses of writing – transactional, poetic and expressive. The study was not linguistic in nature, however, and its observations about the nature of written language were rather general.

All the above reports deal with a single discrete stage in the overall developmental trajectory. Only a handful of studies survey writing development across the years of schooling. Notable in this respect is the longitudinal study by Loban (1976), who followed the same population of 211 students from kindergarten to year 12 in American schools. In the UK, the *Crediton Project* (Wilkinson et al. 1980) mapped the written language of children through to adolescence, using traditional grammar to document grammatical changes in their writing of narrative, autobiography, argument and explanation. Romaine (1984) offered a sociolinguistic account of language development in childhood and adolescence in which she traced aspects of the emergence of literate language.

The development of writing has been studied from a number of different perspectives: the 'mechanics' of spelling, handwriting and punctuation (e.g. Moats 1995; Ehri 2000); the composing process (e.g. Graves 1983); the uses of writing (e.g. Britton et al. 1975); writing difficulties (Newcomer and Barenbaum 1991; Johnson 1993; Edwards 2003); cognitive and metacognitive strategies (e.g. Labbo and Teale 1997; Zimmerman and Risemberg 1997); and motivational issues (e.g. Bruning and Horn 2000; Graham and Harris 2000). Hyland (2002) has provided a useful overview of research into writing, grouping the studies into those that are 'text-oriented', 'writer-oriented' and 'reader-oriented'. While acknowledging the insights provided by such researchers, we note that there is relatively little written from a linguistic approach to writing development, identifying growth as evidenced in learners' actual use of language.

Linguistic descriptions of writing development tend to fall into two major categories: structural and functional, the former being concerned with morphology and syntax at the sentence level and the latter having regard for how grammatical choices realize meaning in different contexts. Early structural studies (e.g. Hunt 1965, 1977; O'Donnell et al. 1967) dealt with such matters as the positioning of adverbials and the frequency of the passive in writing at different ages. Harpin (1976) and his colleagues, alluded to above, used measures of development such as sentence length, clause length, subordination, non-finite constructions and pronoun use. His findings indicated a decrease in the use of personal pronouns in the writing of older children and an increase in the length of clauses, including enhanced numbers of subordinate clauses, as well as longer sentences in the writing of older children. Around the same time, Loban (1976) similarly reported a greater use of embedding and dependent clauses, an increase in the length of sentences, and an extended vocabulary in older writers.

Perera's study (1984, 1990) was arguably the most significant survey of growth in children's writing in its day. She used a simple framework for linguistic analysis of written texts, based first, on the organization of the subject matter of the text ('chronological' or 'non-chronological') and second, on the relationship of the writer to the subject matter and the reader. Within this framework, she discussed writing development at the level of the morpheme, phrase, clause and sentence, right through to cohesive relations and global coherence at the discourse level. She also used the functional category of Theme, found in the SFL grammar, an important tool for analysis of written language, to be explained more fully below. Perera characterized her study in terms of growth in grammatical structures, drawing on Quirk's descriptive grammar (Quirk et al. 1972). Much of what she described resonates with our own study and we have referred to her work in this book. Thus, she noted an early reliance in young writers on simple clause structures and clause relations, simple lexis, use of personal pronouns and the active voice, while she recorded a steady development towards greater complexity in clause types and clause relations, expanded lexis, greater use of modals and use of the passive voice.

A recent large-scale empirical study of the linguistic characteristics of writing in 13- and 15-year-olds by Myhill (2008a and b) ranks as one of the most significant investigations to date into development in adolescent writing. Based on her detailed grammatical and text-level analysis of personal narratives and arguments, Myhill distinguishes between those texts which display a more 'spoken', chaining quality and those which are more 'written' (evidenced by, for example, greater use of subordination). She also differentiates those texts which use simple declarations with little awareness of reader expectations from those which are more highly elaborated and display a better sense of anticipated audience. In particular, like Perera, she points to the use of non-finite clauses in more mature writing and suggests they are a resource for explanatory or reflective detail in argument, and for descriptive and emotional contextualization in narrative. She also finds that more successful writers pay greater attention to the shaping of the text, for example, displaying flexibility in creating the opening of sentences in various ways to guide the reader. A distinctive feature of her study is her claim that it is possible to think of linguistic development in terms of 'three developmental trajectories: from speech patterns to writing patterns; from declaration to elaboration; and from translation to transformation'. The developmental pattern thus suggested implies a steady movement away from the grammatical organization of speech to that of written language, and this accords in many ways with the claims we shall make about the emergence of writing ability. Myhill's study is of interest in that she goes beyond structural description to consider function and meaning. However, the study is restricted to a narrow age range, and it does not take into account the different curriculum areas and range of genres we consider. Finally, it does not elaborate on the interpersonal dimension of writing development, so that it has less to say of how attitudinal expression develops as children mature.

A functional linguistic approach

While some of the studies above draw selectively on specific elements of a functional model, we endeavour to offer a comprehensive account building on the potential afforded by Halliday's multifunctional, multistratal model of language (e.g. Halliday and Matthiessen 2004). Such a model is concerned not so much with developments in syntax and structure *per se*, but with the relationship between linguistic form and the meanings being realized by those forms in context.

The project on which this book is based investigated the writing of students from early childhood through to late adolescence across three areas of the curriculum – English, history and science – involving a number of social purposes for writing in academic contexts. Halliday's model of language (e.g. Halliday and Matthiessen 2004) focuses on the relationship between texts and their contexts, investigating how the choices we make from the language system both act upon, and are constrained by, the social context. The model draws on functional studies of the development of the mother-tongue in infancy and early childhood (Halliday 1975, 1993; Oldenburg 1986; Painter 1999). These studies explain development in terms of the functions that language serves in enabling the learner to achieve social goals such as getting needs met, establishing and maintaining relationships and reflecting on experience. In late infancy these functions tend to coalesce into the three 'metafunctions' that characterize the adult language: resources for representing our experience of the world, resources for establishing and maintaining relationships in interaction and resources for forming text.

On entry to schooling the child experiences challenges involving all three metafunctions. The field of experience changes from the familiar and everyday to increasingly generalized and abstract knowledge; relationships with others become more diverse; and the mode of communication now requires a transition to written language. A functional model enables us to explain how these contextual shifts impact upon the child's developing grammatical system.

In the movement into literacy, children move into 'a new, more abstract mode', requiring that they 'reinterpret their experience' in a new way (Halliday 1993: 109).

Our study builds not only on Halliday's functional description of language development but on the work done within SFL by Martin and colleagues (e.g. Martin and Rothery 1986; Christie and Martin 1997; Unsworth 2000; Martin and Rose 2003, 2008) in investigating the social purposes for using language in school contexts. Here we will mention only a few studies representative of SFL contributions in the fields of science, English and history – the subjects on which we focus in this study.

Seminal work in science is reported in three important volumes: *Talking Science* (Lemke 1990), *Writing Science* (Halliday and Martin 1993) and *Reading Science* (Martin and Veel (eds) 1998). In subject English, functional studies have focused on the demands of writing various types of stories and responding to literary works (e.g. Rothery and Stenglin 2000). Macken-Horarik (2006) has also examined ways students discuss literary texts at the secondary level. With reference to history, a number of studies have been undertaken by Coffin (e.g. 2006 a and b), Coffin and Derewianka (2008a and b), Derewianka (2007), Martin (e.g. 2002, 2003), Schleppegrell et al. (e.g. 2004) and Veel and Coffin (1996), all investigating the nature of historical discourse and the particular challenges of learning to research and write history.

The present study

While previous SFL research into the language demands of schooling has been extensive and detailed, there has not been any attempt until the present study to provide a comprehensive and systematic study of development from childhood through to adolescence in a range of curriculum areas across a variety of genres employing all three metafunctions.

The texts used in the present study for the most part are drawn from studies we have both undertaken into writing development over the last 20 years in primary and secondary schools, including a major research study funded by the Australian Research Council (2004–06), devoted more specifically to secondary schooling. On occasion we have used texts from other sources – including the projects of research students and texts judged as exemplary from the Higher School Certificate in New South Wales – and in such cases we have acknowledged this. The total database consists of some 2000 texts. Despite the reasonably large database, the numbers of texts discussed in each chapter are relatively small, because the nature of the analyses we have used does not permit discussion of a large number of texts. We have chosen representative texts, in that they are characteristic of similar texts by children of the various ages cited. However, they are chosen, in addition, because they were assessed as being good – or at least promising – by their teachers or examiners, thereby providing a benchmark of what is possible at each phase of development. While we have documented the contexts in which the texts were produced, we have not sought to intervene in those contexts by specifying the nature of the task. Rather we have simply collected whatever was being produced by the students in the course of their studies. We make no attempt to draw conclusions based on a detailed analysis of the context of production of the texts. Our focus here is on the texts themselves. We have reproduced the texts as the children wrote them, though we have corrected spelling and punctuation on occasion, in the interests of reading them more easily. Texts in the corpus have been analysed in great detail using an SFL framework and these analyses inform our observations about the texts included here.

In the light of our analyses, we shall propose the presence of four developmental phases in learning to write, the first of which covers the years from about 6 to about 8 years of age, the second from about 9 to 12 years of age, the third from about 13 to 15 years, and the last from 16 to 18 years on, leading into adulthood. Depending on their subsequent work and other life choices, many people go on to develop their writing capacities in new and demanding ways beyond their school days, so it is not suggested that the process stops simply because formal schooling concludes. The phases are to be understood flexibly, so that it is not claimed that all students should pass in some kind of lock-step manner from one to another, while the distinctions between the phases are often blurred, such is the nature of human development generally. Moreover, it should be borne in mind that what constitutes success in each of the phases does depend in part on the field of knowledge involved, so that linguistic resources are deployed rather differently when writing science, history or English.

The theoretical framework

At this point, we will spend some time describing the theoretical framework for the study, drawing on the functional theory of language as outlined primarily by Halliday and Matthiessen (2004). As mentioned previously, SFL theorizes language in terms of the relationship between the meanings being made in a particular context and the linguistic resources which have evolved to realize those meanings. In looking at language development, researchers using a functional model are interested in the increasing range of contexts within with children are likely to participate as they grow older, the kinds of linguistic demands which these contexts make on children, and the types of linguistic resources the learners need to develop if they are to operate successfully in these contexts.

We can conceive of context at two levels: the *context of culture* and the *context of situation*. Martin (1997) sees genres as social practices operating at the level of culture. The notion of genre is concerned with how a text is organized to achieve its social purpose. The purpose of 'telling what happened', for example, is typically realized in a recount genre which has a characteristic structure of Orientation ^Events ^(Re-orientation).[1]

At the level of the specific situation within the culture, we find the contextual variables of *field* ('what is going on?'), *tenor* ('who is involved?') and *mode* ('what role is language playing?'). A particular combination of these variables is referred to as the *register*. Given a set of register variables, we can predict that certain choices will be made from the language system.

Resources in the language system cluster into the three *metafunctions* referred to previously: the *ideational* metafunction (language for representing our experience and the relationships between aspects of experience); the *interpersonal* metafunction (language for interaction with others); and the *textual* metafunction (language for the forming of coherent and cohesive texts).

We can represent the relationships between these various elements diagrammatically as in Figure 1.1. Note that the ideational metafunction can be further divided into the experiential metafunction (how language organizes experience) and the logical metafunction (logical relations between elements).

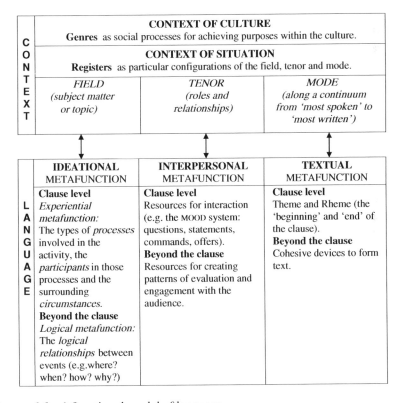

FIGURE 1.1   A functional model of language

To take an example from our study, we could explain the language features of a particular text in terms of:

- the social purpose that the text serves in the culture (e.g. to discuss both sides of an issue – one of the *arguing genres*) and hence its characteristic structure (e.g. Issue ^ Perspectives ^ Position);
- the *register* (e.g. the *field* of history, in particular the debate around responsibility for World War II; the *tenor*, in particular the judgements being made and the attempts to align the reader; and the *mode*, in particular the use of written academic discourse).

Given these contextual features, we could now describe how the related choices from the language system are functioning to create certain ideational, interpersonal and textual meanings.

We will proceed to outline each metafunction in greater detail:

- the ideational function of language (how the clause represents a 'slice of experience' and how we combine clauses in various ways to construe logical relationships);
- the interpersonal function of language (how elements of the clause create patterns of interaction and evaluation);
- the textual function of language (how the beginning of the clause ('Theme') is used to guide the reader through the text; and how cohesive links are created at the discourse level).

In addition we will look at the phenomena of grammatical metaphor and lexical density.

A. The ideational function of language

As learners move from the more familiar, everyday contexts of home and early school to contexts where knowledge is increasingly technical, abstract and specialized in the later years of schooling, they need to expand their linguistic resources in order to represent the kinds of experience encountered in these contexts.

The clause level: Processes, Participants and Circumstances

At the level of the clause, we are concerned with how language represents our experience of the world (sometimes called the *experiential* metafunction):

- the various kinds of *processes* that are engaged in;
- the *participants* in those processes;
- and the *circumstances* surrounding those processes.

Processes

Different Process types represent different aspects of experience, as outlined in Table 1.1.

Table 1.1   Types of Processes

Process type	Aspect of experience	Example
Material Processes	Doings and happenings in the material world – 'outer' experience	We **went** to the bus.
Behavioural Processes	Physiological and psychological behaviour	The crowd **gasped**.
Mental Processes	Processes of consciousness – 'inner' experience	They **realized** that she was right. (cognition) I **liked** the beds and the lounge room. (affect) We **noticed** that a big wave was coming. (perception)
Verbal Processes	Processes of 'saying' and 'meaning'	'Stop!' **cried** a commanding voice.
Relational Processes	Processes of 'being' and 'having' creating relationships between elements of experience	I **was** really excited. Cody **had** a kind heart but no money.
Existential Processes	Existing	In ancient times, there **was** a minotaur.

Processes are typically realized in the grammar by verbal groups. These can take the form of a single item:

*they **waited***

or a number of items:

*they **had waited***
*they **had been waiting***
*they **could have been waiting***

Sometimes, Processes can realize a causative function:

*the changes **wrought** by the events of WWII*
*the use of propaganda **encouraged** them to join the War effort*

Participants

Each Process type involves a different set of Participants. In a material Process, for example, the key Participants are the *Actor* and the *Goal*:

We	*found*	*a cave.*
Actor	Process: material	Goal

Participants in describing relational Processes express the thing being described (*Carrier*) and the description (*Attribute*):

The water	*was*	*flat.*
Carrier	Process: relational (attributive)	Attribute

Participants are typically realized in the grammar by the nominal group. Nominal group structures can be very simple, consisting of a single *Headword*, for example, 'dungeons':

dungeons
Headword

The Headword can be expanded through premodification:

dark	*dungeons*
Premodifier	Headword

and through postmodification, using an *embedded phrase*:

dark	*dungeons*	*[with creepy cobwebs]*
Premodifier	Headword	Postmodifier (phrase)

or an *embedded* clause:

dark	*dungeons*	*[[in which experiments were carried out]]*
Premodifier	Headword	Postmodifier (clause)

Sometimes the Headword in the nominal group is an adjective. Note in this example that the adjective is modified by a Postmodifier containing two embedded clauses – one inside the other:

extremely	*glad*	*[[to see the Presbyterian church*
		[[built a couple of years later.]]]]
Premodifier	Headword	Postmodifier

Participants can also be realized by other grammatical resources such as embedded clauses (particularly in relational Processes):

An eclipse	is	*[[when the earth or Moon blocks out the light of the Sun.]]*
Participant	Process: relational	Participant

Embedded clauses are referred to as being 'rank-shifted' – they do not operate at the level of a ranking clause but rather function at the group level.

Circumstances

Circumstances provide information about such details as 'how', 'when' and 'where'. Circumstances are typically realized in the grammar by adverb groups or prepositional phrases. Table 1.2 illustrates some of the more common types of Circumstances.

Table 1.2   Common Circumstance types and their realization in adverbs and/or prepositional phrases

Circumstance	Example: adverb	Example: prepositional phrase
Time	*recently*	*in those days*
Place	*elsewhere*	*in the cave*
Manner	*quickly*	*with surprising haste*
Cause		*in honour of their god*
Angle		*according to Darlington*
Role		*as Pharaoh*
Concession		*despite their many losses*

Together these resources for representing experience (Processes, Participants and Circumstances) form the system of *transitivity*.

In Text 1.1 we observe how language constructs experiential meanings in the science text of a young writer.

Text 1.1   Recount of a science experiment (excerpt)

First we soaked 50 beans.
Then we filled both bottles with the soaked beans
and put a little water in the bottom of each.
Next we put the cap tight on one of the bottles
and left the other open.
Finally we shook the water over the beans.

We can identify simple nominal groups representing concrete Participants (*50 beans; both bottles; soaked beans; the cap; the water*) and material Processes (*soaked; filled; put; left; shook*). Circumstances are primarily of place (*in the bottom of each; on one of the bottles; over the beans*) though the genre also requires the use of Circumstances of manner (*with soaked beans; tight; open*).

This contrasts with the representation of experience in Text 1.2, an extract from a report written by a girl aged 15/16.

Text 1.2   Down Syndrome

Down Syndrome is a chromosomal disorder [[that affects the genetic make up of human beings]]. Ultra sounds can pick up abnormalities in the foetus, but further testing needs to be done to confirm Down Syndrome. There is also a blood test [[that can be performed]]. This tests the mother's blood for abnormal levels of 3 chemicals, which indicates the risk of the baby [[developing Down Syndrome]]. The only definite way [[to diagnose Down Syndrome for sure]] is [[to perform an amniocentesis]].

Here the grammar generalizes about the disorder, beginning with a definition (containing an embedded clause):

Down Syndrome	*is*	*a chromosomal disorder disorder [[that affects the genetic make up of human beings]].*
Participant	Process: intensive	Participant (definition)

Nominal groups are relatively complex, often with pre- and postmodifiers:

The only definite	*way*	*[[to diagnose Down Syndrome for sure]]*
Premodifier	Headword	Postmodifier

Representation now involves technicality (*chromosomal disorder; foetus*); abstraction (*abnormalities*); and less common Circumstances (*for abnormal levels of 3 chemicals; for sure*).

Beyond the clause: Types of clauses and clause combinations

As they mature, students use a greater variety of clause types and combine these in different ways, allowing them to construe more complex kinds of relationships between meanings. Halliday and Matthiessen (2004: 309) refer to this as the *logical* metafunction.

We can describe the relationship between clauses in terms of the degree of interdependency and/or in terms of the semantic nature of the relationship created.

Dependency relations between clauses

It is often the case that a sentence consists of a single, independent clause. When two clauses are combined, their relationship might be one of equal status:

*The sealed cans are lightly cooked **and** heated.*

or unequal status with one clause dominant and the other dependent:

*It does not stop growing **until** it reaches the ovary.*

Table 1.3 lists some typical conjunctions relating clauses of equal dependency and conjunctions relating clauses of unequal dependency.

Table 1.3 Conjunctions realizing equal and unequal dependency

Equal dependency	Unequal dependency
and	while
but	when
so	until
not only . . . but also	since
either . . . or	whereas
and meanwhile	instead of
otherwise	if
and yet	unless
	although
	despite

Dependent clauses can sometimes take the form of non-finite clauses:

*The Japanese were kept in Vietnam **to maintain law and order**.*
*It shows the inhabitants of the island, **revealing more about their appearance, clothing, possible occupations and social class**.*

or non-defining relative clauses:

*Then we heard of this place called Illawarra, **which turned out to be perfect**.*

Logical relations between clauses

Another way of understanding the relationship between clauses is in terms of the kinds of logical meanings constructed. There are two basic groupings:

1. where one clause expands on the meaning of another, creating relationships of, for example, addition, exemplification, cause, time, condition and concession:

Initiating clause	Expanding clause
The Moon doesn't disappear completely	*when there is a lunar eclipse.*
Ultra sounds can pick up abnormalities in the foetus,	*but further testing needs to be done to confirm Down Syndrome.*

2. where one clause projects another, as with processes of saying and thinking:

Projecting clause	Projected clause
He states	*that the fleet is Theran.*
We can understand	*that Therans had advanced building and architectural skills.*

More complex combinations of clauses can involve a variety of relationships of expansion and projection as well as equal and unequal dependencies:

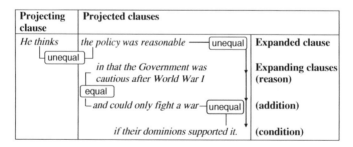

FIGURE 1.2 Various types of interclausal relationships (from Text 5.5)

Whereas children's talk often contains intricate combinations of clauses (mainly linked by 'and', 'but' and 'so'), when children start to write there is a regression to single clauses and simple combinations. In later childhood and early adolescence we see a flourishing of various types of clauses and clause combinations, however full control over the logical resources needed for the kinds of complex reasoning required in later schooling does not develop until well into adolescence.

B. The interpersonal function of language

As students move from childhood to adolescence, their use of interpersonal resources develops and matures – from the unmediated expression of personal feelings and emotion through to more judicious evaluation of behaviour and phenomena based on institutionalized norms. While young learners generally lack a strong sense of authorial identity in their writing and a sensitivity to the needs of an unknown, distant reader, older learners are more able to establish an authorial presence and engage with diverse perspectives and possibilities.

The clause level: The MOOD *system*

In the Hallidayan tradition, interpersonal meanings at the level of the clause are primarily concerned with resources for making statements, asking questions, giving commands and making offers. While these are important when considering the kind of interaction in the oral mode, analysis at this level is not particularly revealing for our purposes. We have therefore chosen to focus on interpersonal meanings beyond the clause.

Beyond the clause: Patterns of evaluation

In our analysis of interpersonal development, we draw primarily on Appraisal theory (Martin and White 2005) – a relatively recent development in SFL, building on elements identified by Halliday such as attitudinal lexis and modality.

Appraisal theory deals with the evaluations people make (*Attitude*), how these evaluations can be upgraded or toned down (*Graduation*), and resources for building the 'authorial self', particularly in dialogic interactions with others (*Engagement*). We can represent these in a simple system network (Figure 1.3):

FIGURE 1.3   The Appraisal system

We will discuss each of the sub-systems in turn.

Attitude

The resources of Attitude (Figure 1.4) are used to express emotional reaction (*Affect*), to evaluate the worth and quality of things and processes (*Appreciation*), and to judge the behaviour of others (*Judgement*).

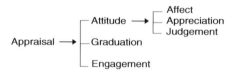

FIGURE 1.4   Attitude

While young children might display some feeling in their writing, personal affective response is not greatly encouraged or rewarded in the writing of older students unless the teacher is fostering an emotional engagement with the subject matter (as in empathetic autobiographies in Chapter 4):

*we were **glad** to set foot on land*

or unless the writer is describing the feelings of others (as in the stories of Chapter 2):

*Every man was **agitated and excited***

The ability to appreciate the quality and significance of things and processes – ideas, literary works, artefacts and the like – is, however, highly prized. In childhood this might take the form of opinions based on personal preferences and predispositions. With the move into adolescence, there is an expectation that the writer's evaluations will display an awareness of the social values of the community, drawing on institutionalized criteria to evaluate, critique and challenge – as evidenced, for example, in the literary response genres of Chapter 3:

*Both stories are made **more interesting and more engaging** through the use of such Gothic elements.*

the interpretations of historical sites in Chapter 5:

*she believes they were a **very religious** society*

and the science explanation and argument in Chapter 7:

*introduced animals themselves could do **great harm** to the natural environment*

> *Some believe that mobile phones **can cause great illness**, while others believe that the phones are **completely harmless**.*

Adolescent writers are also required to make relatively dispassionate judgements of people's behaviour with regard to such factors as their moral or ethical conduct, their abilities, their tenacity or their distinctiveness. Again, such judgements need to be made against an awareness of culturally valued attributes. Evaluation of human behaviour is particularly salient in genres such as:

- reviews, where the capacity of the author or artist is critiqued (Chapter 3):

  The people who were involved in this movie quite obviously have an amazing talent

- character analyses in literature (Chapter 3):

  Atticus is not racist or discriminatory

- historical biographies (Chapter 4):

  Galileo was bold enough to say that Aristotle was wrong

- and expository texts that evaluate the authority and trustworthiness of the cited authors (Chapter 5):

  Kennedy is also an expert on diplomacy, international relations and military strategy.

Graduation

The strength of feelings, opinions and judgements can be raised or lowered through the resources of Graduation, either by using an intensifying adverb:

  *The murmuring of the crowd was **extremely** intense*

or by selecting a graded lexical item:

  *The sacrifice at Gallipoli was **enormous**.*

A meaning can also be made more forceful by quantifying:

  *That would have been **lots** of fun*

. . . or by emphasizing extent:

> *Australians **all over the world** will be commemorating the 90ᵗʰ anniversary of the*
> *Gallipoli campaign*
>
> *He was killed by a machine gun bullet through the heart, **less than four weeks after his***
> ***arrival.***

While younger writers tend to make a point by using high levels of intensification:

> *This book is **brilliant** . . .*

older writers display a more subtle and varied use of Graduation resources:

> *The reflective and reminiscent tone of the last stanza conveyed to me, personally, the*
> *importance of experience, and **to a certain degree**, risk taking in my journey of life in*
> *this world.*

Engagement

Resources in the engagement system enable the writer to construe an authorial presence by adopting a particular stance. One strategy is simply to make 'bare assertions', referred to as *monogloss* ('single voiced'):

> *'Blue Hair Day' is a fantastic book for young children.*

In the writing of younger students, such assertions are commonplace. As the students get older, however, they become more sensitive to the need to engage with other perspectives and possibilities. We refer to this as *heteroglossic* ('multi-voiced'). The Engagement system, therefore, consists of monoglossic and heteroglossic options (Figure 1.5).

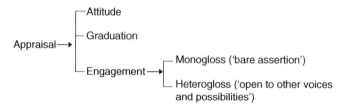

FIGURE 1.5 The Engagement system

Heteroglossic resources enable writers to position themselves in particular ways with regard to the assumed values of the imagined reader and the values of the relevant discourse community. This might involve aligning or disaligning themselves with certain attitudes, anticipating the value position of the reader, trying to persuade the reader to adopt a particular point of view, demonstrating an awareness of alternative views, and being more or less open to negotiation.

Text 1.3 is an excerpt from an exposition written by an adolescent girl. In attempting to align the reader with her position, she draws on several Appraisal resources.

Text 1.3   Appraisal in an exposition on the conditions in Gallipoli

Engagement with other perspectives and possibilities	*The conditions in Gallipoli tested the endurance of all involved. Winters were freezing cold and muddy but by mid year the weather had become extremely hot and soldiers had to suffer plagues of disease-carrying flies and fleas. There was never enough water and food was hardly consumable. One soldier, Ion Idriess, recalls "I wrapped my overcoat over the tin and gouged out the flies, then spread the biscuit, held my hand over it and drew the biscuit out of the coat. But a lot of flies flew into my mouth and beat about inside. I nearly howled with rage" Worse than this, the hygiene conditions were abominable, toilets were open pits and corpses lay rotting in no-mans-land.*

Graduation of attitude

Attitude:
Judgement
Appreciation
Affect

Even in this relatively brief passage, we observe the writer making extensive use of Appraisal resources – though there is still potential for development in terms of a more nuanced use of interpersonal strategies.

C. The textual function of language

The textual function of language is perhaps the most critical for learners to master as they move from the dynamic and spontaneous oral mode into the more reflective, crafted written texts of schooling. In oral interaction, the learner is supported by others in the joint construction of meaning whereas in the written discourse, the writer takes sole responsibility for the construction of monologic text. Such contextual factors influence the choices made from the language system.

The clause level: Theme and Rheme

As children move from the relatively brief turns of spoken language into the writing of extended text, they are faced with the challenge of how to organize the discourse to make it accessible to the remote reader. In English, we tend to use the beginning of the clause to signal our point of departure. Halliday and Matthiessen (2004) refer to this as the Theme of the clause. Here we will focus on a particular aspect of Theme – the development of the topic of discourse.

In spoken language we do not carefully monitor the thematic development of the conversation – the pace is too quick and different interactants interrupt and change topics. We can also exploit the resources of intonation and stress in indicating salience. In writing, however, we have time to sit down and reflect on how the text is developing. We draft and redraft our texts and craft and polish them. In the process, whether consciously or unconsciously, we are attending to the flow of information in the text and how this contributes to the coherence. In Text 1.5 for example, the writer immediately signals the point of departure: a salad spinner.

Theme	Rheme
A salad spinner	*is a device [[designed to dry lettuce]].*

The Theme is a cue to the reader: 'This is what I'm talking about'. The rest of the clause, or the Rheme, provides the new information.

The following clause continues this pattern:

Theme	Rheme
It	*consists of a small plastic basket inside a bowl with a lid.*

The next clause then shifts topic slightly, picking up on *the lid* which has been introduced in the previous Rheme:

Theme	Rheme
The lid	*has a handle on top . . .*

We can track the various patterns of thematic development, either in terms of maintaining the topic or shifting the topic in various ways. This is referred to as *thematic progression*:

A salad spinner	is a device designed to dry lettuce.
It	*consists of a small plastic basket inside a bowl with a lid.*
The lid	*has a handle on top . . .*

Sometimes writers choose points of departure that are not like the simple topics above. A writer might choose, for example, to place a dependent clause in Theme position:

Theme	Rheme
As the crank is turned slowly by hand	*the basket spins rapidly.*
To stop the basket spinning	*you can tip the spinner*

or a prepositional phrase:

Theme	Rheme
For each turn of the crank and large gear,	*the basket and small gear turns many times*

These are referred as *marked Themes*, when a choice has been made to begin with something other than the Subject of the clause (Halliday and Matthiessen 2004: 67) in order to foreground a particular angle.

In conversation, personal pronouns dominate as Theme choices (Halliday and Matthiessen 2004: 73) and we notice this pattern in the early written texts of young children (as in Chapters 2 and 4). As students begin to write increasingly lengthy texts, however, they need to be able to manipulate the flow of information in various ways, using the beginning of clauses to alert the reader to how the text is unfolding. Skilful use of Theme position continues to develop even at tertiary level (e.g. Hewings and North 2006). As we shall see in Chapter 5, the shaping of written texts extends beyond the clause level up to the level of discourse, where the writer has to monitor the organization of the whole text to ensure its coherence.

Beyond the clause: Cohesion

In the early years of infancy and childhood, learners are heavily supported by other interactants in the give-and-take of oral interaction. Meanings are jointly constructed in face-to-face conversation. There is generally no need for explicitly naming items as they are visible in the surrounding setting. In Text 1.4, a conversation between a mother and a young child as they work together on preparing a salad, we can observe that the exchange consists of a number of short turns where the mother is answering questions, providing vocabulary items, and completing utterances. Rather than refer to items by name, they use 'pointing words' such as *this* and *it*, creating a link between the text and the physical setting. This is referred to as *exophoric* ('pointing outwards') reference.

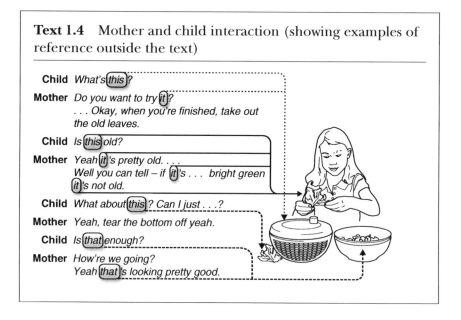

Text 1.4   Mother and child interaction (showing examples of reference outside the text)

Child	*What's this?*
Mother	*Do you want to try it?* *. . . Okay, when you're finished, take out the old leaves.*
Child	*Is this old?*
Mother	*Yeah it's pretty old. . . .* *Well you can tell – if it's . . . bright green it's not old.*
Child	*What about this? Can I just . . .?*
Mother	*Yeah, tear the bottom off yeah.*
Child	*Is that enough?*
Mother	*How're we going?* *Yeah that's looking pretty good.*

We could compare this text with Text 1.5 – an explanation of how a gear system works – typical of those written by students in later adolescence. The writer now is not able to rely on other interactants to help develop the meaning. He must try to anticipate what the reader – distanced in time and space – might want to know. No assumptions can be made about shared experience. The text needs to be able to stand on its own, independent of any external setting. Reference links must now be internal to the text (or *endophoric* – 'pointing inside').

Text 1.5   Explanation of how a salad spinner works

A salad spinner is a device designed to dry lettuce. It consists of a small plastic basket inside a bowl with a lid. The lid has a handle on top, which when rotated spins the basket and lettuce inside. Salad spinners work on the principle of gears. The crank on top turns a gear, which is connected to another gear that turns the basket.

As the crank is turned slowly by hand the basket spins rapidly. For each turn of the crank and large gear, the basket and small gear turns many times causing the basket to spin faster than the crank. To stop the basket spinning, you can tip the spinner so that the basket rubs against the wall of the bowl. This provides a large force due to sliding friction that is far from the pivot point of the spinning basket, producing a torque which quickly slows the basket's spinning.

The writer of this text has used a range of cohesive devices (Halliday and Matthiessen 2004: 534) to create links within the text:

- the personal pronoun *it* refers back to the *salad spinner*;
- the determiner *the* refers back to *a lid* – it has been introduced as new information (*a lid*), but can now be taken for granted (*the lid*);
- the relative pronoun *which* refers back to the *handle*;
- the comparative *another* refers back to the *gear* mentioned previously;
- the demonstrative *this* refers back to a sequence of clauses (*you can tip the spinner so that the basket rubs against the wall of the bowl*).

The writer also creates cohesion through the careful selection and patterning of lexical items, in this case a 'part-whole' pattern: the *salad spinner* consists of a *basket* inside a *bowl* with a *lid* which has a *handle*. The spinner has a system of *gears* – a *small gear*, a *larger gear* and a *crank*. In a different context, a writer might have employed a class-subclass pattern, building up a taxonomy of different types of gears: spur gears, helical gears, bevel gears, worm gears and the like.

Learning to make a text internally cohesive and independent of any supportive setting is a significant challenge for young learners accustomed to relying on the physical environment and conversation partner to assist in the construction of meaning. The challenge, however, extends into late adolescence, where students need to be able to recognize and construct cohesive links between complex and abstract elements of a text. As in the final example above, for instance, a link has to be established between *this* and a stretch of text, often extending for several sentences. Cohesion can also be created by using an abstract term such as *principle* to summarize a sequence of clauses (Francis 1994):

Salad spinners work on the principle of gears.

The crank on top turns a gear, which is connected to another gear that turns the basket. As the crank is turned slowly by hand the basket spins rapidly. For each turn of the crank and large gear, the basket and small gear turns many times causing the basket to spin faster than the crank.

Research into reading development indicates that cohesion is key factor in comprehension, with adolescents who fail to perceive the global unity of text struggling with reading at the secondary level, particularly in the case of non-narrative texts (MacLean and Chapman 1989). Our research suggests that cohesion is also an important feature in the development of writing from early childhood through to adolescence, with different demands arising according to the genre and the level of abstraction.

Mastery of the textual metafunction involves learning how to create texts that are cohesive, coherent and well-crafted. Contrary to the belief that children's writing development is completed in the primary years, our research shows that developing control over the written mode continues well into later adolescence.

Grammatical metaphor

Halliday (in Halliday and Matthiessen 1999) has identified a phenomenon which he believes to be the key indicator of language development as students move from childhood into adolescence and beyond. He calls this *grammatical metaphor*. In the language of children and in conversational interaction, experience tends to be construed congruently – processes, for example, are realized as verbal groups, participants are realized as nominal groups, and circumstances are realized as adverbs or prepositional phrases:

clause ('literal')		
The basket	*spins*	*rapidly*
'what?'	'action'	'how?'
nominal group	verbal group	adverbial group

In the adult language, particularly in the written mode, we are likely to find such an expression realized not as a clause but compacted into a nominal group:

nominal group ('metaphorical')			
the	*rapid*	*spinning*	*of the basket . . .*
	'how?'	'action'	'what?'
	↘	↘	↘
	adjective	noun	postmodifying phrase

As a result, the 'action' meaning is now realized as a noun (*spinning*), the 'how' meaning is realized an adjective in the nominal group (*rapid*) and the 'what' meaning is no longer a participant in the clause but simply a postmodifier (*of the basket*). There is thus a mismatch between what we would typically expect (i.e. the 'literal') and the unexpected realization of these meanings (i.e. the 'metaphorical').

The recognition of this interplay between form and function is made possible precisely because SFL provides us with a stratified model of language which allows for meanings to be realized in unexpected grammatical forms. Derewianka (1996, 1999, 2003) investigated the emergence of grammatical metaphor in a longitudinal case study spanning some ten years. Her findings show that while lower level types of grammatical metaphor start to develop in late childhood, it is not until adolescence that the more complex types appear. The work of Christie (1998, 2002) confirms that in the earliest years students' writing shows only congruent realizations of experience; but that by the upper primary years some non-congruent grammatical formulations will appear, at least among the most able pupils; and that by the mid-secondary years, successful writers will have achieved considerable control of non-congruent realizations, although it is equally apparent that many students struggle with it. Teachers tend to reward the emergence of non-congruent forms, for it is in these that the abstraction, technical statements and arguments so critical to secondary education are realized.

Control over grammatical metaphor is central to success in secondary schooling. It is intimately involved in the building up of technicality – the specialized knowledge of the different disciplines. It also enables the development of argumentation, providing resources for the accumulation, compacting, foregrounding and backgrounding of information and evidence so that the argument can move forward. It is not simply a matter of style – an 'optional extra' to render a text more 'sophisticated'. Rather it is fundamental to the very nature of educational processes in the higher levels of schooling – the construal of experience into specialized domains and the reasoning about experience in abstract, logically developed terms.

The forerunners of grammatical metaphor can be seen in the writing of young children when they start to use embedded clauses, downgrading a full clause to part of the nominal group. In the following example, the child has used a single clause containing a nominal group with two embedded clauses:

> *In the ancient times there was **a minotaur** [[that was very nice and kind // and lived in a cave]].*

Alternatively, this could have been written as three full clauses:

> 'In the ancient times there was a minotaur.
> He was very nice and kind
> and he lived in a cave.'

The use of embeddings is a first step in learning to compact information. With the advent of adolescence, we find an increasing tendency to integrate and compress:

Metaphorical: information compacted into a single clause	Congruent: information distributed across three clauses
1. *This lack of plants may be one of the sources of the lack of stability in the creek bank and the large amount of erosion.*	1. 'Because there aren't many plants 2. the creek bank is not very stable 3. and there is a lot of erosion.'

In the above example, the 16-year-old student had written in a previous sentence that a great amount of native vegetation had been cleared. This 'process' is now taken for granted and is construed as a 'thing' – *this lack of plants* – a causal factor resulting in two outcomes, also construed as 'things': *the lack of stability in the creek bank* and *the large amount of erosion*. Nominalization of processes is a major factor in being able to manage the reasoning required in the secondary school.

At this point it is opportune to clarify our use of the terms *nominalization* and *grammatical metaphor*. In most cases, we have used the terms interchangeably. However, there is a distinction to be made. At a basic level, nominalization is a broad, overarching term that can be used to refer to the phenomenon of construing various meanings in nominal form. Not all nominalizations, however, involve grammatical metaphor. The probe for grammatical metaphor is to ask whether it is possible, in this particular instance, to unpack the nominalization to a plausible, congruent alternative. The word *organization* in the following example could not be unpacked and is therefore not metaphorical – it is simply a nominalization of the verb 'to organize':

> *This is a great organization.*

In the following example, however, it would be possible to imagine a more spoken alternative, construed as a clause rather than as a nominal group:

Grammatical metaphor	Congruent alternative
The success of the party was due to **her great organization**.	The party was a success because **she organized things so well**.

In this case, the nominalization involves grammatical metaphor. In the metaphorical version, both the 'literal' and the 'metaphorical' are in play. The writer could have chosen the congruent but has opted instead for the metaphorical.

Lexical density

In English we distinguish between lexical items and grammatical items. Lexical items are the content words, generally nouns, adjectives, verbs and some adverbs (Halliday 1985):

> Then **suddenly** he **remembered** a **story** which **Christopher Robin** had **told** him about a **man** on a **desert island** who had **written something** in a **bottle** and **thrown** it into the **sea** . . .

The grammatical items include such categories as articles (*the, a*), prepositions (*in, on, by*), pronouns (*he, him, it*), auxiliary verbs (*had told, is playing*), conjunctions (*and, when*), and demonstratives (*this, those*).

In conversation, we tend to use fewer lexical items – generally because there is no need to name something if we can see it in the surroundings. In writing, however, we need to build up the information through the language itself, so we tend to include more lexical items. Writing is therefore more lexically dense.

We can measure the lexical density by counting the number of lexical items per clause. In the conversation above between the mother and child, for example, there are typically one to three lexical items in each clause:

		Lexical items
Mother:	*Do you **want** to **try** it?*	2
	*Okay, when you're **finished**,*	1
	***take out** the **old leaves**.*	3
Child:	*Is this **old**?*	1
Mother:	*Yeah it's **pretty old**.*	2
	*Well you can **tell** –*	1
	*if it's . . . **bright green***	2
	*it's not **old**.*	1

An excerpt from Text 1.5 demonstrates how the lexical density increases in written text, in this case between three and nine lexical items per clause.

		Lexical items
i)	As the **crank** *is* **turned slowly** *by* **hand**	4
ii)	the **basket spins rapidly**.	3
iii)	For each **turn** *of the* **crank** *and* **large gear**, *the* **basket** *and* **small gear turns** *many* **times**	9
iv)	**causing the basket** *to* **spin faster** *than the* **crank**.	5

Halliday (1985: 61–8) recommends counting the number of lexical items in a passage of language and expressing these as a ratio of the number of clauses involved. This establishes the lexical density found in a text.

Organization of the chapters

The following chapters are organized in terms of development in writing in three areas of the curriculum: English, history and science. The three subjects are of interest to this study because they offer contrasts: the meanings of English, history and of science all differ, for the three broad areas of inquiry address different aspects of human experience, identify and answer different questions and build different understandings about the world. The same linguistic system is drawn upon and deployed in different ways to create the discourse patterns of the three subjects and hence to realize their meanings. All three subjects provide a good basis for tracking the developmental trajectory involved in learning to write from early childhood to late adolescence.

Chapters 2 and 3 canvass development in the writing of key genres in subject English. In Chapter 2 we consider the story genres of recounts and narratives, written to entertain and record events in a chronological sequence. Chapter 3 examines development in responding to literary texts and works in other media, from the personal responses of early childhood and the reviews of later childhood through to the character analyses and thematic interpretations of adolescence.

Chapters 4 and 5 observe writing development in history. In Chapter 4 we deal with the genres encountered in the writing of history in early to late childhood: those ordered chronologically (including recounts of various kinds as well as simple, time-based explanations) and those that are not ordered chronologically (including studies of historically significant sites and periods). Chapter 5 turns to those genres needed by students of history in early to late adolescence, where they need to interpret, explain, argue and discuss.

Chapters 6 and 7 investigate development in students' writing of scientific genres. In Chapter 6 we explore how students' writing develops through the genres of observing, experimenting with and documenting natural phenomena while in Chapter 7 we look at those genres concerned with classifying and describing, with explaining how and why, and with discussing issues that arise in school science.

Table 1.4 provides an overview of Chapters 2 to 7.

Table 1.4   Overview of curriculum areas and related genres

ENGLISH			HISTORY		SCIENCE	
Chapter 2	**Chapter 3**	**Chapter 4**	**Chapter 5**	**Chapter 6**	**Chapter 7**
Recounts; Narratives	*Personal response; Review; Character analysis; Thematic interpretation*	*Recounts; Empathetic autobiographies; Biographical recounts; Historical accounts; Site studies; Period studies*	*Site interpretations; Factorial explanation; Consequential explanation; Exposition; Discussion*	*Procedural recounts; Demonstration genres; Research articles; Field studies*	*Reports; Explanation; Discussion*

The final chapter – Chapter 8 – summarizes our conclusions regarding the ontogenesis of writing development and proposes pedagogical implications.

Note

[1] See notation section in the front of the book for an explanation of symbols used.

Chapter 2

Writing Stories in Subject English

Introduction

Contemporary curriculum statements stress that English aims 'to enable students to use, understand, appreciate, reflect on and enjoy the English language in a variety of texts and to shape meaning in ways that are imaginative, interpretive, critical and powerful'. (New South Wales Board of Studies 2003b: 12). The same document states that in English, students 'learn about the power, value and art of the English language for communication, knowledge and pleasure' and that they 'engage with and explore texts that include the literature of past and contemporary societies'. (New South Wales Board of Studies 2003b: 7).

The National English Curriculum for England and Wales, Stage 3 (Qualifications and Curriculum Authority 2007: 1), declares 'English is vital for communicating with others in school and in the wider world. . . . In studying English, pupils develop skills in speaking, listening, reading and writing that they will need to participate in society and employment. Pupils learn to express themselves creatively and imaginatively and to communicate with others confidently and effectively.' Such statements about English, while common, can obscure what have been and remain, significant debates.

English emerged as a distinct subject in the late 19th century, and since then it has generated more heated debate than any other subject in the school curriculum. That is partly because of the status and significance attaching to English as the national language in the English-speaking world and the manner in which discussions of the subject are often linked to public debates about the economic welfare of nations. Economic prosperity, goes this argument, is dependent on the presence of a well-educated work force, and in this context performance in English is essential. Other arguments of a less utilitarian nature, associated with the English teaching profession rather than the wider community, have concerned the importance of English for children's personal development and for self expression. Some arguments have reflected the legacy of (Arnold 1869; Sutherland 1973) who first advocated the values of teaching literature for its civilizing or refining influence, while other arguments that emerged over the 20th century revealed the influence of progressivist and/or constructivist models of the curriculum and the learner,[1] whose impact was to diminish the role of a literary heritage, stressing instead the values of personal expression and the reading of rather eclectic selections of texts. By the end of the century cultural studies had also had some impact, apparent, for example, in the adoption of texts from popular culture, including visual ones. As several studies have shown (e.g. Peel et al. 2000; Kress et al. 2005; Christie and Macken-Horarik 2007; Locke 2007), by the start of the 21st century, there was no one model of English, for English had proliferated several models.

It is because of this tendency to produce many different models rather than one relatively stable one that English has been termed a subject with 'horizontal knowledge structures', in contrast with the 'hierarchical knowledge structures' of science (Bernstein 2000: 155–74). (See Christie and Martin 2007 for discussion). Subjects with horizontal knowledge structures create 'segmented' discourse patterns, where these are not closely related, and the learning of one confers no necessary advantage in learning another.

For the purposes of school English, while children are required to write a variety of texts across the years of schooling, at least two broad families of genres are involved, each with its distinctive 'gaze' or preoccupations. They are *stories,* written for entertainment and for pleasure, and as contributions to verbal art, and *response genres,* written to appraise and respond to other texts. Both genre types are very privileged texts in English, valued for the opportunities they offer children to articulate values, attitudes and beliefs. We shall examine response genres in Chapter 3, turning here to stories, more particularly narratives and recounts.

Narratives and recounts

Of all the text types found in English, stories are the most enduring. The reasons are not hard to see, for even at the pre-school teachers regularly read stories to young learners, and when they take their first steps in writing they are often invited to write 'stories', though the texts produced are often rather rudimentary. Stories are in any case ubiquitous throughout an English-speaking culture, found in television and film, CDs and websites, picture books and novels. Stories are also profoundly part of the oral culture, as Labov (Labov and Waletsky 1967) among others has noted, while it has been suggested that learning to narrate about experience in talk prepares young children for narrating about experience in writing, hence assisting the development of literate capacities (Michaels 1986). Overall, from kindergarten to Year 12 (or its equivalent), students are constantly exposed to stories and they are often asked to write them as part of studying subject English, for stories represent important sites in which many attitudes, values and beliefs are expressed.

Stories constitute a family of text types, having features in common, as well as differences, and they are hence deemed 'agnate', where this involves adoption of two useful perspectives – typological and topological. The typological perspective acknowledges features distinctive to a given text type, while the topological perspective 'takes into account overlaps and similarities (between text types) and locates items on gradients of similarity along various parameters' (Coffin 2006a: 46). Several story types are written in English, and they may draw on fields of personal experience or imagined, even fantastic, experience. We have selected narratives and recounts because they are the most commonly written story types in the English programme. Rothery (1991) identified other written stories, while Plum (1988) identified several spoken ones.

The schematic structures of narratives and recounts

In the SFL tradition adopted in this book, all stories have an orientating stage, all have some temporal sequence of event, and all have some kind of closure (Martin and Plum 1997). The greatest variations are found in the 'middle' of the text, since the problem or complication found in a narrative is not found in other stories, while patterns of evaluative response and/or reflection upon event also vary. Though the patterns of evaluative language differ, evaluation of some kind is critical to a successful story, for as Labov (Labov and Waletsky 1967) suggested of oral stories, it is this which gives 'point' to the telling of the tale.

Table 2.1 displays details of the schematic structures of narratives and recounts.

A narrative may have an *Abstract*, though this is optional. Both genres must have an *Orientation* which introduces character(s) in a setting of time or place (or sometimes both), and beyond that, they differ. A narrative introduces a problem – the *Complication*, and this is followed by an *Evaluation*, in which response to and/or reflection on the Complication is provided (though evaluative language can occur in other elements). The narrative ends with a *Resolution*

Table 2.1   Schematic structures of recounts and narratives (based on Martin and Rose 2008)

Genre	Elements of structure
Narrative	(Abstract)*
	Orientation
	Complication
	Evaluation
	Resolution
	(Coda)
Recount	Orientation
	Record
	(Reorientation)

* Brackets indicate an optional element.

where the problem is solved, and an optional element – *Coda* – offers commentary. As for the recount, its 'middle' has events in temporal sequence, referred to as the *Record*, and it has an optional concluding element, the *Reorientation* which 'rounds off' the text, normally returning the protagonists to the point whence they came. *Comment* on the events occurs prosodically, and across the text, rather than falling in a distinct element of schematic structure.

Table 2.2 A sample of stories: narratives and recounts and their fields and age and sex of writers

Text	Genre and field type	Sex and age of writer
2.1 'Werribee Park'	Recount (personal)	Girl aged 6/7 years
2.2 'The Minotaur'	Narrative (imaginative)	Boy aged 7/8 years
2.3 'The Aqua Knight'	Narrative (imaginative)	Boy aged 8/9 years
2.4 'The Day I nearly got smashed on the rocks'	Narrative (personal)	Boy aged 11/12 years
2.5 'The Greedy Man'	Narrative (imaginative)	Girl aged 12/13 years
2.6 'The Fairy Realm'	Narrative (imaginative)	Girl aged 13/14 years
2.7 'A robbery in Paris'	Narrative (imaginative)	Boy aged 15/16 years
2.8 'The Footy'	Recount (personal)	Girl aged 13/14 years
2.9 'The Beginning'	Recount (imaginative)	Girl aged 17/18 years

Table 2.2 identifies the nine stories we shall discuss, selected because they offer a sample across the years of schooling from age 6 to 17 or 18. Only three are recounts, one of which draws on an imaginative field, while the narratives mainly draw on imaginative fields, though one draws on personal experience. Narratives appear more frequently in our data than recounts. We have indicated the probable ages of the writers of the texts, for while we know the ages of some, we are not sure of others. Hence, knowing the school years in which the children were writing, we have given estimates, a practice we adopt in all other chapters.

First we shall briefly summarize the changes in written language that emerge in learning to write stories, drawing on the SFL theory (Halliday and Matthiessen 2004) and Appraisal theory (Martin and White 2005), both introduced in Chapter 1.

Developmental change in learning to write narratives and recounts

Even very young children, aged 6–8 years, often reveal a sense of the requirements for written stories. They can create reasonably orthodox stages of the target genre, showing an awareness of their role in the unfolding of a tale.

In addition, with the probable exception of Text 2.1, the simplest of all the texts we shall examine, the texts considered provide evidence of how young story writers express values of various kinds, to do, for example, with kindness to others, courage in the face of danger, the virtues of peace over rivalry, or perhaps the excitement of meeting the new in life.

The simplicity in young children's first stories is evident in the congruent grammatical expression of clauses, involving minimal experiential meanings, realized in elementary nominal groups, verbal groups and prepositional phrases, and simple topical Themes, as in this clause, displayed to reveal its analyses:

We	*went*	*to Werribee Park*
nominal group	verbal group	prepositional phrase
Actor	Process: material	Circumstance: place
Theme	Rheme	

Adverbs are not typically found among young writers, apart from those of intensity, though others appear by about age 9.

Process types, while various, always include a significant number of material Processes to build action, as in the instance just displayed, though existential Processes can be used to introduce characters:

*In the ancient times there **was** a minotaur. . . .*

Clause patterns are also very simple, so that equal clauses are the most common, linked by additive or temporal conjunctions:

then we went to the bus // we got our lunch // and ate it all.

Where a dependent clause appears in stories by young writers, it will be one of time:

***When we got off the bus** // we went in the mansion.*

Very young texts, like the recount from which the last two clauses were drawn, are lexically 'thin' (Perera 1984; Halliday 1985), for their language patterns are closer to those of speech than those of writing, though there are variations, about which we shall say more below.

Important developmental changes commence by late childhood to early adolescence when children are aged 9–12 years of age and when grammatical metaphor tends to emerge (Aidman 1999; Halliday and Matthiessen 1999; Derewianka 2003). This appears first as a nominalization as in:

*After an hour of **trudging** through the dark and depressing forest . . .*

More congruently this would read: 'After they had trudged through the dark and depressing forest'. . .

Experiential meanings expand as the resources of nominal groups, verbal groups, prepositional groups and adverbs are exploited more fully and attitudinal meanings are also enlarged. Moreover, clause types and their interdependencies become more varied and intricate. For example, the following sentence from a child aged 9, shows skill in creating a series of interconnected clauses. The first clause initiates, and the second extends on this, while the others are variously dependent (as marked):

The king stepped off his carriage
and the very moment [[he did]] the crowd gasped
as they saw (clause of time, which also projects*)*
their great ruler and beloved king stride onto the wooden platform (projected clause)
to announce the two duelists [[who would serve the offering]] (clause of purpose)

In fact, where the first dependent clauses in stories are of time, those of reason, purpose, condition and concession tend to emerge later, sometimes in children aged 8, though more typically in the period from about age 9 to 12 or 13 years. The latter finding is supported by earlier studies of Harpin 1976, Loban 1976 and Perera 1984.

In addition, topical thematic progression becomes more varied, so that writers often 'pick up' what is written towards the end of one clause (referred to as *New Information* (Halliday and Matthiesen 2004: 87–92) and then foreground it as *Given Information* in a later one, helping to build unity across a text:

*Last summer holidays my family and I went on our holidays to **South West Rocks.***

I was really excited because we always have so much fun there.
***In South West Rocks** the surf isn't too rough . . .*

At least one other way in which a different pattern of thematic progression is facilitated occurs when a dependent clause is placed in an enclosed position, making it Theme:

It was really hot on the rocks so << ***when we finished lunch***>> *Nic turned to Mum //*
and said. . . .

In an unmarked way this would read: 'It was really hot, so Nic turned to Mum when we finished lunch and said . . .'

An enclosed clause in Theme position can occur by age 8, though it is more common from age 9 on.

Attitudinal expressions, while very simple in the earliest stories, often involve a mental Process of affect:

*I **liked** the beds and the lounge room,*

becoming more varied as children reach late childhood, when they draw on an expanding vocabulary with which to express meanings, building values of Appreciation and of Judgement, giving vigour and colour to their stories. One instance drawn from the narrative by a boy aged 9, already cited above, offers positive Appreciation of the qualities of fresh sea air (expressed using adverbs of intensity to 'scale up' the meaning), said to be:

***so** fresh, **so** pure [[that you could almost taste it]]*

By mid-adolescence when children are aged 13–15 years, at least among successful writers, the grammatical patterns are quite varied, while meanings are often expressed using grammatical metaphor to build abstractions. Non-finite dependent clauses and some elliptical clauses can appear, the latter in particular contributing to increased lexical density. The vocabulary also expands, so that experiential and attitudinal meanings are 'fused':

*we **trudged** our way to Richmond station **with squelching shoes and dripping hair**.*

When successful students are aged 16–18 years their stories exploit a range of lexicogrammatical resources for the construction of abstract meanings in stories, and they can deploy these resources in artful ways. Sometimes, students in adolescence 'over write', in that they can display more elaborate patterns of language than older writers, for they are still learning to control what they do. Lexical metaphor is often used, sometimes in fact with considerable skill. One student of 17 or 18 for example, writes metaphorically, and in the first person, of the imagined experience of a baby about to be born, hearing the sounds of others around her mother's body:

Voices break into a thousand colours in front of me, forming pictures and shapes that I can only imagine exist on the outside.

The general shift developmentally in the writing of stories as young people move from childhood to adolescence, is psychological and attitudinal, in that they achieve enhanced skills in building abstraction and generalization, and in exploring aspects of human motivation and behaviour.

Finally, in completing this overview of developmental changes in story writing, we should refer to the issue of lexical density, introduced in chapter 1. According to Halliday (1985: 80) a 'typical average lexical density for spoken English is between 1.5 and 2, whereas the figure for written English settles down somewhere between 3 and 6, depending on the level of formality of the writing'. With two exceptions, the lexical density in our stories settles at about 3 by late childhood to adolescence, hovering thereafter between 3 and 4. The exceptions are Text 2.2, by a boy aged 6, whose lexical density is 3.7, and Text 2.7, by a boy aged 15 or 16, whose lexical density is 7. On the face of it, both seem surprising, the former because it seems unusually dense for a young child, the latter because it represents a density level greater than the other texts examined. However, both can be explained. Text 2.2 has only seven clauses, and it remains an impressive, if juvenile, effort. Text 2.7, while longer (34 clauses) makes rather excessive use of its lexis, and this increases the overall lexical density; a more mature writer would be a little more restrained. We shall display the overall statistics for the lexical density of all our stories later.

Two stories of early childhood

Stories by young writers make considerable use of unmarked topical Themes, as in recounts of personal experience, like Text 2.1, and most are realized in the personal pronoun *we*, though there is one marked instance that commences the Record (*when we got off the bus*). The use of *we* is exophoric (referring to things outside the text) and this is not uncommon in recounts of personal experience, even by older writers, though one aspect of learning to control written language more generally will involve mastering endophoric reference (referring to things inside the text). The excessive reliance on the personal pronoun *we* is one measure of the immaturity of this young writer, for an older child, also writing of personal experience, would show greater facility in deploying other Themes. Despite its simplicity, it is a complete instance of a recount, and one of the first texts the child had written.

Text 2.1   A class visit to Werribee Park

Orientation	*We went to Werribee Park*
Record	***when we got off the bus*** *we went in the mansion. I liked the beds and the lounge room and the stairs after that we went to the garden and I liked the flowers and the colours. Then we went to the bus we got our lunch and ate it all. Then we went to see the animals and we saw lambs sheep ducks a kangaroo emus goats camels water buffalo pigs guinea pigs zebras*

(Continued)

Text 2.1—Cont'd

> *rhinoceros and after that we played on the swings and then we went*
> *to the island and we climbed the island and Mandy and I climbed it and*
> *the mud was all slippery and we had to come down and go on to the top*
> *and we found a cave and there was a door in the cave and there was steps*
> *on the island and nearly everyone went into the cave and Stephen and*
> *I was the monster and it started to rain*

Reorientation   *so we went home and all of us were tired.*

---

* Werribee Park is a tourist attraction outside the Australian city of Melbourne.

The use of the dependent clause:

when we got off the bus // *we went in the mansion*

is of interest because it is the only such clause in a text whose clauses are otherwise equal. Such young texts rely on simple clauses, linked mainly with additive and temporal conjunctive relations, though there is one instance of the consequential *so*, marking the start of the final element.

Theme and Reference in Text 2.2 are different from in Text 2.1, reflecting a different field and a different genre. Here the demands of a narrative of imagined experience come into play, for this is an attempt at verbal art, and it has a value position involving Judgement of the proprieties of good behaviour towards others. As we noted above in introducing narratives, the Orientation introduces characters in some setting, and here both physical and psychological considerations are relevant in building interest. Significant information should ideally be provided about character and/or event, which sets up expectations that are later overturned. The writer of Text 2.2 understands the requirements when he uses a marked Theme of time and an existential clause to commence his story, using an embedded clause to 'flesh out' the information.

Text 2.2   The Minotaur

Orientation	*In the ancient times there was a minotaur [[that was very nice and kind //* *and lived in a cave]]*
Complication	*but one day he stepped on a magic spot and turned bad so he started to kill the dwarfs and people*
Resolution	*and one day a witch came along and turned him good again and made everything alive again.*

The central character is introduced with a *presenting reference* – **a** *minotaur* – and there are subsequent uses of *presuming reference,* so-called because it presumes in the reader the knowledge established with the presenting instance – *he stepped* . . .; *so **he** turned bad.* A second presenting reference introduces the other character – **a** *witch* – and a final use of *him* refers back to the *minotaur* (Martin 1992: 93–156). Reference works well in this text, partly because it is very short. Among older children, writing at greater length, reference often causes difficulties (Perera 1984: 241–3).

The embedded clause in the opening element is of interest developmentally. According to Painter (1990: 96–8), with respect to oral language, and Derewianka (2003: 191) with respect to early writing, embedded clauses may provide an 'entry point' to abstract expressions in language development generally, because they involve 'uncoupling' the usual ranks, in this case a clause, and embedding it within the nominal group structure. Such embedded clauses, they suggest, may be considered 'protometaphorical', disposing children, in time, towards more extensive uses of abstraction, including – much later on – grammatical metaphor. While such observations are relevant for an overall awareness of ontogenetic development, it is likely that in early narratives, use of embedded clauses to introduce characters is learned from the stories read to children.

A marked Theme of time introduces the second element:

*but **one day** he stepped on a magic spot // and turned bad // so he started to kill the dwarfs and people*

and a similar marked Theme introduces the last element.

Text 2.2 has no Evaluation element, but the child nonetheless expresses attitude. The resources of lexis, intensity and conjunction, as well as some repetition, are all involved. Positive Judgement about the *minotaur* is suggested in the Orientation:

he was very nice and kind (intensity and lexis),

while subsequent events in the Complication, heralded with the adversative conjunction (*but*) set up an unexpected event, leading to negative Judgement about what happened:

but he turned bad // so he started to kill the dwarfs and people.

Finally, in the Resolution a positive Judgement is offered of the witch:

who turned him good again // and made everything alive again.

These expressions contribute to the moral position of the text, suggesting that the good should triumph over the bad: a not uncommon moral position adopted by writers of narratives in the adult world. Even in an early narrative this young writer demonstrates ability to offer a culturally valued moral position.

Two narratives of late childhood

By late childhood successful story writers display creative language to build imagined worlds, as in Text 2.3, by a child of 9, the tale of a brave knight who overcomes adversity, displaying valour in the process. The Orientation has a good control of vocabulary and it builds a lot of action, using a range of verbal groups realizing material Processes, while it also exploits the resources of nominal groups, prepositional phrases and some adverbs to create the account. It is in fact an exercise in building verbal art, whose attitudinal values express Appreciation of events, some Affect to do with the feelings of participants in the story, and some Judgements of their behaviour.

Text 2.3   The Aqua Knight

Orientation *The waves [[crashing on the shore of Aqualand]] would make you think the*
(extract only) *waves were roars from Neptune, which blew the <u>fresh</u> sea air which at*
Aqualand was <u>so fresh, so pure</u> [[that you could almost taste it]]. The crowd
came parading down to the beach towards the <u>sacred</u> rock pool for the offering
[[that was in honour of their god, Theorise]]. The crowd was <u>waiting, waiting</u>
for the offering to begin. The offering didn't consist of special food for the god.
It was duel on the beach. Every man [[standing on the <u>scorching</u> sand]] was
<u>agitated and excited</u>, because they wanted to know who the two duelists [[that
were going to serve the offering]] would be. This offering had happened every
20 years in the city of the land, Aquarius. The murmuring of the crowd was
<u>extremely intense</u> and it <u>sounded as if it were a volley of rifles going off</u>. The
king sat in a <u>heavily decorated</u> carriage with dancers [[<u>swirling // and</u>
<u>twirling</u> around him]] while trumpets <u>blasted with sound.</u>

This child is excited with the possibilities of language for pleasure and for artistry, when, for example, he uses repetition:

> *the fresh sea air which . . . was **so fresh, so pure** [[that you could almost taste it]]*
> *the crowd **was waiting, waiting** for the offering to begin,*
> *with dancers **swirling and twirling** . . .*

and lexical metaphor:

> *the waves . . . would make you think **the waves were roars from Neptune** . . .*
> *the murmuring of the crowd . . . . . . **sounded as if it were a volley of rifles going off**,*

and some grammatical metaphor:

> *the king sat in **a heavily decorated carriage**. . . .*

More congruently the latter would read:

> 'The king sat in a carriage which had been decorated heavily.'

The text is very long (149 ranking clauses)[2] and we can reproduce only a little of it. Thus, the writer makes frequent use of marked Themes of time to introduce new phases in the story, as when the loss of a famous knight is announced:

> ***While getting his armour on** // **to test try it a month ago** // a wave came crashing down on him // and then he was sucked away. . . .*

Another example, cited above, occurs using nominalization:

> ***After an hour of trudging throughout the dark and depressing forest**, as quick as a flash something had dropped from the forest roof. . . .*

Other marked Themes appear, as in this one realized in a Circumstance of place:

> ***Into his scabbard** it (i.e. a sword) went . . .*

At several points adverbs are used to create a heightened sense of the feelings of participants in the story:

> *Only one person said **sorrowfully** that a funeral must be announced*
> *They were relieved when they **exhaustedly** returned to the Aqualands*

and occasionally the young writer creates his own adverb:

> *Everyone wondered **anticipatingly** what he was doing.*

This young writer displays considerable interest in using adverbs of manner to create his imagined world.

Clause types and interdependencies (one instance of which we cited earlier) are intricate:

Every man standing on the scorching sand was agitated and excited (initiating clause)
because they wanted to know (clause of reason that projects)
who the two duelists [[that were going to serve the offering]] would be. (projected clause)

One further development is the use in this text of a dependent clause of time in an enclosed position, in order to make it thematic:

He held up his hand // and **<<as soon as this happened>>** *a temple rose out of the sand. . . .*

The tale concludes as the knight vanishes into the sea, his brave deeds accomplished and his glory recognized by all:

Next, he said, 'Farewell, oh people of the Aqualands!' and disappeared under the foam.

Text 2.4, by a child aged about 11, is the only narrative we have selected drawn from personal experience. (It has 50 ranking causes.) It also deals with overcoming adversity. The writer understands he must advise his reader of relevant information in order to lead up to the problem – namely that he is threatened by a strong wave. Among other matters within his Orientation, he tells us, using some negative polarity, that:

the surf **isn't** *too rough but the beaches have lots of rocky outcrops so everyone is always very careful . . .*

The writer's own pleasure in the holiday is established early, expressing Affect, and his Appreciation of events is made clear, where adverbs of intensity heighten the feelings, thus 'scaling up' the attitudinal values involved.

Text 2.4   The day I nearly got smashed on the rocks

Orientation	*Last summer holidays my family and I went on our yearly holidays to South*
(extract only)	*West Rocks. I was really excited because we always have so much fun there.*
	In South West Rocks the surf isn't too rough but the beaches have lots of
	rocky outcrops so everybody is always very careful to swim away from them.

The holiday setting having been established, the writer progresses to the Complication, in which he is revealed to be at some risk. Part of the Complication and the Resolution are reproduced. The language is generally simpler (and less dense) than that in Text 2.3, and this may be because the story is of personal experience, not imaginative.

Text 2.4—Cont'd

Complication (extract only)	*Once we had finished our lunch, my sister and I jumped into the water thinking that we could swim away from the rocks quickly because the water was flat and we were good swimmers. But **little** did we know that the reason [[the water seemed calm]] was [[because it was actually pulling more water back from under the surface // to make a bigger wave]]. **When we noticed that a big wave was coming**, we tried desperately to swim away from the rocks so we wouldn't be crushed.* *My sister succeeded to do this but I was stuck stranded, trying to swim to shore.*
Resolution	**After a while** *I noticed that [[the only way I could survive]] was [[to dive under the water]]. So I took a deep breath, dove under the water.* ***When I noticed the wave had passed*** *I sprung back up and noticed I was still alive.*

The writer compresses information relevant to the crisis he faced when he uses clause embeddings:

> *the reason [[the water seemed calm]] was [[because it was actually pulling more water back from under the surface // to make a bigger wave]].*

Embedded clauses do not necessarily create grammatical metaphor, though there is evidence of grammatical metaphor in this expression, for when we unpack this, it reads:

> 'the water seemed calm // because it was actually being pulled back from under the surface // to make a bigger wave'.

A similar expression appears later, again with use of embedded clauses, where causality is captured in *the only way [[I could survive]]*:

> *the only way [[I could survive]] was [[to dive under the water]]*

This, more congruently would read:

> 'I could survive // only by diving under the water.'

Compressing the information into the clause embeddings turns the events into 'things' – relatively abstract phenomena, around which the events unfold. It may be significant that such abstract formulations of experience appear at the point of crisis in the story: they highlight the danger the young writer faced. If the Resolution seems a little 'flat', this is to be explained by the fact that this is a young writer still learning to handle the tools of written English. Nonetheless, the writer is shown to have faced a difficulty and succeeded:

> *When I noticed // the wave had passed // I sprung back up // and noticed // I was still alive.*

The story reaffirms a principle often expressed in stories: that of the value attached to individuals who face hardship, and triumph over it.

Thus far, we have traced developments in the writing of stories – mainly narratives – from early to late childhood. Before proceeding to examine three narratives of adolescence, we shall briefly review what has been argued. In writing their first stories young children use a congruent grammar, creating simple clauses with simple nominal and verbal groups and simple prepositional phrases. Where they use a dependent clause, it will be one of time. By late childhood when children are aged about 9 to 12 years, they display growing facility in a number of ways: clause types are more varied (the range of dependent clauses extends) and their interdependencies become more intricate; nominalization emerges as the first step in grammatical metaphor; texts achieve enhanced lexical density as the resources of nominal and verbal groups are expanded, while prepositional phrases and adverbs – especially those of manner – provide more circumstantial information; experiential and attitudinal expression are overall much enriched, while texts achieve enhanced overall direction and organization because of more confident control of Theme. Where these developments have occurred, children are ready to meet the demands of the secondary school experience of writing stories.

Three narratives of early adolescence

Texts 2.5, 2.6 and 2.7 are narratives of adolescence. The first two, by girls aged 12/13 and 13/14 years respectively, are fairy tales, and both have very clear ethical or moral positions. (The texts were written in different schools, in different Australian states, so there was no connection between the writers.) Text 2.5, *The Greedy Man*, concerns a man who is initially poor but good, and who is rewarded for helping a pixie. However, he grows greedy with his newly acquired wealth, and is punished, after which, having truly repented, he is restored to his good fortune. Text 2.6, *The Importance of Unity*, concerns the *fairy realm*, where different fairy clans fight amongst themselves, demanding powers they do not naturally hold. After being given extra magical powers, they find themselves still not happy. A good fairy intervenes and they come to see that it was better not to strive for what was not naturally theirs, and to live instead at peace. Text 2.7, by a boy aged 15 or 16, is quite different in character, for it concerns a robbery in contemporary Paris, and it lacks the strong moralizing quality that marks the other two narratives, seeking instead to create a sense of the atmosphere and life of Parisian streets and their inhabitants.

All three texts use language creatively and imaginatively. Texts 2.5 and 2.6 are more successful than Text 2.7, for the latter suffers from a tendency to 'over write', alluded to above. The writer has yet to learn to control his sometimes exuberant use of language, though his text is of interest for its developmental significance. The writer is in a sense 'flexing his linguistic muscles' as he comes to terms with writing creatively.

Text 2.5 (with 74 ranking clauses) reveals developing facility with building a narrative structure like that found in Text 2.2, showing considerable ontogenetic development. Consider for example, an extract only from the Orientation of Text 2.5, in which two surprisingly named characters are introduced. Considerable detail is devoted to establishing the principal character – *Cody* – offering Judgement of his qualities:

he had a kind heart

and Appreciation of his circumstances:

he had nothing to eat but a stale piece of bread.

Text 2.5 The Greedy Man

Orientation (extract only)	*A poor man [[named Cody]] once roamed the beautiful green hills and the dusty paths of the countryside, thousands of years ago. Cody had a kind heart but no money and nothing [[to eat]] but a stale piece of bread.*
	A few months passed and the weather began to turn bad. **On one moderately cold day** *Cody was walking along a curvy path when he tripped and fell flat on his face and came at eye level with a pixie. This pixie introduced himself as Zucchini and gave Cody an offer [[he couldn't refuse]]. Zucchini told Cody that if he could give him shelter during the winter then he would give Cody 10 bags of gold.*

The prototypical manner of introducing a character is employed, using a nominal group with embedded clause:

a poor man [[named Cody]],

while in other ways the resources of nominal groups are exploited to build experiential detail as in these examples:

the beautiful green hills and the dusty paths of the countryside,
a stale piece of bread,

and circumstantial information is also expanded

*Cody . . . roamed . . . the hills . . . **thousands of years ago***
***on one moderately cold day** Cody was walking*
*Cody was walking **along a curvy path.** . . .*

The grammar is congruent, though the clause interdependencies are quite varied, and the text reveals the developmental gains made by this student, in her first year of secondary education. She has used her language to build an imagined world, in a manner not yet available to the writer of Text 2.2. She establishes early important information about her two protagonists. Even the information that the weather was *moderately cold* is relevant, for as the story unfolds the weather deteriorates, so Cody's efforts in protecting Zucchini are, by implication, the more meritorious. Cody is duly rewarded, receives his castle, marries and has two children, and all goes well for some time.

The crisis comes, as Cody mistreats his wife and servants. Notable here are two marked Themes, expressed in non-finite clauses (one of time, the other of manner). Judgement of his behaviour and some Affect are involved, while a dependent clause of condition foreshadows the punishment that awaits Cody:

***if he didn't ease off on his wife** then he would lose everything including his family.*

Text 2.5—Cont'd

Complication
(extract only)

*It was time for [[Cody to learn his lesson]]. **While parading around his castle**, he tripped and came face to face with Zucchini. Zucchini gave him a warning telling him that if he didn't ease off on his wife, children and servants then he would lose everything including his family. Cody agreed to change and he did, for about two days, and then the trouble started again. **As threatened**, Cody lost everything and was not angry at Zucchini because he deserved his punishment. He was however at a loss on what to do. So again he roamed the country a poor man with no money.*

Above, we cited an example of a non-finite clause in Theme position in a text by a 9-year-old. Use of non-finite clauses, often, as here, to commence a sentence, while found in late childhood, is more commonly a feature of stories in adolescence (Perera 1984: 235):

> **While parading around his castle** // *he tripped and came face to face with Zucchini.* **As threatened** // *Cody lost everything. . . .*

Cody is punished by being exiled, until, overcome by remorse, he is allowed to resume his life with his family, and we are told, using emphasis to reinforce or 'scale up' the point:

> *He was extremely grateful at being given a second chance and he never did a horrible thing again.*

The general moral of the piece is apparent, and its principal value in Appraisal terms concerns Judgement of the proprieties of behaving well towards others.

Text 2.6, while also very judgemental, is a more ambitious piece of writing, reflecting the skills of a slightly older writer. (It has 213 ranking clauses.) While its overall schematic structure is not very different from that of Text 2.5, its language is rather different, in that it deals much more with abstract experience – even its title is an abstraction. Its vocabulary is much richer and it makes use of grammatical metaphor, not present in Text 2.5. Its values concern the importance of living in unity and harmony with others, where these involve Appreciation of certain events, and Judgement of the ethics of particular behaviours. The Orientation and opening, only, of the Complication are displayed.

Text 2.6   The Importance of Unity

Orientation	***The World of Fairies***
	Once upon a time there were fairies. <u>Fairies of all colours and shapes. There were</u> <u>the Rainbow Fairies, the Flower Fairies and the Celestial Fairies. All the clans</u> <u>had a different job [[to do]] in order for them to live peacefully. The Rainbow</u> <u>Fairies kept the magic of the rainbow and all its colours alive. The Flower Fairies</u> <u>helped the flowers bloom and spread. And the Celestial Fairies were in control of</u> <u>the sun, moon and the changing of the seasons. They all lived in the Fairy</u> <u>Realm, under the command of their Queen, Narcissa, and her family.</u>
Complication (extract only)	*The Fairy Realm <u>lived in peace for many years. But <<**as time went on**>> the</u> <u>separate clans began to fight. The Rainbow Fairies were jealous of the other</u> <u>clans' long life. The Flower Fairies were jealous of the other clans' power, which</u> affected the giants' world as well. <u>But the most curious jealousy was that of the</u> <u>Celestial Fairies, who were jealous of the other fairies' commonness. The Celestial</u> <u>Fairies were so few and so well known [[that they were bound to their city in the</u> <u>clouds, the last of a dying race]].</u>*
	(*Continued*)

Text 2.6—Cont'd

Complication *The Queen tried to bring peace back to the realm and reduce the fighting.*
(extract only) *But she did not succeed, meanwhile the clans were becoming more and more*
*violent, plotting even to kill each other. **After a particularly vicious attempt on***
***the life of one of the Celestial Fairies, Rowena**, the Celestial Fairies held*
a meeting, a meeting [[that none of the other clans or even the Queen knew
existed.]]

This writer strives to create verbal art, using her language in creative ways to
construct a sense of her imagined world, sometimes, for example, in the use of
a one-clause sentence:

Once up a time there were fairies.

sometimes in elliptical expressions:

Fairies of all colours and shapes.

sometimes in deliberate repetition:

There were the Rainbow Fairies, the Flower Fairies and the Celestial fairies.

The rest of the opening offers several expressions of Judgement concerning
the propriety of the fairies' behaviours, all of them positive, for the intention
is to capture a sense of the harmony or order that initially prevails. This
harmony and good order are then challenged in the Complication, subverting
the reader's understandings and expectations, for the Judgement becomes
negative: *the separate clans began to fight.*

The text displays a significant resource for building experiential information
not found in the earlier texts. It is that of nominal groups in apposition, used
to elaborate upon experiential information, providing more detail. (Halliday
and Matthiessen 2004: 68). Two examples appear in the text extract cited, the
first of which elaborates by providing a name, while the second elaborates on
the information:

*After a particularly vicious attempt on the life of **one of the Celestial Fairies,***
Rowena**, the Celestial Fairies held **a meeting, a meeting [[that none of the other
***clans or even the Queen knew existed]]**.*

According to Perera (1984: 293) ability to extend the nominal group in such a
way is 'a late grammatical acquisition which is generally more common in writing than in speech'. Macken-Horarik (2006) suggests such nominal groups in

apposition are one mark of successful secondary students of English, allowing the writer to elaborate upon experiential information in enriching ways.

As the tale unfolds, the fairy clans receive new powers, though they are not happier. They eventually learn they were better as they were, rather than striving for what was not naturally theirs. One fairy refers to the fact that they have been given the gift of long life and are now living longer. Their number is rising uncomfortably, causing over-crowding, and she declares, using grammatical metaphor:

Our newly extended lives are causing our population to rise like never before.

Expressed more congruently this sentence might read:

'We are now living much longer than before // and therefore there are more of us.'

One other extract only can be used from Text 2.6, drawn from the Resolution, of interest for its expressive uses of language giving vigour to the tale. Rowena, assisted by her unicorn, Sparkle, intervenes to stop argument and restore order. Appreciation of Rowena's actions and Judgement about the propriety of certain behaviours are both involved.

Text 2.6—Cont'd

Resolution   *'Stop!' cried <u>a commanding voice</u> from the door. Rowena was riding Sparkle into the Great Hall. <u>A ringing silence followed her, until nothing could be heard but the clattering of Sparkle's hooves on the white marble floor.</u> Once she reached the throne where the Queen sat, <u>she slid gracefully off Sparkle's back,</u> bowed to the Queen and turned to face her watchful audience. 'You have discovered the problem yourselves, and you have also answered it,' <u>she called out in clear, ringing voice,</u> 'The way [[you were]] was perfect for the running of the Realm and your lives. But if you try to become something you're not, nothing works, the whole chain is broken.' The Fairies all looked at Rowena, <u>her dark brown hair falling around her face, which wore a hard, blazing look,</u> and <u>realized that she was right.</u>*

Note how rich the language is in such expressions as:

a clear commanding voice;
a ringing silence;
the clattering of Sparkle's hooves on the white marble floor;

she slid gracefully off Sparkle's back;
her dark brown hair falling around her face;
a hard blazing look.

All such expressions are attitudinally 'infused' (Martin and White 2005: 143), in that experiential and attitudinal values are enmeshed. Compare, for example, the use of *a commanding voice* with 'a loud voice', which is what might have been written, or indeed *a clear ringing voice* with 'a loud voice', and we can see how much richer are the lexical choices made to build the evaluative qualities, and hence also the qualities of verbal art.

Text 2.7 uses language evocatively to create the atmosphere on a summer evening in Paris, and the text (with 34 ranking clauses), while promising, is not entirely successful. At times the meaning is a little confused, partly because of a rather excessive use of participial expressions, though this is compounded by other, rather awkward expressions. We display extracts from the Orientation. The writer seeks to suggest the bustle and excitement of Paris streets, so that the Appraisal values are mainly those of Appreciation of the city and its people.

Text 2.7   A robbery in Paris

Orientation (extract only)	The <u>warm, summer</u> air <<so easily associated by many with the chirruping of swallows, <u>lazy</u> swaying of leafy trees and <u>merry</u> frolicking of <u>laughing</u> children>> had only in the last few minutes begun to dissipate into the <u>sharp, icy chill</u> of European evenings – regardless of what time of year it happened to be. **In the short of things**, the <u>still-frantic</u> Avenue des Champs-Elysées << bustling with <u>fashionably-dressed</u> shoppers and <u>astute-looking</u> business men and women>> was actually very far from singing birds, laughing children – although the street was admittedly lined with straight rows of green foliage.
	It was an afternoon very much like any other. The sun dipped with <u>surprising</u> haste into narrow gaps between high, shuttered buildings, throwing broad shafts of orange light across the bitumen at the frequent intersections of the boulevarde with adjoining avenues and side-alleys. **On the sidewalks and amongst the <u>hectic</u> whirl of traffic**, people were to be observed going about their everyday lives: everything was as it should have been, even if //what was viewed by Parisians as normality// rarely counted as such elsewhere.
	No building within view was as <u>outrageously</u> suited to its surroundings that afternoon than an <u>ancient yet very well-maintained</u> turret of an establishment //signed 'Musée des Oeuvres Mondials'//. The museum was squeezed in so tightly between a major traffic junction and a substantially more modern and cramped café //that one wondered how the narrow museum could ever possibly sustain its own weight.//

The sense of colour and movement can succeed at times, though at other times the writer seems to lose control:

> *The sun dipped with surprising haste into narrow gaps between high, shuttered build-ings throwing broad shafts of orange light across the bitumen at the frequent intersections of the boulevarde with adjoining avenues and side-alleys.*

The latter would have been better expressed, for example, had the writer said:

> 'The sun dipped with surprising haste into narrow gaps between high, shuttered buildings, throwing broad shafts of orange light across the bitumen **at points** where the boulevard intersected with adjoining avenues and side-alleys.'

Elsewhere the vocabulary choices are a little odd, as in the advice that:

> *no building was as **outrageously** suited to its surroundings that afternoon . . .*

The writer is playing with his language, experimenting with ways to build a lively picture of the scene, though no very adequate closure is achieved, so that the point of the tale becomes lost, and no obvious purpose emerges:

> *In the midst of the city night, five <u>young, slender</u> men, <u>remarkably uniform</u> in appear-ance, <u>stealthily slithered</u> past. Emerging from the side-avenue on the corner of which [[the museum was situated]], they directed their steps towards its <u>rather unspectacular</u> entrance: glass doors with a thin, gold frame – much like any other of the <u>expensive</u> stores or museums in the vicinity.*

The young men disappear into the museum, emerging shortly after, and we are told:

> *They were followed almost instantly by a <u>beefy</u>, moustached man of around fifty years, who emerged holding a CV-radio device.*
> *"Cambrioleurs!" he shouted, <u>evidently in a panic.</u>*

Here the story stops, without adequate closure. The writer displays some skill, suggesting that with assistance he might well go on to become a compe-tent story writer.

Two recounts of adolescence

Texts 2.8 and 2.9, written by girls, aged 13/14 and 17/18 respectively, are very different in character, for the former involves a field of personal experience, while the latter is about the imagined experience of birth. Text 2.8, reproduced in full, makes clever use of language to create an ironic account of the writer's attendance at a football match, dwelling with some humour on the uncomfortably cold and rainy weather and her reactions to the behaviour of others.

Text 2.8   The Footy*

Orientation

Sue and I left my house and headed for the tram stop [[that's on Sydney Road.]] We were both <u>psyched up</u>, because the Pies were to play the Dockers – a game [[the Pies were <u>sure to win</u>, despite their many losses]].

We were there at the tram stop, destined for the MCG, wrapped up in our Magpies' scarves and beanies . . . <u>in six degree weather</u>! The tram was approaching, <u>more slowly than usual</u> and we were <u>eager</u> [[to get inside away from the cold.]] We found a window, sat down and <u>sighed</u>. **Then to <u>our disappointment</u>,** *the rain came, and I means <u>lots of</u> rain! We <u>sighed again</u>. – the day was going to be long.*

Record

*We arrived at the MCG and joined the queue. We got inside and <u>miserably</u> scanned the scene for a place [[to sit]]. **<u>After much conflict with Sue</u>,** it was me [[who had to ask // whether all the seats were allocated.]] The man in the MCG staff uniform was <u>a hefty and solid looking man with a stern expression</u> [[moulded onto his face]]. **Nimbly** I asked where we could sit. His <u>stern</u> face turned <u>sour</u> and he <u>barked a few unclear words</u>, which I understood as 'anywhere but under the shelter!' I looked <u>helplessly</u> at the seats [[that weren't under the shelter]]. It was still raining, the seats were wet and piled up along the barrier were a <u>loud group of drunken Pies supporters</u> who << **even though the game had not yet started**>> were <u>yelling insults</u> out to the umpires and team staff. We made our way to our seats, directly behind the goals, yet as far away from the <u>loud drunken</u> group as possible.*

The game was about to start when <u>large and heavy</u> hailstones began to pound us. There was a <u>large noise of murmuring and squealing</u> from the crowd in the stadium. Then the hail subsided and it poured rain. The horn [[announcing the first quarter]] sounded. Sue and I <u>tried to seem excited</u> even though we were <u>dripping wet and freezing cold</u>. **In the second quarter,** *I <u>gave in</u> and forked out the money to pay for some disposable raincoats.* **Despite the rain,** *the game was <u>excellent</u>.* **Even though the Magpies led most of the way,** *<u>the group [[hanging off the barrier]] only shut their mouths to get a breath</u>.*

Reorientation

At the end of the game << *after we <u>proudly</u> screamed out our team anthem*>> *we <u>trudged</u> our way to Richmond station with <u>squelching</u> shoes and <u>dripping</u> hair. We caught our train and tram and got home, <u>drained of all energy</u>. We were seeking only one thing – a hot shower!*

---

* Incidentally, the football referred to is Australian Rules Football, which excites much interest among its fans, especially in the city of Melbourne, the birthplace of this football code. The two teams referred to are famous, while the MCG is the 'Melbourne Cricket Ground'.

Theme patterns are skilful, contributing in no small measure to the overall structuring of the text. Most Theme choices are unmarked, identifying the writer and her friend, and this is particularly important in the Orientation where the physical and psychological setting of the narrator and her friend are established. One marked Theme (expressed in a Circumstance of manner) appears towards the end of the Orientation, helping to foreshadow the negative events that follow:

> *Then,* **to our disappointment** *the rain came.*

In the Record there are five marked Themes, all helping to shape the directions taken, and all contributing to the overall attitudinal expression:

> **After much conflict with Sue** *it was me who had to ask . . .* (Circumstance of time)
> **Nimbly** *I asked . . .* (Circumstance of manner)
> *who <<* **even though the game had not yet started** *>> were yelling insults . . .*
> (clause of concession)
> **In the second quarter** *I gave in . . .* (Circumstance of time)
> **Despite the rain** *the game was excellent* (Circumstance of concession)
> **Even though the Magpies led most of the way** *// the group [[hanging off*
> *the barrier]] . . ..* (clause of concession)

Finally the Reorientation starts with a marked Theme, made up of a Circumstance of time and a clause of time:

> **At the end of the game** *<<* **after we proudly screamed out or team anthem** *>>*

The writer displays facility in the Record, where she 'packs in' a great deal of experiential information. Consider for example, her nominal group structures, which are expanded in more than one way:

> *(we) headed for* **the tram stop [[that's on Sydney Road]]**
> **a game [[the Pies were sure to win despite their many losses]]**
> *we scanned* **the scene for a place [[to sit]]**
> **the man [in the MCG uniform]** *was* **a hefty and solid man [with a stern expression**
> **[[moulded onto his face]]]**
> *it was* **me [[who had to ask//whether all the seats were allocated]]**
> **large and heavy hailstones** *began to pound us.*
> *I looked helplessly at* **the seats [[that weren't under the shelter]]**
> *there was* **a large noise [of murmuring and squealing from the crowd]**
> **the horn [[announcing the first quarter]]** *sounded*
> **the group [[hanging off the barrier]]** *only shut their mouths*

Attitudinal values are cleverly infused through the text, so that a strong sense of pleasure in the game, discomfort at the conditions, and disapproval of the drunks is distributed throughout. This is a story for pleasure and entertainment, written with verve.

Text 2.9 (consisting of 102 ranking clauses), is an unusual recount, partly because (unlike most recounts that we have collected) it is of imagined experience, and partly because it is written in the present tense. It is entirely built on metaphor, as it offers an account of birth as a journey, tracing the development of the baby and its eventual entry to the world. It has no Orientation, consisting only of the Record, and unlike all other stories reviewed in this chapter, its temporal sequence is achieved not by overt temporal connection (i.e. with clauses and circumstances of time), but by building with the lexis an urgent awareness of time passing while the baby prepares for birth, impatiently conscious of movements beyond the confines of the uterus. The rows of dots indicate where text is omitted. The attitudinal values are mainly those of Appreciation of the process of birth and Affect or feelings experienced because of this. Overall, the language is used artfully, so that one senses this is a writer using her language strategically to create an effect.

Text 2.9   The Beginning

Record
(extracts only)

They come and go, <u>these voices like pendulums swing near and far, so close</u> <u>[[that I feel as if their melodic sounds are directed solely at me]]</u>, yet, at times, <u>distant as if I am but a bubble in a turbulent tide, rushed past the commotion</u> <u>and excitement of their world. It is as if their music resonates around me.</u> <u>The ever present, ever constant percussion surrounds me, its beat my only</u> <u>companion in my isolated world of darkness.</u> I have grown, each cell dividing, a multiplying array of tiny proportions. Movements are constricted, as always I force my arms and legs outward as my patience, ever-decreasing, is momently. (momentary??)

. . . .

Only the voices outside return me to consciousness, <u>they provide colour in my</u> <u>lost and blackened environment. Voices break into a thousand colours in front</u> <u>of me, forming pictures and shapes [[that I can only imagine exist on the</u> <u>outside]].</u>
An <u>uneasy feeling is washed over me</u>, like an ocean of <u>confusion I taste the salty</u> <u>tang of change.</u>
***No longer guided by my own mind and thoughts alone**, <u>I feel this dark world</u> <u>has plans of its own. I am merely the prisoner of this moist and dark cell, my</u> <u>captor has become restless. I am no longer wanted</u>* . . . .

. . . .

<u>She screams! The world beyond is in turmoil</u>, <u>the voice is screaming in pain.</u> ***As if responding to this external distress*** *<u>the confines of my soft walls become</u> <u>rigid, concrete panels which constrict my every movement. I am forced</u> <u>downwards again, through a tunnel of despair, foreign sensations and</u> <u>constricting muscle.</u>*

Record (extracts only)	*This new landscape [[I have journeyed towards]] is unlike my former residence. . . . . . A light appears beyond my head. I am being pushed in regular motions towards the bright end of normality. Towards the screams, towards the blinding dry and cold light.* *My travels have brought me to a place of frightening possibilities[[where the unknown is my greatest exploration]]. [[To discover // what lies in the world of voices and colour]] is a new journey. I am pulled from my cocoon of muscle and raised high above the voices, my discomfort at this new landscape's condition could only be mirrored by that of the woman screaming. I look at her face [[whose cries have ceased]] as she gazes upon me and I realize that this is not the end, it is merely the beginning.*

At times the writer 'over writes', straining a little to achieve her effect, though the language is often skilled, evoking a sense of the baby's passage to the *beginning*. Several features of the text show an older writer, attempting to produce verbal art:

its skilled use of the present tense, a notoriously difficult tense choice for writing stories in English:
they come and go these voices;
its occasional use of singular clauses to emphasize or sharpen:
she screams!
its artfully simple series of largely unmarked topical Themes, contributing to the measured way in which the text unfolds:
only the voices outside . . . they provide colour . . . voices break into . . .;
its uses of metaphor both lexical and grammatical, building the attitudinal values of Appreciation and Attitude and Affect:
these voices like pendulums swing near and far;
I feel as if I am but a bubble in a turbulent tide;
their music (i.e. the voices heard) *resonates around me*;
the ever present, ever constant percussion;
its beat my only companion in my isolated world;
a place of frightening possibilities;
the world of voices and colours;
its uses of non-finite clauses . . .
rushed past the commotion and excitement of their world;
each cell dividing;
forming pictures and shapes that I can only imagine . . .
its elliptical clauses . . .
its beat my only companion in my isolated world of darkness;
its nominal groups elaborating on experiential information:

a multiplying array of tiny proportions,
the ever present, ever constant percussion.

The text appeals to some familiar values in an English-speaking culture about the importance of new life, while the metaphorical use of birth as a beginning to be celebrated, though not new, is handled with some skill.

Lexical density

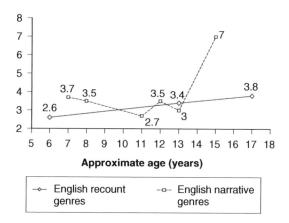

FIGURE 2.1   Lexical density in a sample of recounts and narratives

Figure 2.1 displays the lexical density counts for the narratives and recounts reviewed. By late childhood children achieve a density of about 3, and density levels between 3 and 4 remain for most writers throughout adolescence. Lexical density is not in itself a reliable guide of students' writing achievements, for the text with the highest count – Text 2.8 – is in many ways the least successful. Moreover, lexical density varies, depending on the field of knowledge as well as the genre, and we shall compare the counts for history and science later on.

Conclusion

We have sought to trace the ontogenesis of written language among students aged 6–17 years with respect to the writing of stories, specifically recounts and narratives. While the schematic structures of both genres remain reasonably constant from childhood to adolescence, the linguistic resources in which these are realized are very much expanded as students mature. Stories are written for entertainment and enlightenment, and as examples of verbal art.

Even the earliest stories (such as Text 2.2) can display language to entertain and to affirm culturally held values, to do, for example, with the triumph of good over evil, or courage in the face of adversity. As children grow older, reaching late childhood and thence adolescence, their expanding control of the grammar of writing unleashes new language resources, used in exploring human behaviour, attitudes and values in increasingly ambitious ways.

The texts we have used were selected because their teachers judged them to be at least satisfactory, and in several cases, good. Not all students achieve in the same ways. Indeed, the evidence available to us is that many experience difficulties with their writing, especially as they move beyond the first steps in which some initial literacy is established. About these matters we shall have more to say in our last chapter. Since English is about more than stories, important though they are, we should turn to the response genres written in English, so that we can provide a more rounded account of what constitutes development in this subject.

Notes

[1] The terms 'progressivist' and 'constructivist' have been often debated in educational literature and different interpretations are frequently offered. Generally, though the origins of the two traditions differ, the two refer to pedagogies which attach importance to self-directed learning, rather than teacher-directed learning. The discussions in Muller 2002 and Christie 2002 and 2004b explore the limitations of such pedagogies.

[2] In the cases of texts where we use only extracts, we shall adopt the practice throughout the book of providing advice regarding the number of ranking clauses. Where texts are reproduced in full, we shall not do this.

Chapter 3

Writing to Respond to and Evaluate Other Texts

Introduction

English attaches particular significance to development of capacity to respond to and evaluate texts, developing ability in students to talk and to write about them, making judgements about them and reflecting upon the values they express. Originally, the texts evaluated were literary, though by the latter part of the 20th century the range of texts had expanded to include other modes of communication, most notably films and television programmes. Today, reflecting the influence of cultural studies, other images such as paintings and cartoons are often included among the texts selected. However, while the English curriculum has expanded to include other media, literary texts remain those most frequently considered, sometimes in their own right, as it were, and sometimes as part of a unit of thematic study (such as World War I) that considers other media as well. Capacity to respond to, and express opinions about, other texts, has had, and continues to have, a particularly privileged status in English studies, mentored from the earliest years in the primary programme, and gaining increased significance, especially at the level of public examinations held in the upper years of a secondary education.

We shall adopt the term *response genres*, proposed by Rothery (New South Wales Department of School Education, Metropolitan East Region (1994)) to refer to the group of text types written in responding to other texts, and while this discussion owes a great deal to her original descriptions, we shall depart in some ways from her manner of characterizing them. The developmental trajectory we have outlined in Chapter 2 with respect to learning to write stories has many parallels with that found in writing response genres. One would expect that, since children are learning to deploy the same linguistic system in learning different areas of the school programme, though the emphases will differ, depending on the genre concerned and the field involved. Hence, the general movement in learning to write response genres is, grammatically, from the congruent to the non-congruent, and semantically, from the immediate to the increasingly abstract. Specifically, in the case of response genres, the movement is from immediate expression of simple affect about text(s) towards eventual abstract reflection on the values expressed in text(s) read or viewed, and judgement about them.

A topology of response genres

We shall recognize four types of response genres: *personal response; review; character analysis* and *thematic interpretation.* These tend to emerge in the order given in children's writing, though the set we are proposing is not definitive, for other texts are written. However, those selected are commonly found in schools, in Australia at least, and examination of these allows useful discussion of the developmental processes in learning to write literary response texts. Thus, personal response genres, outlining one's immediate feelings about a text, appear early, while reviews emerge in late childhood to adolescence, and they involve some synopsis of events in the text as well as statements about its qualities. These tend to disappear after early adolescence. Beyond that, character analyses involve some discussion and evaluation of a character in a text, and they tend to appear in the mid-secondary years. Thematic interpretations emerge in the senior years, and they involve abstracting away from the immediate details of texts(s) examined and constructing reflections and/or abstract statements about experience as understood through the lens of the texts concerned. In contemporary English curricula, such thematic interpretations often involve considering three or more texts – verbal and visual – and discussing these in the light of the overall theme offered students for discussion.

Figure 3.1 attempts to capture the topology of response genres concerned.

The range of response genres, once mastered, is available to older writers to use freely. Reviews of films and books for example – by far the commonest response genres in the wider community – appear regularly in the pages of the newspapers, and they are thus often written by adults. Moreover, personal

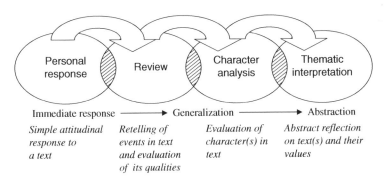

FIGURE 3.1 A topology of representative response genres in English

response genres, offering quick attitudinal comment on a book, film or play, may be produced by writers of any age – perhaps in personal letters and even e-mail messages. Rothery (New South Wales Department of School Education, Metropolitan East Region 1994: 149) suggested that personal responses were common in the junior secondary English programme, though our data suggest they are commonly a feature of English in the earlier years. Apart from reviews and personal response genres, the other two that Rothery identified were *critical response* and *interpretation genres*. A critical response genre discusses a text with a view to rejecting it, or at least some aspects of it. Like Rothery we have no evidence that students write such critical genres in the junior years of secondary school, nor in the senior years – at least in the Australian system.

What we do have evidence for is the thematic interpretation genres we have already alluded to, and these differ from those described by Rothery as interpretations, though there is some similarity. For Rothery, the interpretation typically is written in response to a question that asks the student to identify 'the message of the text', and this is 'taken at face value', so that the student is inducted 'into an acceptance of the values embedded in the text' (New South Wales Department of School Education, Metropolitan East Region 1994: 148). The thematic interpretation genres that we have identified certainly involve students in interpretation, where this means adopting some value position or idea, in the light of which the text(s) must be interpreted and evaluated. This may involve interpreting the 'message' of texts as Rothery suggested, though it is the overall theme (be that 'Gothic' themes' in texts, or perhaps the notion of 'change' in human affairs) that motivates much of what is written. In addition, more than one text is commonly selected, where these include verbal and visual examples. As for the character analyses, while they were not identified by Rothery, we have evidence for them, normally in the mid-secondary years, though they can appear in the upper secondary school as well. They seem to fall somewhere between the reviews on the one hand, with their tendency to summarize details of events in book or film and judge the text's overall quality, and on the other hand, the thematic interpretations, which have a much more abstract character, established by reference to an overarching theme.[1]

As Figure 3.1 is intended to suggest, the various genre types overlap, for while they have different schematic structures, they all have in common a preoccupation with evaluation of text(s). We shall proceed by drawing on the general observations made earlier about developmental growth in writing, while focusing on instances of response genres, and in particular, on the emergence of attitudinal expression in these, using the resources of Appraisal, also introduced earlier.

Table 3.1 displays the response genres we have selected, and details of the writers. All the texts, with one exception, were written as class assignments, some taken home, others written in class time. The exception is the last text, which is an examination script published in a set of scripts produced for the information of students and teachers (New South Wales Board of Studies 2006:

Table 3.1 A selection of response genres

Genre	Text(s) discussed and evaluated	Age and sex of writer
3.1 Book review	*Blue Hair Day* by James Maloney	Girl aged 8/9
3.2 Personal response	*Rowan of Rin* by Emily Rodda	Boy aged 9/10 years
3.3 Book review	*Strange Magic* by Elizabeth Beresford	Boy aged 11/12 years
3.4 Book review	*Sally's Story* by Sally Morgan	Boy aged 12/13 years
3.5 Film review	*Who Framed Roger Rabbit?*	Girl aged 12/13 years
3.6 Character analysis	Atticus Finch and Scout in *To Kill a Mockingbird* by Harper Lee	Girl aged 14/15 years
3.7 Character analysis	Antonio from *The Merchant of Venice* by William Shakespeare	Boy aged 15/16 years
3.8 Thematic interpretation	*The Curious Incident of the Dog in the Night-time* by Mark Haddon	Girl aged 17/18 years
3.9 Thematic interpretation	*Frankenstein* and *Buffy the Vampire Slayer*	Boy aged 15/16 years
3.10 Thematic interpretation	Several texts grouped under the general rubric of *The Journey*	Girl aged 17/18 years

102–14). It is included because it was rated by the examiners as a 'High range' text, providing us with a measure of what counts as excellence in writing response genres at the senior level.

A selection of response genres

The writing of response genres is variously scaffolded in the early primary years, principally through use of teacher questions to guide writing (e.g. 'Did you like this novel? Who was your favourite character and why?'). Sometimes children write responses after interacting with a moderator and other students through 'book raps' – asynchronous discussions set up on the Internet by a moderator (Simpson 2003). In general, young children seem not to write response genres independently before the age of about 8 or 9, and sometimes not till they are 10.

Personal response genres and reviews

Table 3.2 displays the schematic structures of personal response genres and reviews.

The schematic structure for personal responses is very simple, while that for reviews is more detailed. According to Rothery, the personal response offers *Response* to, and *Observation* about, the text concerned and these two elements operate interchangeably and recursively. Quite often in fact, the genre offers more Response than Observation, as is true of Text 3.1 to be examined below. The review genre has three elements: the *Context*, which provides essential contextual information about the text, its type of work (e.g. novel, play) and

Table 3.2 Schematic structures of personal response and review genres (after Rothery in New South Wales Department of School Education, Metropolitan East Region (1994))

Genre	Elements of structure
Personal response	Response/Evaluation
Review	Context
	Text Description
	Text Judgement

sometimes its setting; the *Text Description,* which introduces characters and some details of the plot; and the *Text Judgement,* which offers the writer's evaluation of the text. Rothery termed this last element the 'Judgement', but we have chosen to use the term 'Text Judgement', to avoid confusion with the term 'Judgement', also used as an aspect of the values recognized in the Appraisal system.

The typical schematic structure of a review has the merit that it gives direction and order to the manner in which the apprentice writer may go about the writing task. While such a claim can be made for the schematic structure of any genre, it holds for the review because the writing of this can prepare the apprentice writer for what is organizationally the more ambitious task in later years, of abstracting away from the text(s) discussed and offering generalizations and or abstractions about them. Details of context and plot are marshalled in an orderly way in the review before a judgement is offered. Beyond the review, the other response genres (character analyses and thematic interpretations) require rather different overall structures which call for an opening element that establishes broad overall directions and/or themes to be developed in later elements. Overwhelmingly, in these latter genres, it is the successful students who create a clear opening element and who build clear overall connectedness to the later elements. These matters will be explored more fully when we examine the other response genres.

A review of childhood

Text 3.1 is a review written by a girl aged 8/9. Two simple instances of positive Appreciation of the book are given, both realized in adjectives, the first in the Introduction, the other in the Text Judgement, where a reason is given for the value expressed, using a dependent clause of reason:

This book is brilliant // because it describes // how the characters feels.

The lexis generally is simple, while relational Processes build description:

*the book **is** about two sisters*

and material Processes build actions:

> *they **have to stop** their grandmother . . ..*

One clause of result occurs in the Description, as well as one of purpose, revealing that the writer already has some facility with using different clauses of expansion to develop her writing:

> *so they take their grandmother to the hair dresser* (dependent clause of result)
> *to wash it out . . .* (dependent clause of purpose).

The choice of the third person to thematize the book and/or characters in a series of unmarked Theme choices (apart from one reference to *I*) helps build a sense of the writer distancing herself from the book being appraised. The young writer has one instance of a nominal group expanded with an embedded clause:

> *two sisters [[who dyed their grandmother's hair blue // without her knowing it.]]*

Overall, the child reveals a clear sense of the purpose of a review, even using appropriate technical lexis:

> *characters; chapter book,*

and offering a recommendation which uses a modal verb:

> *I **would** recommend it to children my age,*

though such verbs are not commonly part of the written language of children so young.

Text 3.1   A review of *Blue Hair Day*

Publishing details	*Title: 'Blue Hair Day'* *Author: James Maloney* *Year: 2003* *Place: Sydney*
Introduction	*I read 'Blue Hair Day' by James Maloney. It is a chapter book. 'Blue Hair Day' is a <u>fantastic</u> book for young children. The illustrator is Leigh Hobbs.*
Description	*This story is about two sisters [[who dyed their grandmother's hair blue // without her knowing it.]] They have to stop their grandmother finding out they dyed her hair so they take grandmother to the hair-dresser to wash it out before it is too late.*
Text Judgement	*This book is <u>brilliant</u> because it describes how the characters feel. I would recommend it to children my age.*

A personal response of late childhood

Text 3.2 discusses the children's novel, *Rowan of Rin*, by the Australian writer Emily Rodda. It uses a series of unmarked topical Themes, several identifying the writer or something of his (*my favourite character*), while its experiential resources involve mental, material and relational Processes. The evaluative lexis is simple, though the range is greater than that of Text 3.1, and this probably reflects the fact the child was a little older, while in varying ways the attitude is heightened, using intensity. Thus, while the evaluative lexis mainly involves adjectives, one familiar lexical metaphor is used:

he always looked on the bright side.

The text reveals positive feelings or Affect about the book:

I liked the book,

and positive Appreciation of its features:

it was well written; my favourite character,

while reasons are given for the positive evaluation of the character, using two dependent clauses of reason:

*My favourite character was Allun // because he was merry // and
(because he) always looked on the bright side.*

Positive Judgement of the writer is given:

Emily Rodda thought of some good ways . . .,

and the writer offers some comparative Judgement about himself and his capacities:

*I would never have thought of putting a stick in the bog to see which way
was safe.,*
and overall there is a sense of amplifying the evaluations made, as for example in:

that would have been lots of fun

Writing of the secondary English programme, Rothery (New South Wales Department of School Education, Metropolitan East Region 1994: 149) argued with some justice that personal response genres are 'depowering' because they ask the student to do no more than offer personal feelings about a text, when English in fact rewards language skills that explain the text, and ideally discuss

---

Text 3.2   *Rowan of Rin* – Emily Rodda

Response/ Observation	I liked this book *and I think it was well written. Emily Rodda was very clever writing the verses and making them fit in. My favourite character was Allun because he was merry and always looked on the bright side. I think Emily Rodda thought of some good ways [[to get up the mountain.]] I would never have thought of [[putting a stick in the bog to see which way was safe.]] My favourite part was [[when the ice cracked and Jon and Rowan went back to Rin.]] That would have been lots of fun.*

---

how it is constructed. We suggest that they may have some value in the primary years, though they should not constitute a major part of the secondary programme. Reviews provide a better model for developing students' evaluative capacities than do personal response texts.

A book review of late childhood

Text 3.3, a book review, has two elements, clearly labelled by the writer, and we have preserved these, since they were provided by the teacher to guide the young writer. As was true of Texts 3.1 and 3.2, the grammar in Text 3.3 is congruent. Apart from several unmarked Themes that identify the book or a character, the Synopsis has several marked Themes of time to signal the start of the stages in the tale. The Process choices realizing experiential information, while various, are for the most part material, constructing events:

*the book **starts** with Joe . . ..*
*he **meets** the Griffin.*

Text 3.3   *Strange Magic* by Elizabeth Beresford

Synopsis of story	*The book starts with Joe, a nine year old boy [[who is fairly shy]] going to visit his aunt Mrs Chatsworth. **While he is on his holiday** he meets the Griffin, a dog-like creature with wings, and finds out that the Griffin has to find some treasure before a certain time (in other words the Griffin has a time limit in Joe's world) which takes him through many adventures.*
	***After a couple of adventures** the Griffin and Joe come across a companion, Grace, which leads to many more wild adventures looking for the Griffin's treasure. **As the last minutes tick away** they find the treasure – some old blue china- in the attic above Mrs Chatsworth's house just before the Griffin has to leave. **After that** everything settles down and it becomes normal days again for Joe and Grace.*

In this element, as was true of Text 3.1, the writer positions himself as (re) teller of events before going on to appraise the book. He is in this sense somewhat removed from the book, in a manner akin to that in Text 3.1.

The second element reveals a rather mixed evaluative response to the book. It uses mainly unmarked Themes, though one marked example occurs, realized in a dependent clause of condition, revealing developing capacity to acknowledge and engage with, the attitudes of others:

> *If I were to recommend this book* // *I would recommend it to people who like to take their time*

Evaluative lexis – adjectives and at least one adverb (*clearly*) – contribute to the overall evaluation, while experientially, several relational Processes of attribution build description creating some positive Appreciation of the book:

> *'Strange Magic' is a good book for eight, nine year olds,*

though this is immediately qualified to some extent:

> *but not for ten, eleven years old because the language is very simple.*

A negative Judgement is offered about the writer:

> *the author can't express her ideas clearly, for example it was difficult to understand who Grace was,*

while a final expression of Affect reveals what the writer thought of the book overall:

> *But overall I can't say that I enjoyed it thoroughly.*

Text 3.3—Cont'd

Evaluation	*'Strange Magic' is a good book for eight, nine year olds but not for ten, eleven years old because the language is very simple. However, I feel that the author can't express her ideas clearly, for example it was difficult to understand who Grace was.* **If I were to recommend this book** *I would recommend it to people //who like to take their time //and ponder over //what the author has said.//* *I do like how the author gives a picture of what the characters are doing at a particular time. For example,* *'Mr Serafin was sitting in front of the window with his feet up on a stool and his hands clasped over his stomach. He had a large blue and white handkerchief over his face and as he breathed in and out the handkerchief went up and down . . . Mr Serafin snorted and*

> *the handkerchief blew right off his face and onto his waistcoat. Mr Serafin was*
> *very fat and quite bald, and sometimes Joe tried to work out where his forehead*
> *and his real head began' (p.6).*
> *But overall I can't say that I enjoyed it thoroughly.*

Two reviews of early adolescence

Texts 3.4 and 3.5 are reviews of a book and a film respectively, and they differ though their schematic structures are similar. The film review makes use of technical language to discuss how the film is made, while the book review confines itself to observations about the details of the characters and the events that shape their lives, offering no observations on the book's style. The difference reflects the relative paucity of a language for discussing literary texts as verbal art which can be a feature of the modern English classroom. Without a language for discussing the ways texts are constructed, students are confined to discussing the details of story and character. Films are an increasingly common aspect of the secondary English programme in Australia and the UK (Kress et al. 2005). Where they are taught, it seems that English teachers introduce a technical language. The reasons for the absence of a technical language in discussions of literary texts are complex, requiring a longer discussion than space allows. Suffice to note that students of English in contemporary secondary classrooms – in Australia at least – often have limited language resources for appraising the texts they read, because the models of English that prevail tend to stress personal feeling or 'empathetic response' (Macken-Horarik 2006) rather than a concern for the language in which attitudes and feelings are expressed. The result is that the book review, while dealing at some length with the details of the autobiographical book, *Sally's Story*, has little to say of the manner in which the book is written (though the writer notes that the book is an *autobiography*). The film review, by contrast, addresses aspects of story and film technique.

Developmentally, Text 3.4 displays many grammatical features consistent with those of a young writer in early adolescence, discussed in our previous chapter. The grammar is congruent, though some lexical metaphors appear:

Daisy and Gladys . . . **try to cover up** *. . . the fact that they are Aboriginal.*

The experiential resources expressed in dense nominal groups and prepositional phrases contribute to the relative density of the text, while Theme choices (two of which are marked) carry the discourse forward clearly. In Appraisal terms, the values expressed mainly realize Appreciation, some of it positive:

This is the story of Sally growing up in a close-knit family . . .

On two occasions the writer seeks to involve, and hence engage with, the reader when she uses the first person plural and a mental Process, building solidarity with her readers regarding the book:

> *we **learn** that family relationships are very important,*
> and
> *we **learn** how her father's war neurosis . . . . deeply affect her family.*

Text 3.4   Review of *Sally's Story* (extracts only)

Context	*'Sally's Story' by Sally Morgan is an autobiography about the life of an Aboriginal girl and her poor family, the Milroys, living in a Perth suburb [[called Manning]] during the 50's and 60's. This is the story of Sally [[growing up in a close-knit family and [[discovering her Aboriginal heritage and [[being proud of her background //while living in a community with racist attitudes]] In the story we learn that family relationships are very important to her, especially her maternal grandmother. We learn how her father's war neurosis and battle with alcohol deeply affect her family.*
Text Description (extract only)	*Sally Milroy lived with her family in a small suburban house. She was the eldest of five children. Her siblings were Jill, Bill, David and Helen. Her mother Gladys and her father Bill also shared their house with Gladys' mother, Daisy. **Throughout the story**, Daisy and Gladys, the 'Mothers' of the family, try to cover up, even from the children, the fact [[that they are Aboriginal]]. This was [[because during the 50's, being Aboriginal was an embarrassment.]]*

The general pattern is sustained for the remainder of the Text Description. Essentially, the text is about the feelings of Sally and her family, and the writer's disapproval of racist attitudes towards Aborigines is obvious. Some limited Appraisal of the book's qualities is offered. Thus, the Text Judgement, which is set out in full, reveals some Affect:

> *I enjoyed the book,*

and some Appreciation of its style:

> *this true story is written in an interesting way,*

while in the last sentence the writer again engages with the potential reader by offering advice that the text is *suitable* for some readers.

Text 3.4—Cont'd

Text Judgement   *I enjoyed this book, which gives the reader the idea of [[what it was like for Sally //growing up in a poor Aboriginal family in Perth during the 50's and 60's]]. This true story is written in an interesting way which helps us to understand the challenges [[faced by Sally and her family]]. 'Sally's Story' is suitable for readers [[that are looking for a rich, zesty, moving story [[to read]] or those [[who are interested in racial and cultural issues]].*

Text 3.5 is a review of *Who Framed Roger Rabbit?*, a movie made with a mixture of 'real life' characters and animation. The Context element is set out in full, and it uses unmarked Themes and various experiential resources to build descriptive statements about the film. Such resources include technical film language:

cartoon backdrops; live photography; animation; light and shadows,

revealing familiarity with some of the skills of film making. The opening element builds positive Appreciation of the film as a work of art, which is said to be made:

very cleverly,

while it has:

revolutionary animation.

Such artistic statements lead to an authoritative Judgement about the director and his capacities, for he is said to be:

award-winning,

Text 3.5   A review of *Who Framed Roger Rabbit?*

Context   *'Who framed Roger Rabbit'? is a combination of cartoon backdrops and characters and real backdrops and characters. It is done very cleverly; the cartoons were drawn and inserted after the live photography was shot. Its revolutionary animation included the use of light and shadows to produce a remarkably realistic effect and had the cartoon characters interact perfectly with the real objects and actors. Who Framed Roger Rabbit? won four Academy Awards in the year 1988. It is directed by award – winning Robert Zemeckis, and set in the year 1947.*

In using the third person the writer again distances herself from the film appraised, and this, together with her use of the technical lexis, gives an authoritative sense to the observations she makes. The lexis is reasonably rich, so that a great deal of the evaluative colouring given by this writer is distributed through the text, and found for example, in such expressions as:

a remarkably realistic effect

or

the cartoon characters interact perfectly with the real objects and actors.

In all of these instances the lexis used intensifies, building Graduation, hence 'scaling up' the values expressed.

An extract only can be produced from the Text Description, where the writer emphasizes the fact that the characters are *REAL*, though they are *still drawings*. . ., having *a strange human/animal element to them*, (and they) *even perform live . . ..*

Text 3.5—Cont'd

Text Description (extract only)	*It's a world where cartoons didn't have to be drawn repetitively in order to become real . . . they WERE REAL. They're still drawings and creations, but they have a <u>strange human/animal</u> element to them, and they even perform live or act in your typical short films.*

In the Text Judgement the writer uses the first person, and offers positive Appreciation of the film. Thus, giving authority to the claims for the excellence of the movie, the writer cites an apparently authoritative source (a website) to construct a Judgement. She then endorses it herself, offering Appreciation of some of the film qualities:

astonishing camera shots,

In addition, a sense of engaging with the potential viewers is suggested with the dependent clause of condition, acknowledging that viewers will have different needs and values:

*a kid of any age would love this movie, **even if they love it for different reasons**.*

Text 3.5—Cont'd

Text Judgement	*I think that this movie is <u>suitable</u> for both children and adults. There are jokes for children and those, 'Wink, wink. Nudge, nudge' ones that*

> *only the adults will understand. The plot is very easy to understand and*
> *the characters are very child friendly, – so a kid of any age would love this*
> *movie, even if they love it for different reasons.*
> *In my opinion, this is an excellent movie; the interaction between the*
> *cartoon characters and the real characters is unbelievable. On the website*
> *www.imdb.com/title/tt0096438 , they say 'Who framed Roger Rabbit?' is*
> *'nothing short of miraculous.' And I, personally, agree with them.*
> *The movie also included a great deal of astonishing camera shots and*
> *angles, which were expertly done. The people [[who were involved in this*
> *movie]] quite obviously have an amazing talent for what they do, and*
> *should continue doing it, because, in my opinion, they could go a long way*
> *(if they haven't already).*

Character analyses

Much earlier in this chapter, we noted that response genres such as character analyses and thematic interpretations have schematic structures whose opening element establishes the broad overall directions to be followed, and later elements are closely linked or interconnected with the opening. This helps give the text an overall sense of unity. A useful method for examining the overall organization of such texts will be discussed in Chapter 5, where we consider expository texts in history, and we examine notions of *macroTheme* and *hyper-Theme*, the former referring to an overarching thematic statement offered to open a text, the latter referring to later thematic statements (typically starting new paragraphs) which link back to the macroTheme. Sufficient to note here that successful students who write character analyses and thematic interpretations by mid- to late adolescence have grasped both the grammatical resources for creating generalization and abstraction and the schematic structures involved in writing such genres.

The tendency, at least among successful students, as they move away from reviews and towards character analyses, is to avoid providing too much plot detail, though offering enough to give some interpretation of character. The movement is towards generalization about character, but by implication at least, (and sometimes explicitly) it often leads to reflection about life. In consequence while all the attitudinal values continue to have relevance in response genres among older writers, Appreciation and Judgement in particular become important, for they are related at times, so that Appreciation of qualities found in texts can lead to Judgement about ethical principles for living. In developing the skills to reflect upon the values found in texts students must develop various interpretative capacities. Such skills require students to deploy their grammatical resources a little differently from the way they do in reviews. Among other matters, they must learn to distance themselves further from the text(s) involved and to demonstrate what texts 'show' or reveal of character and/or human values. Where 'showing' verbs sometimes realize verbal processes, though elsewhere they realize identifying processes, as we shall see.

Table 3.3   Schematic structure of character analyses

Genre	Elements of structure
Character Analysis	Character Presentation
	Character Description
	Character Judgement

Table 3.3 introduces the schematic structure for character analyses. The opening element of a character analysis is the *Character Presentation,* where the character of interest is introduced; the *Character Description* provides description of the character, where the skill is to do so by offering some interpretive details. The *Character Judgement* concludes by offering some final judgement about the character.

We will briefly consider extracts only from two character analyses, one an analysis of Atticus and Scout in Harper Lee's novel, *To Kill a Mockingbird,* the other of Antonio in *The Merchant of Venice.*

The opening element of Text 3.6 offers generalizations about the novel and about two of its central characters. In Appraisal terms, these create positive Appreciation of the characters and of the way they *hold our interest,* and then Judgement of the ethically correct nature of Atticus' behaviour in the book.

Text 3.6   A character analysis of Atticus and Scout in *To Kill a Mockingbird*

Character Presentation (extract only)	*To Kill a Mockingbird' by Harper Lee contains* believable *characters which we* can relate to *and characters who also* hold our interest. *Two* interesting *and* believable *characters are Atticus and Jean Louise Finch (Scout). Atticus Finch is a middle-aged lawyer who lives in Maycomb county in the 1930's with his two children Jem and Scout and Calpurnia – an African-American housekeeper. Atticus' main role in the novel is defending Tom Robinson – an African American man who* was wrongly accused *of raping a white woman. Atticus is also* a role model to his children and teaches them wisely and honestly *about the world [[in which they live]] Atticus is a* believable *character because* he has opinions [[that differ from the opinions of society]]. He is not racist or discriminatory like the majority of Maycomb's residents. "The one thing that doesn't abide by majority rule is a person's conscience".*

The lexis is attitudinally rich in expressions such as:

believable characters; role model; teaches them wisely and honestly.

In order to explore the proposition that the characters are *believable*, the writer relies on, and asserts, some culturally valued attitudes about parents who are:

good role models,

and have the courage to hold:

opinions [[that differ from the opinions of society]].

These assertions made, the writer goes on to develop support for them, and the language begins to reveal features not found in the reviews considered above, and not typically found among younger writers. That is because this writer has moved to offering interpretations of character in developmentally different ways. Thus, several verbs are used (realizing different processes), demonstrating how the writer interprets events and characters' reactions to them, the first in the Character Presentation, where the verb *show* creates an unusual relational Process of attribution,[2] used to suggest how an action of Atticus reveals an aspect of his character:

> *(Atticus) is compassionate and stands up for what he believes in, although he is not aggressive. This **shows** when confronted by the antagonist of the novel . . .*

Later in the Character Description (not displayed), a mental Process with a first person Participant actively engages the reader to share the view of Scout's world.

> *we **can see** that (Atticus) is a loving, caring and respectable father.*

Then, in the same element, another mental Process is used twice to interpret for the reader Scout's view of world:

> *(Scout) **realizes** that the world [[she lives in]] is harsh and unfair.*
> *(Scout) **realizes** that the majority of Maycomb is racist.*

This capacity to argue what texts and their events and/or characters' behaviours reveal, is an essential aspect of the interpretative tasks involved in writing response genres of the later years of adolescence. Text 3.7, about *The Merchant of Venice*, uses similar resources, though in other ways it differs from Text 3. 6. The Character Presentation in Text 3.7 offers a generalization about the character of Antonio and the play. Changes said to occur in *Antonio's character* are held to lead to Judgement about what *major themes* are in the play.

Text 3.7   A character analysis of Antonio from *The Merchant*
of Venice

Character **Presentation**	*In this essay I have chosen to do a character study of Antonio.* *I will discuss his changes in his character in the light of one of <u>he major</u>* *<u>themes in the play – reasoning and emotion.</u> In the play Antonio <u>let his</u>* *<u>emotion overrule his judgement, thus causing Shylock to let his</u>* *<u>judgement overrule his emotions, leaving it all to</u> Portia to bring emotion* *and reason together.*

The object of the Character Description is to provide detail about Antonio and
the other characters to support the generalization made. Hence this element
offers a claim, using a dependent clause of concession:

> **Although the play seems to centre around Antonio,** *in fact he has very little*
> *influence over the play as he is reliant upon Shylock's mercy.*

This is to set up one possible interpretation of the play's events with a view to over-
turning it. In this sense the writer commences an argument about Antonio and
from this position goes on to develop his case. In other words, he adopts an authorial stance, and from this stance he offers a positive Judgement about the character of Antonio, using strong evaluative lexis, which 'scales up' the values involved:

> *he is portrayed as a compassionate, generous, admired, beloved merchant.*

As was true in the culturally valued characteristics ascribed to Atticus, here the
reader, by implication, is invited to subscribe to, and hence engage with, the
values attributed to Antonio. It is notable too, that the young writer says of all
these qualities in Antonio that they *can be seen*, in a conversation not cited here
from the play. Like the writer of Text 3.5, this writer refers to what actions and
words 'reveal' of characters, as a part of building his case.

Text 3.7—Cont'd

Character **Description** (extract only)	*"The Merchant of Venice" is named after Antonio because everything* *revolves around him: can he pay the bond? will he lose his life? can* *he restore things back to normal? and so on. <u>Although the play seems to</u>* *<u>centre around Antonio, in fact he has very little influence over the play</u>* *<u>in general, as he is reliant upon Shylock's mercy and Portia's wit to</u>* *<u>decide whether he shall live or die.</u> Antonio is portrayed in the play as <u>a</u>* *<u>compassionate, generous, admired, beloved</u> merchant, as can be seen in* *the following conversation: (a quote follows)*

The Character Description is developed further, making extensive use of quotations from the play (too many in fact, so that the associated discussion is a little under-developed). Space will not allow that we display these. Instead, we shall select from the Character Description, noting the success with which the opening marked Theme is realized in a clause of purpose, guiding the reader's understanding, while the subsequent sentence uses a showing Process (*shows*) to help elaborate the general argument being made:

> **To enable Bassanio to win Portia**, *he will himself pay interest on a loan, rather than let his best friend lose his dearest hopes. This* **shows** *how [[Antonio's emotion has erased rational thinking]].*

Here the process realized in 'shows' is held to be relational identifying, because the Participant 'this' is held to be Token for (or evidence for) the notion that Antonio has lost rational thought (the Value).

Finally, having reviewed other aspects of the play and the character of Antonio, the writer produces his Character Judgement, in which he makes a strong assertion about what he has *shown*, where the process is a verbal one, with which the writer is declaring his position:

Text 3.7—Cont'd

Character Judgement   *Through this character study of Antonio* **I have shown** *how Antonio changes through the play- from <u>over-generous</u> at the beginning, to <u>depressed</u> when his ships are lost, to <u>relieved</u> at the end. Although his emotions guided him in the predicament, <u>Portia was able to get him out of it through her wits and cunning logic.</u>*

Statements such as that in the first sentence, particularly involving use of the verbal Process *show*, represent strong propositions of a kind that do not admit qualification or challenge. They are used by writers who wish to 'proclaim' a position in terms that 'suppress or rule out alternatives' (Martin and White 2005: 98). The interpretative response genres of late adolescence require capacity to offer such strong statements.

Thematic interpretations

Thematic interpretations bear some relationship to character analyses, since they are topologically closely related. The difference is that while character(s) may be evaluated as part of pursuing the overall theme in the text being written, it is this theme, rather than an interest in character, that is the primary

Table 3.4 Schematic structure of thematic interpretations

Genre	Elements of structure
Thematic interpretation	Thematic Interpretation/Preview of Elements
	Element Evaluation
	Reiteration of Theme

motivation for the response genre that is written. Table 3.4 displays the schematic structure for thematic interpretations.

In the *Thematic Interpretation/Preview of Elements*, a main theme is stated and the elements (essentially evidence) to be examined in its support are indicated. In the *Element Evaluation*, as the name suggests, the various arguments adduced in support of the theme are discussed and since there are generally several, this element is recursive. The final element – the *Reiteration of Theme* – reconfirms the overall theme.

Of the three we have selected to examine, Text 3.8 is not completely successful, though it has some features making it of interest to this discussion. Some of these features are like those of a character analysis, in that it identifies characters and evaluates their actions, though the difference is that it offers an overall evaluation of the novel and its themes, rather than dealing only with the characters. The discourse in the opening element is quite abstract, much of it

---

Text 3.8 *The Curious Incident of the Dog in the Night-time*

Theme identification/
Preview of elements

Mark Haddon's novel The Curious Incident Of The Dog In The Night-time DEMONSTRATES *that people's perceptions of the world are often hindered by a lack of understanding and empathy. Christopher's individual perception of his ideal world was uniquely displayed in the novel. The novel explored many relationships of deception between characters as well as false illusions. These relationships DEMONSTRATED the physical, psychological and emotional aspects of the characters' worlds, including perceptions and understandings between characters. There were many barriers between characters [[that hindered their relationships and understanding of particular situations [[that were occurring around them]]]. Ed acted as a barrier that intercepted between Christopher and his mother Judy and hindered their relationship and Judy's impatient and low tolerated personality* kept her from an understanding and empathizing with the son. Though many characters* DID NOT SHOW *the quality of empathy, Christopher displayed sincere empathy when he held Wellington in his arms after he had been killed.*

* The student presumably meant the character had a low tolerance or was intolerant

building Judgement about the ethics of certain behaviours, and it is notable that three showing Processes (displayed) are used to suggest what the story 'reveals'.

Abstract nominal groups abound in the text, some using grammatical metaphor, and creating abstract participants:

people's perceptions of the world; a lack of understanding and empathy.

Apart from the relational identifying Processes, as in:

Mark Haddon's novel . . . . DEMONSTRATES [[that people's perceptions of the world are often hindered by a lack of understanding and empathy]],

abstract material Processes suggest metaphorically how the novel examines characters:

*The novel **explored** many relationships of deception between characters as well as false illusions*
*Christopher's individual perception . . . was uniquely **displayed** in the novel.*

and

*Christopher **displayed** sincere empathy when he held Wellington . . ..*

Subsequent elements in the text seek to take up matters relevant to exploring the overall theme, not all of them always well handled. The first Element Evaluation, for example, commences with the claim, challenged by the teacher, for it is in fact difficult to sustain:

Perceptions of the world are usually distorted by false illusions and lies.

In other ways, Text 3.7 displays awkward expressions at times, reflecting the fact that the writer was still learning to control her written language. We need look at it no further.

The two remaining thematic interpretations are rather different in character, for they both require that the writers address more than one text, in the name of a selected theme given them, in Text 3.9 by the teacher, and in Text 3.10, as part of a public examination in New South Wales. The exercise involved in the writing of Text 3.9 was no doubt intended as preparatory to developing the skills needed at the public examination. The English programme involved (New South Wales Board of Studies 2007) adopts overarching themes, in the name of which students study a range of different texts. About this more will be said below when we consider Text 3.10.

Text 3.9 examines what the teacher had referred to as 'Gothic' themes, and students were asked to 'compare how the two composers of the two texts, Mary

Shelley's *Frankenstein* and the animated television series, *Buffy the Vampire Slayer,* used the Gothic to convey their stories'. We set out here the opening element of Text 3.9. The text begins with a rhetorical question regarding *elements of the Gothic genre* in the two texts, followed by an assertion that there are *many techniques* used to create the texts while *four main elements* are provided in summary. Each of these is later discussed in detail in the next stage in the schematic structure. Positive Appreciation of the qualities of the two texts is particularly at issue, and of their *two composers.*

Text 3.9   'Gothic themes in *Frankenstein* and *Buffy the Vampire Slayer*'

Theme identification/ **Preview of elements**	*How have both Joss Whedon and Mary Shelley effectively used elements of the Gothic genre to add meaning and characterize their tales? There are many techniques used by both composers which can be compared and used to answer such a question. Four main elements I will outline and compare are: the use of strong emotions, dramatic tension, the use of a typical evil and good theme and also the use of strange and mysterious realms. These elements I believe have been used effectively by both composers and have resulted in two very different and yet in some ways the same, compositions.*

Primarily this is a statement about the Gothic qualities said to attach to two works of art. In referring to the *four main elements* claimed to be involved in constructing the two texts, the writer has established his overarching macroTheme, around which the subsequent text will unfold through its stages. In each stage, the writer pursues each of the elements that have been foreshadowed.[4] Each is introduced so that a reference is made back to the opening stage in the text, displayed above, while also looking forward to what is to come. The skill is in offering first a statement of the Element, and then providing detail from the texts to support it. Once again, it is interpretation that is at issue, this time in the light of the overall theme of *the gothic,* and in a manner that echoes some of the linguistic resources noted above in Texts 3.6 and 3.7, the writer employs mental and verbal Processes to indicate how WE CAN SEE matters that illustrate the theme. The first Element is reproduced in full, and only extracts from the others are given. We have identified the instances where the reader is told what we CAN SEE or what we are SHOWN or OBSERVE, or what is IMPRESSED UPON US. These are all of critical importance in guiding the reader's interpretation, and are indicated.

Text 3.9—Cont'd

Element 1	*In both **Buffy the Vampire Slayer** and **Frankenstein**,* WE CAN SEE *examples of strong emotions used throughout. Spike's love for Drusilla causes him to take <u>dramatic measures and risk even his own life to benefit her</u>. **Also, in the episode 'Some assembly required' [[which copied the Frankenstein theme]],** WE CAN SEE the love between the monster and his incomplete wife. **In Frankenstein** <u>strong</u> emotions form a large point of the story in allowing us to engage in the book by reading of the <u>intense</u> emotions between characters. "Hateful day when I received life" (p. 133) were the writings of the monster in Frankenstein,* SHOWING *us the depression and sadness [[which is a critical part of the gothic genre]].*
Element 2	*Dramatic tension also plays a large part in both compositions, <u>enthralling the audience and enticing us to hang on</u> to every word of the story to discover the leadings of such drama. **In both Frankenstein and Buffy,** WE OBSERVE a classic 'damsel in distress' theme. **In the episode 'School hard',** Buffy is the saviour and the hero to her friends and mother, however, in Frankenstein, the 'damsel', being either Clerval or Elizabeth, was not saved as is accustomed to such a setting, this however further* IMPRESSES UPON US *the Gothic elements of disappointment sadness and horror.*
Element 3	*One of the main elements of both Buffy and Frankenstein [[which obviously classifies the compositions as 'Gothic']] is the use of a 'good and evil' theme. The appearance of heroes and villains in both puts forward this theme, and it is added to by the classic struggle between the two for domination . . . . <u>although Frankenstein struggles to undo evil, he himself created such horror and is unable [[to save the ones [[he loves]]]]</u>.* WE CAN SEE *this in <u>the death of innocents</u> such as William, Clerval, Justine and Elizabeth.*
Element 4	*The use of strange realms and unusual settings in both compositions also plays a <u>vital</u> role in the classification of both under the Gothic genre. **In the episode 'School Hard'** Buffy climbs into the roof to reach others **and in the episode 'Some assembly required'** WE WERE WITNESS TO dark dungeons [[in which experiments were carried out of <u>the most gruesome manner</u>]]. Also **in Frankenstein** there is lots of travel to unknown realms and many locations such as the ice caves, where* WE SEE *the Gothic setting helping to influence the feel of the story.*

Apart from the many instances where the writer interprets the text by engaging the reader with what is SHOWN or what we CAN SEE, various abstract material Processes help build the sense of an interpretation of events:

*In Frankenstein strong emotions **form** a large point of the story . . .*

*Dramatic tension also **plays** a large part in both compositions,*

*One of the main elements of both Buffy and Frankenstein which obviously **classifies** the compositions as 'Gothic' . . ..*

*The use of strange realms and unusual settings in both compositions also **plays** a vital role in the classification of both under the Gothic genre.*

The text concludes, bringing together the various elements examined, reconfirming the qualities with which WE CAN SEE how the Gothic has been used in the two texts.

Text 3.9—Cont'd

Reiteration of Theme	*Overall the use of Gothic genre in both compositions HELPS US TO UNDERSTAND better the happenings of the works. The Gothic genre is used effectively by both Joss Whedon and Mary Shelley to add empathy and further meaning to their compositions. Both stories are made more interesting and more engaging through the use of such Gothic elements as I have explained. **After reading Frankenstein and viewing Buffy** WE CAN SEE how these Gothic elements have changed the way || that both compositions are experienced by the audience||.*

Text 3.10, the examination script, is the longest text examined in this chapter and it cannot be reproduced in full.[5] While it bears some relationship to Text 3.9, it is by an older writer and it reveals a level of abstraction not found in the latter. To some extent, of course, this reflects the nature of the task, which we briefly explain. Over the period 2005–07, later extended to cover 2006–08 (New South Wales Board of Studies 2006) a major *Area of Study* was established as part of the senior English syllabus, devoted to *The Journey*, taken up by all students. A number of texts are studied, some drawn from the literary canon, such as *The Tempest*, others of a factual rather than literary character such as Melvyn Bragg's *On Giants' Shoulders*, others being films like *Life is Beautiful*, and poetry by Robert Frost and many others. The mix is deliberately eclectic, and it reflects the influence of cultural studies, whose interest in popular culture, initially well intended, has often been to trivialize much educational endeavour (Maton 2006). We have considerable reservations about the English studies involved, documented elsewhere (Christie and Humphrey 2008), since the themes adopted are often rather facile, and the actual engagement with the texts is often superficial. Nonetheless, since students must now write such texts, it is important that we examine them for what they reveal of writing development. In fact, many of the observations we have now made about the language abilities required for writing in late adolescence, as in Text 3.9, hold true for Text 3.10.

The notion of *The Journey* is intended to capture some sense of a transformative journey experienced by the student in studying the selected texts. It may be understood as an 'imaginative journey', a 'physical journey' or an 'inner journey'. The writer of Text 3.10 chose the imaginative journey. The wording of the question makes clear that it is the overriding theme that is of concern for evaluative purposes, and the evaluation offered must reflect on the lessons learned by the student:

> *To what extent has studying the concept of imaginative journeys expanded your understanding of yourself, of individuals and of the world?*

In answering this, students were asked to consider at least three texts, two of which were prescribed, and one was of their own choice.

In a rhetorically clever move the writer of Text 3.10, well aware of the metaphor involved, generalizes about the *Journey* in her opening element, when she declares that:

> *The journey, especially in the imaginative sense, is a process [[by which the traveller encounters a series of challenges, tangents and serendipitous discoveries // to arrive finally, at a destination and/or transformation.]]*

This is a definition, and it becomes the central organizing theme (the macroTheme) around which the text is written. Moreover, the lexis carries rich evaluative significance, so that attitude is diffused throughout the text. One further point of some significance is the manner in which the texts to be discussed are said to *SHOW* benefits claimed for the *Journey*, where the writer uses strategies like the writer of Text 3.9:

> *Melvyn Bragg's* (work) . . . *SHOWS how individuals can influence others* . . . while *the importance of self growth* (revealed in a Japanese film) *has increased my understanding of myself,* (and Frost's' poem) *has increased my understanding of myself.*

Text 3.10 *The Journey*

Theme identification/ Element preview	*Studying the concept of imaginative journeys has expanded my understanding of myself, of individuals and of the world in several ways. The journey, especially in the imaginative sense, is <u>a process [[by which the traveller encounters a series of challenges, tangents and serendipitous discoveries //to arrive finally, at a destination and/or transformation.]]</u>* **In the context of individual journeys,** *Melvyn Bragg's depiction of science as a collective journey in* On Giants' Shoulders *SHOWS <u>how individuals can influence others and mankind through their journeys</u>. The importance of self growth as a result [[of overcoming obstacles //as highlighted in the Japanese anime,* Spirited Away,]] *has increased my understanding of myself, with this transformation portrayed on a global or universal scale in Robert Frost's* The Road Not Taken.

The next stage is the longest and it is here that the selected texts are evaluated, each in turn. We shall reproduce only extracts, drawn from each Element, noting that the behaviours of scientists (Element 1), the central *persona* in the Japanese film (Element 2), and of the poet Robert Frost (Element 3) are very much to the fore. In all these elements, aesthetic statements about the works reviewed (Appreciation) tend to lead to reflection on what the writer has learned about herself and her life (Judgement).

Text 3.10   The Imaginative Journey

Element 1   On Giants' Shoulders *depicts the individual lives and achievements of 12 scientists as a collective imaginative journey over the last 2500 years.* **In portraying their separate profiles as one story in a chronological line up,** *Bragg delineates <u>the concept of a cumulative and ongoing journey</u>, reflected in his thesis[[that science is 'an extended kind of continuous investigation']]. It is through this that <u>I personally have learned the importance of individuals interlinking with others to achieve a greater end, and influencing or inspiring others, as inherent in the concept of scientists standing on 'giants' shoulders'.</u>*

Element 2   Spirited Away *offers a more personal lesson in regards to the concept of journeys, through the transformation of a persona who overcomes obstacles in the course of her journey. The medium of Japanese anime is particularly <u>pertinent</u> for imaginative journeys because of its <u>fantastical</u> possibilities and ability to remove the responder from everyday inhibitions . . . . . . This text <u>widened my scope in understanding myself, as it views challenges not as obstacles, but as opportunities for growth through testing and awareness of actions.</u>*

Element 3   **On a more global or universal scale,** *however, Robert Frost's* The Road Not Taken *was most <u>valuable</u> for study. This poem encompasses an imaginative journey in terms of retrospection and an inner one as well. The text pivots on the conceptual metaphor of life as a journey, and therefore, symbols and metaphors play a <u>central</u> role in conveying Frost's meaning. . . . . . . The reflective and reminiscent tone of the last stanza <u>confirms</u> the <u>value</u> of the journey[[that 'made all the difference']], and conveyed <u>to me, personally, the importance of experience, and to a certain degree, risk taking in my journey of life in this world.</u>*

Like Text 3.9, Text 3.10 uses a number of abstract material Processes to indicate what is revealed in the texts:

On Giants' Shoulders **depicts** *the individual lives and achievements . . ..*
In **portraying** *their separate profiles as one story in a chronological line up,*
Bragg **delineates** *the concept of a cumulative and ongoing journey,*
reflected *in his thesis that science is 'an extended kind of continuous investigation'.*
This poem **encompasses** *an imaginative journey . . .*
The text **pivots** *on the conceptual metaphor of life as a journey . . .*

Overwhelmingly Text 3.10 deals in abstract observations about life, as that is revealed in the texts studied and appraised.

The final element, the Reiteration of Theme, is a statement about what the writer has learned of some culturally valued principles for living, concerning such matters as the importance of addressing *challenges* faced in life, or being part of *a great quest in the search for collective knowledge*, though there are others. Such values, by the way, while no doubt laudable, are culturally very widely accepted in an English-speaking culture, so that here, as in the other response genres we have discussed, the student endorses and promotes some well established ethical positions.

Text 3.10—Cont'd

| Reiteration of Theme | *Thus, the study of the concept of the imaginative journey has expanded my understanding __significantly__ of myself as defined through challenges: of individuals as part of a __great__ quest in the search for collective knowledge; and of the world as an experience [[not to be missed]]. It is __equally significant__, also, that the journey's power [[to explore endless possibilities // and offer obstacles]] paves the way to the aforesaid rewards- whether they be tangible or intangible, real or imagined.* |

Text 3.10 is the most abstract of the response genres we have examined, and while the writer seems at times to 'over write' as in the final sentence, whose meaning is actually not very clear, the rhetorical structure overall is very cleverly constructed.

Lexical density in the response genres sampled

Figure 3.2 displays lexical density in the response genres we have sampled. Even the response genres of childhood, like Texts 3.1 and 3.2, achieve a lexical density of about 3. Beyond that, in late childhood to adolescence, they reach densities that vary somewhat, so that Text 3.4, for example, written by a student aged 12/13 years, has a density count of 6, while the next three – Texts 3.5, 3.6 and 3.7 – hover around 4 or a little over. The last three – those of late adolescence – have high counts, the final one, Text 3.10, being particularly dense with a count of 8.9. Halliday's general advice, earlier noted, was that the typical density level for written English falls between 3 and 6, depending on the formality of the text.

What is of interest here is that while the general shift in density that we remarked in Chapter 2 with respect to stories also occurs in the writing of response genres, the tendency is for response genres to be generally denser than narratives or recounts. Thus, the first story we examined in Chapter 2, Text 2.1, had a density of 2.6, lower than the earliest response genre, though

School Discourse

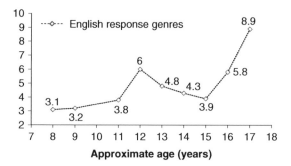

FIGURE 3.2   Lexical density in a sample of response genres

the first narrative (Text 2.2), which was very short, had a density that was more or less in accord with the early response genres. Around late childhood to early adolescence, with the exception of Text 3.4, the counts are not dissimilar, while by mid-adolescence, they are generally greater, and by late adolescence, the highest density count (Text 3.10) is greater than that for the story by a student of a similar age (Text 2.9), whose count was 3.7. The highest count for a narrative, by a student aged 14/15 was 7. The differences reflect differences in fields and in genres: texts that appraise other texts use denser lexis than do many stories, for the fields appear to require this, while the particular preoccupations with evaluation create very abstract genre types.

Conclusion

This chapter has reviewed developmental processes in learning to write response genres. The developmental processes discussed parallel those considered with respect to the writing of stories in Chapter 2. There is a movement from early grammatically congruent texts towards more non-congruent texts across the years of late childhood to mid-adolescence and beyond. Since response texts involve expressions of attitude with respect to other texts (both verbal and visual), we have chosen to review the developmental process with particular reference to the resources of Appraisal. Early response writing normally involves simple Affect, though Appreciation (to do with the qualities of texts) and Judgement (to do with writers, or sometimes their characters) can also appear in early texts, expressed in simple lexis, such as adjectives. By late childhood to early adolescence, when the range of available language resources has begun to enlarge, children show greater versatility to realize aspects of Appreciation of texts and of Judgement, either of writers, or of the values their characters represent, while Affect, though not lost, is less common. As the available lexical resources – at least in successful writers – grow richer and more varied, more nuanced value positions emerge, such that appreciation of the aesthetic qualities of texts is often blended with – or alternatively, leads to – judgements about ethics and principles for living.

Notes

[1] At the time of writing this chapter, two Australian researchers, Wendy Morgan and Mary Macken-Horarik, were researching and describing other types of response genres produced by senior students studying English at an advanced level, though they had yet to produce any publications about them. The texts emerged after work in an English syllabus in the state of Queensland that sought to develop a range of alternative reader positions in response to selected sets of texts, verbal and visual. While different in character from the thematic interpretations discussed in this chapter, their linguistic patterns reveal similar capacities for abstract expression of experience.

[2] Certain relational Processes – which can be realized in a variety of lexical verbs – have the character of conflating process and Attribute, for example, 'it smells', 'it counts', 'it shows'.

[3] Relational identifying processes are quite various, and they are realized in many lexical verbs. (Halliday and Matthiessen 2004, 234–5). The relationship set up in such processes is that of Token and Value, where in many cases two nominal groups are involved. However, in this case the Value is expressed in an embedded clause.

[4] The text has been discussed in some detail in Christie and Dreyfus 2007.

[5] Extracts from the text are reproduced with the kind permission of the student who wrote it, Ms Jenny Lee. A longer discussion of the text may be found in Christie and Humphrey 2008.

Chapter 4

Reconstructing the Past: Recording and Describing Historical Events

Introduction

Chapters 4 and 5 will trace developments in learning the linguistic resources needed to reason as a historian, and hence to perform successfully in school history at different stages. The two chapters sit between the chapters on English and on Science. This is not entirely accidental as history has been torn between the humanities and the sciences from its early beginnings. As this has a bearing on the expectations placed upon students caught up in the 'history wars', we will spend some time on the Janus-headed nature of history before looking at how it is recontextualized in schools.

When history entered the academy as a discipline in the 19th century, it argued for a place as a science alongside the natural sciences. Ranke, in the early 19th century, for example, was influential in proposing that history involved a disciplinary procedure dealing with archivally-based scholarship in a critical, strictly accurate and 'colourless' manner, documenting 'the past as it actually occurred' (Gilderhus 2003: 46). While this more positivist view persisted throughout the decades, other historians such as Ranke's student Burkhardt and his contemporary Nietzsche saw history not as an objective reporting of 'the facts' but as necessitating interpretation, judgement and even a creative leap (Curthoys and Docker 2006: 71–5). Scientific history, it was suggested by Beard (1934: 225), was unable to account for history's 'imponderables, immeasurables and contingencies', for it is not subject to the same principles of investigation, and the phenomena it studies are not capable of such investigation. It was acknowledged that historians bring to the act of interpretation their own prejudices, retrospective understandings and world-views. Among other matters, this has led to recent debates over who owns history (Clendinnen 2006) while the postmodernist turn promotes a problem-atized, self-conscious 'New history', recognizing many truths and many voices, and perhaps therefore no 'final truths'. Curthoys and Docker (2006) see this 'doubleness of history' as part of history's very nature:

Western historical writing possesses a doubleness that means it is always as it were off-balance; it exists in a strange, often contradictory and confused, space between history as rigorous scrutiny of sources and history as part of the world of literary forms. (2006: 116)

On the one hand, history is seen by some as one of the liberal arts: the study of human beings, with all their unpredictability and individual motivations. On the other hand, others propose what are deemed stringent historical methodologies in order to produce a systematic body of knowledge based on careful examination of source material, logical analysis and attention to reliability and validity. In this view, while history, unlike science, is not amenable to the construction of universal laws based on repeatable experimentation and with the ability to predict future outcomes, it nonetheless obtains knowledge by chains of reasoning from sources, using trained judgement to investigate provenance and authorship and ascertain the meaning, reliability and veracity of sources (Macintyre and Clark 2003).

At the level of school history, our data contains traces of all the above positions: history as a collection of undisputed facts woven into a stable grand narrative peopled with key historical figures; history as the struggle of minorities; history as the story of local, familiar individuals and contexts; history as a chain of simple, self-evident cause-and-effect sequences; history as the complex interaction of entangled factors; history as the exacting interrogation of sources of evidence; history as plurivocal and contested.

As a result of this, as suggested earlier, history can be understood as a study with 'horizontal knowledge structures' (Bernstein 1999), meaning that it proliferates many discourses, many topics and many methods for dealing with the social events and movements that constitute its general terms of reference. In such a situation, knowledge is 'segmented' (Maton 2007), creating topics and discourses that are not closely related as in the hierarchical knowledge structures found in science, to be discussed in Chapters 6 and 7. In this sense, history is closer to subject English than to science, and as we shall seek to demonstrate, for school purposes, it produces a range of text types, some more closely related than others, their collective effect, while intended to apprentice students into history, leading to a variety of ways to address historical events and to reason about them.

History as a school subject

In early childhood schooling, history-related activities involve simple recording and/or description of events, and the events recorded are often personal and to do with immediate experience. By late childhood to early adolescence some capacity to deal with experience beyond the immediate emerges, so that children can research and record historical sequences of events apart from those in which they have participated: to this extent they become more detached, able to produce some sustained sequences of events, while reflecting on causes and effects in history. They also show emerging skills in description of historical sites and/or periods of history.

Some empathetic understanding of human actions and behaviour appears in writing history by late childhood to adolescence, and attitudinal expression becomes more important as students develop, for it is necessary to the interpretive skills that are valued in historical studies in the secondary years. By adolescence, history has generally become a discrete subject in the curriculum, and among other matters, students are required 'to demonstrate an understanding of chronology through an increasing awareness that the past can be divided into different periods of time' (Qualifications and Curriculum Authority, UK: *History at Key Stage 3* (Unit 1: What's it all about? ND p. 1)). Students are expected to research and write about events and issues in the often remote past in a reasonably dispassionate manner. Interpretation of events and their consequences becomes important, and students are required to provide evidence for historical arguments, often demonstrating an understanding of conflicting views, while reflecting on the ethical and moral implications of events and actions in history (New South Wales Board of Studies HSC History Extension Stage 6 Syllabus, 1999).

Figure 4.1 provides a topological account of a representative range of genres of history from childhood to adolescence, though it is not suggested that the full range of potential history genres is covered. The progression outlined in Figure 4.1 builds on and extends developmental accounts and descriptions provided by Martin (2002), Coffin (1997, 2006a) and Martin and Rose (2003, 2008) whose pioneering contribution is gratefully acknowledged.

In this chapter, we shall identify two families of history genres found in childhood to early adolescence, both of which we shall suggest are foundational in history studies. The first is a *chronological* group including *recounts, empathetic autobiographies, biographical recounts* and *historical recounts*[1] and *accounts*. The other family consists of *non-chronological genres*, including *site* and *period studies*. (Other non-chronological genres found in adolescence, alluded to here, will be considered more fully in Chapter 5.) The chronological group help build a capacity to (re)construct sequences of events in time, of the kind that we introduced in Chapter 2 with respect to English. Empathetic recounts have the same schematic structure as the recounts of personal experience, though they involve children in writing empathetically of the lives of persons in history, imaginatively creating aspects of the past. Biographical recounts depict significant events in the life story of a key historical figure. Historical recounts chronicle a sequence of past events regarded as historically important. Historical accounts, in addition to recording events in an historical sequence, identify causal links between them. Biographical recounts, historical recounts and accounts are all described by Coffin (2006a).

The non-chronological genres of site and period studies occur frequently in our corpus, though they have not received much attention in other studies.[2] The former refers to texts that identify a site of some historical significance, revealing some of its important features. The latter refers to texts that take a period of history and describe the character of the period, though there is no attempt to build a sense of temporal event within the period. Both site and period studies investigate and document aspects of sites and periods significant for their historical qualities, thus creating an awareness of the need to understand historical contexts and to describe them adequately. Where the chronologically constructed texts involve temporal sequence of events, and later some sense of cause and effect, the site and period studies are essentially descriptive, and while they pose some challenge in terms of how to order the descriptive detail, they are grammatically simpler than the chronologically ordered texts.

As students grow older, they learn to handle more than sequence of events in time, simple causation and simple description, for they move to explanation, discussion and argument. The genres involved in these activities include: *site interpretations,* which interpret the significance of an historical site; *factorial* and *consequential explanations,* whose purpose is to explain historical change; and *expositions* which involve writers in taking a stance and arguing an historical issue. Finally, in the senior years, students of history need to develop historiographical skills, testing and evaluating the reliability and truthfulness of various historical sources, leading to examples of *historiographical exposition* and *discussion.* All these will be considered in Chapter 5.

Figure 4.1 attempts to summarize the shifts in learners' control of the genres of history canvassed in these two chapters, first from the chronologically ordered recounts of early childhood to those that offer some simple sense of cause and effect, and second from the non-chronologically ordered explorations of historical settings in time and space of childhood to the more complex genres of interpretation and explanation in mid-adolescence, and finally to various types of argumentation in later adolescence.

Writing history from childhood to early adolescence

From childhood through to early adolescent writing of history, we can observe general developments in language growth similar to those outlined in the previous chapters.

With regard to experiential meanings, there is a move from predominantly material and relational Processes to a greater range of Process types realized in more complex verbal groups, representing a greater range of tense choices;

	Early Primary	Mid Primary	Late Primary	Early Secondary	Mid Secondary	Late Secondary
	(6–8 yrs)			(9–12 yrs)	(13–15 yrs)	(16–18 yrs)
Chronological	Recount of personal experience		Empathetic autobiography	Historical account		
			Biography			
Non-chronological			Period study		Factorial explanation; Consequential explanation	
			Site study		Site interpretation	
Rhetorical					History exposition and discussion	
						Historiographical exposition and discussion
	Chapter 4				Chapter 5	

FIGURE 4.1 Development in control of the genres of history from early primary to late secondary

a shift from simple nominal groups to those containing a variety of modifying elements, including complex embeddings; and progression from an emphasis on Circumstances of time and place to a much richer array of circumstantial information realized both in adverbs and rich prepositional phrases. Most importantly we see the emergence of grammatical metaphor by late childhood to adolescence, which greatly expands the young adolescent's meaning potential, allowing the writer, for example, to construe time and cause within the clause rather than being restricted to congruent realizations between clauses. For the purpose of writing history in particular, the developmental pattern from childhood to adolescence involves steady emergence of capacity to (re)construct the historical past in increasingly abstract ways, learning to generalize about movements, trends, even long periods of time, laying the foundation for interpretation and argument in later adolescence.

Relationships between clauses show development from simple combinations of clauses of equal status towards more intricate clause interdependencies by early adolescence. The range of dependent clause types expands, moving from those of time and reason to those of manner, purpose, result and condition, while non-finite clauses (sometimes in Theme position) and non-defining relative clauses also emerge by late childhood. All such developments are potentially available to use in creating the history genres of secondary experience, though how the various resources are deployed depends on the genre type concerned.

Interpersonally there is a shift from very simple evaluation in childhood towards greater and more varied evaluation in late childhood to adolescence. Simple expressions of Affect in early childhood are realized in adjectives, while the emergence of modality and an expanded attitudinal lexis by early adolescence contribute to expression of Appreciation of events and movements in history. Judgement of human actions and behaviours, while sometimes expressed in early history texts such as biographies, is a more significant feature of those of adolescence.

In terms of control of textual resources, we see early texts organized very simply, typically relying on repetitive use of personal pronouns in topical Theme position and sometimes uncertain uses of endophoric reference (also referred to in Chapter 2, with respect to writing stories). Later developments lead to texts that are marked by an increasing range of thematic choices, an enhanced control of endophoric reference and a better understanding of ways to marshall and order information, though the particular manner adopted depends on the genre involved.

A sample of history texts from childhood to early adolescence

Table 4.1 outlines the history texts from childhood to early adolescence considered in this chapter, beginning with the chronologically ordered genres (*personal recount, empathetic autobiography, biography* and *historical account)* and ending with the non-chronologically ordered genres of *period studies* and *site studies.*

Table 4.1 A sample of recount and period/site study genres in history from childhood to early adolescence

Text	Genre	Sex and age of writer
Chronological		
4.1 Our visit to the museum	Recount of personal experience	Boy aged 6/7 years
4.2 Letter from an early settler	Empathetic autobiography	Boy aged 11/12 years
4.3 Galileo	Biographical recount	Boy aged 11/12 years
4.4 The Vietnam War	Historical account	Boy aged 12/13 years
Non-chronological		
4.5 Egyptian houses	Site study	Boy aged 10/11 years
4.6 Pioneers	Embryonic period study	Boy aged 6/7 years
4.7 Medieval life	Period study	Boy aged 7/8 years
4.8 Ancient Rome	Period study	Boy aged 12/13 years

Chronologically ordered genres in school history

The family of recount genres provides students with contexts to develop one of the core skills in school history – the ability to select significant events and order them in a chronological sequence. While this might appear to be a fairly rudimentary achievement, Coffin (2006b: 207) cautions that even adolescents can find it difficult to handle chronological order and represent the duration of historical periods.

Recounting personal experience

Children's early recounting of past events takes place in talk, generally scaffolded by older interactants. In their first year or two of schooling students are encouraged to notice changes – in their own lives and in the lives of their immediate family and community. They sequence incidents in chronological order by recounting recent personal events. The field is typically oriented towards specific, familiar persons engaged in recent incidents over short spans, using everyday language relating to time, change and place.

Text 4.1 is a recount of personal experience (similar to that introduced in Chapter 2, where the schematic structure was introduced) written by a young boy of 7/8 years, and although experientially the items discussed are historical phenomena, this is technically not a 'history' text, being concerned with a class visit to a museum. However, the text displays evidence of a child learning to sequence events in a manner valued in history, using instances of marked Themes of time to stage aspects of the recount and to give overall direction to the text. He also offers some evaluative comment on what was observed in the museum, revealing developing capacity to introduce simple attitudinal expression. The text has two elements, an Orientation and a Record, while it lacks any Reorientation.

Text 4.1   Our visit to the museum

Orientation   *Yesterday* we went to the museum.

Record   *We saw antique bikes and insects, mummy cases and a skeleton.*
The _funnest_ part was the magic mirrors.
We saw the old chemist.
When we got to the Aboriginal part
I saw a canoe.
It had a fishing net and a spear and a knife.
When we were in the bird section
you could press a button
and hear the sound of each bird.

The thematic development of the text is dominated by the use of personal pronouns (*we, I, it, you*), as we also saw in Text 2.1, the early recount discussed in Chapter 2. Significantly, however, there are, even at this early age, a Circumstance of time:

Yesterday

and two dependent clauses of time as marked Themes:

When we got to the Aboriginal part
When we were in the bird section

that provide a temporal framework for the events. Such resources will become increasingly important in later years.

The experiential content refers to the immediate past (*yesterday*) and to a brief sequence of activities involving material Processes, using the simple past tense (*went, got*) and mental Processes of perception (*saw, hear*) – reflecting the sensory nature of the experience. Participants are specific and concrete, realized in simple nominal groups such as:

the museum
a canoe
the bird section.

An empathetic autobiography

Text 4.2 is another recount, though this one creates what is termed an *empathetic autobiography*, in which the writer assumes the identity of a settler in a 19th century colonial community in Australia writing to a family member about his recent life. Coffin (2006a: 6) notes the controversial nature of such texts in that they can be interpreted as simply requiring the use of imagination and feeling in approaches to history teaching that emphasize 'empathetic understanding'.

The text shows considerable developmental advance on Text 4.1, for this is written by a boy in late childhood, aged 11/12 years, and already passing into the second of our suggested developmental phases, when there is considerable expansion in children's resources for writing.

Developments in terms of expressing experiential meanings include:

• an expanded range of resources for referring to time;
• nominalizations of temporal phenomena;

- diversity in tense choices showing capacity to shape a sense of historical period by shifting the time focus at different points in the text;
- dense nominal groups and rich adjectival groups.

A greater diversity of clause choices and combinations is apparent, in particular non-defining relative clauses and non-finite clauses.

The range of Appraisal resources being drawn upon has expanded, including empathetic affect, revealing an ability to identify with the feelings of others in different historical contexts; evaluation of the period and setting; and engagement with alternative perspectives, in this case reporting events from the point of view of an early settler. The writer in Text 4.2 is not drawing on personal experience but providing imaginative experience, gained from research, which he turns into a credible tale, intended to capture the 'spirit' of the period. Attitudinal expressions are mainly of Affect (to do with how the man felt) and Appreciation (to do with evaluations of events in his life as a settler).

Only excerpts are shown. The original text was 52 ranking clauses long.

Text 4.2   Letter from an early settler (excerpts from longer text)

Orientation   *Minnamurra House*

Dear Cousin Bruce,

It's been a while since I last wrote to you so I'll refresh your memory about the sorts of things [[that have happened since our arrival in Jamberoo]].

Record   **As you know**, *we came out on The Earl of Durham in 1839 – a <u>tiring</u> voyage and we were <u>glad</u> to set foot on land. Our first thought was [[to settle in]]. We tried Mittagong and Windsor which had been recommended by some friends but we found them <u>much too cold</u> for our liking. Then we heard of this place called Illawarra <u>which turned out to be perfect</u>. Uncle Sandy and I each bought 300 acres adjacent to each other on the Minnamurra River.* **On our way down to Illawarra by horse**, *we came across the Woodstock Mill – three storeys high and one hundred feet long. It was a <u>fine</u> flour and timber mill with a brewery and piggery.*

We sent our furniture down to Kiama on a cedar schooner. **In those days** *there was no jetty causing us a <u>big inconvenience</u> [[getting our goods ashore by rowboat]]. It was a <u>glorious</u> sight [[to see the new jetty built recently]] but <u>heartbreaking</u> [[to see it destroyed by a <u>violent</u> storm soon after]].*

When we arrived *we built our house and our barn, which was used in 1840 for the first Presbyterian services in Jamberoo. I was <u>extremely glad</u> [[to see the Presbyterian church [[built a couple of years later.]]]] . . . .*

Today *Jamberoo is a <u>hustling and thriving</u> village. The main changes [[I have noticed]] in my time here is [[that it has changed from a cedar logging area to a farming community with dairying and wheat products]] . . . .*

I even have an acre sown to wheat.

Reorientation	*I'm a very busy man these days. . . . Life is <u>not in the least dull but always busy and exciting</u>. Margaret and I are well. Looking forward to hearing [[what's happened at home]].*
	Kind regards,
	Robert

Given the nature of the topic, it is not surprising to find personal pronouns (*I, we*) in Theme position, though there is now a much stronger progression through time with temporal clauses and Circumstances as marked Theme:

In those days *there was no jetty*
When we arrived *we built our house*
Today *Jamberoo is a hustling and thriving village.*

Time features prominently in the experiential content of the text. In contrast to the earlier texts where progress through serial time was signalled either implicitly or through temporal conjunctions, now the text unfolds in episodes, marked with Circumstances referring to specific dates:

we came out on The Earl of Durham **in 1839**
and our barn, which was used **in 1840** *for the first Presbyterian services in Jamberoo*

and more general expressions of time:

It was a glorious sight [[to see the new jetty built **recently**]]
[it was] heartbreaking [[to see it destroyed by a violent storm **soon after**]]
I was extremely glad [[to see the Presbyterian church [[built **a couple of years later.**]]]]
I'm a very busy man **these days**.

The timeframe has shifted to longer stretches of time, but is not yet dealing with the abstract periods that characterize history in the secondary school ('the Reformation', 'the Ming Dynasty').

In addition to the phrases and adverbs realizing temporal Circumstances, time is now construed through a variety of other resources such as numeratives in the nominal group:

Our **first** *thought was [[to settle in]].*
our barn, which was used in 1840 for the **first** *Presbyterian services in Jamberoo*

and verbal groups – either through the lexical verb Processes that realize temporal meanings such as 'commencing', 'continuing' and 'concluding':

> When we **arrived**
> it has **changed** from a cedar logging area
> A store **was started up** in the village

or through phasal verbs:

> which **turned out** to be perfect

Significantly, time has been nominalized:

> the sorts of things [[that have happened since our **arrival** in Jamberoo]].
> The main **changes** [[I have noticed]] in my **time** here is [[that it has changed from a cedar logging area to a farming community with dairying and wheat products]]

A greater range of tense choices allows for more subtle distinctions in terms of the duration and relative timing of the actions:

> I'**ll refresh** your memory;
> we **came out**;
> which **had been recommended**;
> Jamberoo **is** a hustling and thriving village;
> I **have noticed**

– a development from the reliance on the simple past tense of earlier recounts.

There is even evidence of a causative Process (**causing** us a big inconvenience), anticipating later developments in explaining history.

Nominal groups have become more dense, including both phrasal and clausal embeddings:

> a fine flour and timber mill [with a brewery and a piggery];
> the sorts of things [[that have happened since our arrival in Jamberoo]]

Adjective groups also include post-modification:

> extremely glad [[to see the Presbyterian church built a couple of years later]]

The emphasis on recounting (virtual) personal experience tends to favour the use of material, concrete participants (places, buildings, people, transport) as opposed to the more abstract, conceptual ones students will need when explaining and arguing in the secondary years.

There is also greater diversity in terms of clause combinations, particularly the use of non-defining relative clauses:

We tried Mittagong and Windsor // **which had been recommended by some friends** . . .
Then we heard of this place [[called Illawarra]] // **which turned out to be perfect.**
We built our house and our barn // **which was used in 1940 for the first Presbyterian service in Jamberoo.**
By now we had a few new neighbours // **who had established themselves at Terragong and Wauchope.**

Unlike the writers of the earlier recounts, the student also uses non-finite clauses (as discussed in Chapter 2):

In those days there was no jetty
causing us a big inconvenience
getting our goods ashore by rowboat.

Empathetic autobiographies are of great interest interpersonally, reflecting history's 'affective turn', with its emphasis on feelings, individual experiences and daily life. Such activities can lead to an appreciation of the individual's physical and psychological experience in historical times (Agnew 2007). A primary purpose, therefore, is to promote an emotional connection with the past, expressed in this case in adjectives realizing Affect:

*we were **glad** to set foot on land*
*I was **extremely glad** [[to see the Presbyterian church [[built a couple of years later]]]]*
*it was **heartbreaking** to see* . . .

Beyond emotional responses, the writer also critically appraises the physical and social conditions of the time, expressing Appreciation of events and phenomena:

*lack of a jetty caused **a big inconvenience**,*
*the new jetty was a **glorious** sight*
*Jamberoo became a **hustling and thriving** village*
*life was **not in the least dull***

At this stage, the empathetic recount steers students towards emotive involvement and evaluation of the material world – a response that is less valued when they need to critique the world of abstract ideas, motives, causes and principles in the later years.

Empathetic autobiographies are quite demanding to write, requiring students to come to a sufficient understanding of the period to create a plausible reconstruction of the time, and adopt the persona of a typical representative of the age. At face value, the writer is simply 'telling his story', but because he is inhabiting an alter-ego, he has become the mouthpiece of a different generation, with different values, life experiences and aspirations. In this way, students are learning not simply to describe but to interpret and to understand that the past can be construed in a variety of ways. This ability to acknowledge different points of view becomes increasingly important in later secondary history, where students are expected to be able to recognize and evaluate alternative perspectives.

A biography

While many of the biographies written by young children are simple recounts of events in the life of a famous person, the more mature biographies evaluate the significance of the person in terms of the values of the person's time and his/her enduring legacy. In the UK, for example, the students are asked 'to make judgements about what makes an individual important and to provide reasons', compiling simple criteria to use in making such judgements (The Qualifications and Curriculum Authority (1997–2008) *History at Key Stage 3* Unit 1: Introductory unit: 'What's it all about?' p. 1).

The typical schematic structure of a biography (see Table 4.2) has an opening element – the *Person Identification* – in which the person is introduced, generally with some indication of why the person is of interest and often locating the person in time and space. The second element – termed *Episodes* – is often recursive, since it describes notable episodes from the person's life. The final (optional) element – the *Evaluation* – provides a concluding evaluation of the person's significance and contribution.[3]

Table 4.2   The schematic structure of biographies

Genre	Elements of structure
Biographical recount	Person Identification Episodes (Evaluation)

Text 4.3 is a biography of Galileo written by an 11/12 year old boy. It begins by naming Galileo and identifying his achievements. It then provides two examples of these achievements: one of his mathematical theories – The Principle of Falling Weights – and one of his astronomical theories, enabled by the

invention of the telescope. The text finishes with a reprise of his contributions both in terms of his intellectual and moral qualities.

The language features at this stage of development are similar in many ways to those outlined above in Text 4.2, though there are some differences, particularly in terms of Appraisal. Where Text 4.2 primarily employed Affect and some Appreciation, Text 4.3 primarily expresses positive Judgement of Galileo himself and of his achievements (*he stood up for what he believed in*), while some negative Judgement is expressed of *other people and the church*, who *rejected Galileo*.

Text 4.3 Galileo (extracts only)

Identification of person	*The reason [[why I am studying Galileo]] is [[because I have been interested in his life – his mathematical and astronomical theories, his <u>ingenious inventions</u>, and the fact [[that <u>he stood up for what he believed in, // even when his thoughts were rejected by the people</u>]]]].*
Episode 1	*The Principle of Falling Weights* **In 1588** *Galileo graduated from the University of Pisa and stayed there to teach mathematics.* **This particular year** <u>*Galileo proved something [['that shattered 2000 years of tradition and earned a great many enemies']]. He challenged Aristotle's theories about the principle of weights.*</u> **Before Galileo made this discovery** *people believed [[what Aristotle had said – // that a heavier object will touch the ground before the lighter object]]. Galileo dropped a 4.5 kg cannonball and a .45 kg cannonball off the Leaning Tower of Pisa. He discovered that even though the cannonballs were different weights, they made contact with the ground at the same time*
Episode 2	*The telescope* **In 1609** *a Dutch lens maker experimented with some lenses. He found out that if the lenses were arranged in a certain order they would magnify and make things seem nearer.* *Galileo heard about this and made the telescope by putting the lenses into a tube. Galileo's first telescopes only magnified things up to three times but Galileo's later telescopes magnified things up to thirty three times.* **With the telescope** *he was able to look up to the stars and discover that the sun was the centre of the solar system. His thought was not believed by other people and the church called him up and put him on trial. He was found not guilty but he wasn't allowed to do anything [[that would make a public disturbance, // like writing books]]. But he did write two more books and made more discoveries before his death.*
Evaluation of person	*The reason [[that I think // that Galileo is remembered today especially by astronomers]] is [[because he invented the telescope // and discovered // that the earth was not the centre of the universe // which Aristotle had claimed to be true]]. <u>He was bold enough [[to say // that Aristotle was wrong]] and defied the church rules of his town and country.</u>*

The two Episode stages begin with marked Themes (*In 1588* and *In 1609*), providing a location in time, though chronology itself is not the main focus of the text. The rest of the Themes tend to select Galileo as the point of departure, with his achievements realized as New Information in Rheme position.

Not surprisingly, given the field, the experiential content of this text privileges mental Processes:

> *Galileo **proved** something [['that shattered 2000 years of tradition and earned a great many enemies']]*
> *people **believed** [[what Aristotle had said . . .]]*
> *He **discovered** that even though the cannonballs were different weights, they made contact with the ground at the same time.*
> *He **found out** that if the lenses were arranged in a certain order they would magnify and make things seem nearer.*

– a feature not noted in the history texts from younger writers where the emphasis is more on the material world. Abstraction is starting to appear at this age, with the nominalization of these processes:

> *even when his **thoughts** were rejected by the people*
> *Before Galileo made this **discovery***

and other conceptual notions such as:

> *He challenged Aristotle's **theories** about the **principle** of weights.*

Biographies provide a context for recognizing the role key figures play in historical change. At this stage, students are not simply recording what individuals have done, but are learning to take on the role of appraiser, interpreting the actions of historical persons with regard to community criteria rather than simply personal reactions (Martin and Rose 2008). The opening stage of the text, for example, sets up the salient values as the background against which the rest of the evaluative meanings in the text will be read: positive Appreciation of the contribution Galileo made:

> *his **ingenious** inventions*

. . . and positive Judgement of his moral and ethical behaviour:

> *he stood up for what he believed in, even when his thoughts were rejected by the people.*

The final stage, then, overtly reinforces the previous positive evaluation by picking up again on Galileo's qualities and achievements:

He challenged Aristotle's theories about the principle of weights.
He was bold enough to say that Aristotle was wrong and defied the church rules of his
town and country.

A further point of interest is the reference to scholarship of others:

. . . *something 'that shattered 2000 years of tradition and earned a great many*
enemies'.

Although the source is not referenced, this is an early example of engaging with others in the discourse community – an important practice in historical inquiry that will take on much greater weight in the later secondary texts examined in Chapter 5.

An historical account

In later childhood and early adolescence, we find a shift from simply 'telling what happened' to 'explaining why things happened'. The text still unfolds chronologically as a series of events, as in the recounts above, but now there are attempts at providing reasons for outcomes. The Australian Government's recent *Guide to the Teaching of Australian History* (Australian Government Department of Education, Science and Training 2007: 5) notes that 'constructing a narrative sequence requires students to reflect on causes, influences, outcomes and consequences'.

The schematic structure of an historical account, displayed in Table 4.3, is similar to that of a recount genre, but rather than simply recording a sequence of past events, the chronicle is infused with causal links – the *Account Sequence* – and the final optional stage provides evaluation of the significance of the outcome – the *Deduction*.

Table 4.3   The schematic structure of historical accounts

Genre	Elements of structure
Historical account	Background
	Account sequence
	(Deduction)

Text 4.4 was written by a 12/13 year old boy, accounting for changes in South-East Asian politics in the lead up to, and during, the Vietnam War.

Key linguistic developments include the strong framework provided by the marked temporal Themes together with cause-and-effect realized primarily through dependent clauses of reason and through the juxtaposition of clauses. The writer is now moving further towards generalization, dealing with groupings such as *civil servants*, and abstraction, particularly in terms of naming 'chunks' of time/space (*its colonial empire*) and concepts (*the Domino Theory*).

Text 4.4   The Vietnam War (excerpts from longer text)

Background	*THE COLONIAL ERA* **In the nineteenth century**, *many European countries established colonies in South-East Asia. France expanded its colonial empire to Indochina.* **In twenty years** *France had a grip on Vietnam, Laos, and Cambodia.*
Account sequence: **Phase 1**	*WORLD WAR II* *The French were defeated by Germany in France while the French colonies were invaded by Germany's ally the Japanese. The Japanese Empire expanded down through Burma, Thailand, and into Singapore, Papua New Guinea and reached for the northern tips of Australia.* **Towards the end of the war** << **when the Japanese were thinking of surrendering** >> *the Americans dropped the first ever atomic bomb on Hiroshima. The Japanese were kept in Vietnam for a few years to maintain law and order until the French could send civil servants to take over.*
Account sequence: **Phase 2**	*THE RISE OF THE VIET MINH* **When the Viet Minh had beaten the Japanese with the aid of the United States**, *the Vietnamese* <u>took pride</u> *and realized that they could become independent. So,* << **when the French came back to rule,** >> *they were confronted with the independence movement of the Vietnamese people. The French tried to fight the Vietnamese but* <u>failed miserably and dramatically because they were using the wrong tactics for the wrong place</u>*. They went out in large groups of men and vehicles in formation. Their tactics were* <u>unable to match the guerilla tactics of camouflage and hit and run</u>*.* *The French left and abandoned their colonial empire.* **While the French were leaving** *the Americans came in, not to claim territory but to help the South Vietnamese to fight the North Vietnamese in fear [[of communism spreading down into the Pacific region]]. Their concept was based on the Domino Theory i.e. communism [[spreading from one country to the next]]. Unfortunately the Americans had problems telling [[who was who, // who was friend // and who was foe]], as only the North Vietnamese wore uniform. The Vietcong* << *(also called VC who were local force rebels [[who fought for communism]])* >> *also wore the same black pyjama like clothes as the civilians.*
Deduction	*Conclusion:* <u>The importance of the Vietnam war in history is [[that it turned Vietnam from a foreign controlled country into an independent, communist country]]</u>*. It also* SHOWED *that* <u>the biggest and richest countries such as America and Russia are not invincible as the Vietnamese proved.</u>

Beyond explaining cause and effect, the writer is also starting to evaluate the significance of factors and outcomes, though much of the language is free of overt attitudinal expression and its tone is dispassionate. Some Judgement is offered of the French who *failed miserably and dramatically* in fighting the Vietnamese, while an overall evaluation of the significance of the war and what it SHOWED is offered in the Deduction.

In terms of its thematic development, this text is similar to the previous ones in that it is governed by marked temporal Themes:

> **In the nineteenth century,** *many European countries established colonies in South-East Asia.*
> **In twenty years** *France had a grip on Vietnam, Laos, and Cambodia.* **Towards the end of the war** << *when the Japanese were thinking of surrendering*>> *the Americans dropped the first ever atomic bomb on Hiroshima.*
> **When the Viet Minh had beaten the Japanese** . . .
> **While the French were leaving** . . .

Ideationally, however, the texts are different. In addition to the various resources realizing 'time', we also find a series of intricately linked clauses – some of time, result and reason – that help create a sense of events and their consequences and/or effects:

> *When the Viet Minh had beaten the Japanese with the aid of the United States,* (dependent clause of time)
> *the Vietnamese took pride*
> *and realized* (projecting clause)
> *that they could become independent.* (projected clause)
> *So,* <<*when the French came back to rule,* (dependent clause of time)>>
> *they were confronted with the independence movement of the Vietnamese people* (dependent clause of result).
> *The French tried to fight the Vietnamese*
> *but failed miserably and dramatically*
> *because they were using the wrong tactics for the wrong place* (dependent clause of reason).

Causality is not always realized overtly, however. At several points in the text it is necessary to infer a causal link from the juxtaposition of events. While this is a common feature of historical writing, in this text the writer does not yet have confident control over the resources to bury reasoning 'within the clause' (see Chapter 5). In the first paragraph of Phase 1, for example, the cause and effect is quite elliptical. A more mature writer might have nominalized the precipitating events and their outcome, making the agency more apparent and allowing a causal link to be made between the events:

Congruent (with implied causality)	Metaphorical (with overt causality)
*The French **were defeated** by Germany in France while the French colonies **were invaded** by Germany's ally the Japanese. The Japanese Empire **expanded** down through Burma . . .*	'The **defeat** of France by the Germans and the **invasion** of the French colonies by the Japanese **led** to the **expansion** of the Japanese Empire . . .'

Sustained cause-and-effect sequences were not present in the texts of early childhood. Although this writer has not yet mastered the resources necessary for mature reasoning (such as nominalization of cause, causative Processes, circumstances of cause, conjunctive causal adjuncts), this account is an important step towards the more complex explanations of the secondary years, to be discussed in Chapter 5.

Compared to Text 4.2, the nature of the field has changed from imaginary participation in a virtual past world to the more detached recording of historical developments. Rather than the everyday experiences of specific people such as the early settler and his wife, in this text we have generalized participants:

the French; the Americans; civil servants

involved in events that span long periods:

the colonial era, World War II, the independence movement.

This ability to package a sequence of activities and events into a nominalized 'chunk of time' is an important developmental step towards abstraction (Coffin 1997: 210).

Not only are the students having to comprehend longer timeframes, they also need to go beyond the local space of their community to represent the movement through geographic territory:

*France expanded its colonial empire **to Indochina**. In twenty years, France had a grip on **Vietnam, Laos and Cambodia**. . . .*
*The Japanese Empire expanded **down through Burma, Thailand, and into Singapore, Papua New Guinea** and reached **for the northern tips of Australia**.*

As we have seen in all the texts so far, an understanding of the relative geographical locations is equally important as an understanding of chronological time. And just as time sequences are collapsed into named periods, disparate geographic locations are brought together into abstract political entities, for example:

its colonial empire, Indochina, South-East Asia

Whereas much of the text deals with fairly concrete entities, there is evidence of some abstraction creeping in:

*. . . to help the South Vietnamese to fight the North Vietnamese in fear of communism spreading down into the Pacific region. Their **concept** was based on the **Domino Theory** i.e. communism spreading from one country to the next.*

Here, *concept* is referring back to the notion of stopping communism by helping the South Vietnamese while *the Domino Theory* refers forward to communism spreading from one country to the next.

the Americans came in, not to claim territory but to help the South Vietnamese to fight the North Vietnamese in fear of communism spreading down into the Pacific region.
↑
*Their **concept** was based on **the Domino Theory***
↓
i.e. communism [[spreading from one country to the next]].

The student is thus starting to use abstractions to create cohesive links in the text – a development which will be taken up more fully in the texts analysed in Chapter 5.

The text ends with an appraisal of 'the importance of the Vietnam war in history', providing reasons for its significance:

It turned Vietnam from a foreign controlled country into an independent, communist country.
It also showed that the biggest and richest countries such as America and Russia are not invincible as the Vietnamese proved.

This is an important step towards assessing the weight and causal force of past events (Coffin 2006a: 140) – an ability that students of history will need when they move into the expository texts of the upper secondary.

Non-chronological genres: site and period studies

As noted above, period and site studies are written by children in childhood and early adolescence. Whereas the chronological genres help students develop an understanding of the build-up of events in a sequence over time, the non-chronological genres shift students into having to deal with description, where they describe either a physical location or a period of time. They express little or no attitudinal values, and since their purpose is primarily descriptive, the particular challenge they offer is in terms of how to marshall and order the description.

The early studies of particular historical sites and periods can be seen as precursors of the genres of mid-adolescence, where students go beyond description of a site or period to interpretation and explanation.

Site studies

Site studies reflect a recent concern among some professional historians that the past exists not only in time but in space:

> Histories representing the past represent the places (topoi) of human action. Knowledge of the past, therefore, is literally cartographic: a mapping of the places of history indexed to the coordinates of spacetime. (Ethington 2007: 465)

The New South Wales History Syllabus Years 7–10 (New South Wales Board of Studies 2003a: 15) defines a site study as:

> an inquiry-based examination of an historically or culturally significant location. Site studies may include an investigation of the school and its surroundings or a visit to an archaeological site, a museum, a specific building, a monument, a local area, or a virtual site available on CD or the internet.

Students examine artefacts to reconstruct the daily activities of the historical group in question and to interpret the social organization and cultural values and beliefs of the particular populace. Furthermore, students are learning to engage with various points of view, recognizing that history is a situated interpretation rather than a disinterested, 'objective' account.

Table 4.4 displays the schematic structure of the site study. The *Site Identification* states the site, while the *Site Description* outlines descriptive detail.

Table 4.4   The schematic structure of site studies

Genre	Elements of structure
Site study	Site identification
	Site description

We have collected site studies in the primary and lower secondary years, including texts, for example, on 'Stonehenge', 'Victorian Architecture', or 'A New Stone Age Village'. The following text was written by a 12/13 year old boy about housing in Egypt. The site identification is located in the heading (*Egyptian houses*) and first paragraph, while the rest of the text provides a description of the site.

Because the writer can no longer rely on the sequential framework provided by the chronological genres, he has to find another way of organizing the information. After his opening element he identifies aspects of the housing, first of the rich Egyptians, and then of the poorer people. The descriptive content is quite vivid at times, due to the elaborations around the nominal group, providing useful detail:

a three-walled room on top of the house // which the family slept in on hot nights.

Text 4.5   Egyptian houses

Site identification	*Much of ancient Egyptian life occurred in their house, which was made of sun-dried mud [[called adobe]] because wood was in short supply in the desert.*
Description of site	*Of course, <<**as it is now,**>> the more wealth or respect you had, the more rooms. A nobleman in Egypt would have three rooms: a reception room, a hallway and private quarters (bedroom). The windows would be covered with mats so that dust, wind and flies couldn't get into the house. Often the walls were covered with wall hangings, which were made out of leather. The floor had tiles and there was also a three-walled room on top of the house, which the family slept in on hot nights.*
	*A commoner's house was usually two or three stories high. The ground floor was for business while the second (or third if they had one) was the living area. **Like the nobleman's home**, the family often slept on top of the house though there wasn't a room there. Sewage was often disposed of in the street or in the Nile. **In a commoner's house,** there wasn't much furniture, just an oil lamp, a cosmetics/jewellery table, clay pots and at least one fly catcher (incense burner).*

The focus here is on description, so we find relational Processes:

*wood **was** in short supply;*
*A nobleman in Egypt **would have** three rooms;*
*The floor **had** tiles;*
*The ground floor **was** for business*

along with detailed participant descriptions, often involving elaborations of various kinds – a development from the simple nominal groups of earlier texts – which, as we noted in Chapter 2, is one mark of a successful writer in adolescence:

Nominal group	Elaboration
their house	*which was made of sun-dried mud [[called adobe]] because wood was in short supply in the desert.*
Three rooms:	*a reception room, a hallway and private quarters (bedroom).*
wall hangings,	*which were made out of leather.*
a three-walled room on top of the house,	*which the family slept in on hot nights.*
[not] much furniture,	*just an oil lamp, a cosmetics/jewellery table, clay pots and at least one fly catcher (incense burner).*

This text does not yet do the type of interpretive work found in the later secondary corpus where the site interpretations provide a much more complex explication of the historical significance of various features of the site. (See Chapter 5.)

Period studies

The period study is similar to the site study, and its schematic structure is set out in Table 4.5. Rather than studying physical settings in the past, the period study describes human activity in a particular segment of time, where the interest is not in temporal events but in detailing the characteristic phenomena and/or activities in a significant expanse of time, such as the 'Roman Empire', or 'Medieval Times', or 'Egypt in the time of the Pharaohs'. Complete period studies have an opening element – the *Period Identification*, identifying the period in question – and a second element – the *Description* – which describes the habitual activities of the inhabitants of the period, or else a specific episode in the period. Many period studies have no Period Identification, providing only Description.

Table 4.5   The schematic structure of period studies

Genre	Elements of structure
Period study	Period identification
	Description

In the three texts that follow, we can observe a progression in ability to describe the characteristic activities of an historical period. Text 4.6, the earliest text of this type in our corpus, and written by a 6/7 year old, is not really an instance of any genre, being only a fragment, though it offers simple observation on a period in history. Its two sentences describe aspects of customary activity in a particular period of time.

Text 4.6   Pioneers

Pioneers used to make their own things even their homes. They had to even clear the land.

Text 4.7, written by a boy of 8/9, is a bit longer and captures several aspects of life in its chosen period – namely medieval times. The text's organization is rather loose, so that it moves a little indiscriminately from one descriptive detail to another.

Text 4.7   Medieval life

Period identification	*Medieval Times*
Description	*Tournaments were often at the village green. The <u>strongest</u> man there was usually the blacksmith. The castle had many parts for example the keep, gatehouse, court and the inner bailey and outer bailey. The lord and the priest were like big bosses over the little peasants, villeins and serfs. **Every Sunday** the peasants had to go to church in their <u>best</u> clothes. **If they didn't** they would be taken before the lord in court.*

The writer shows confidence in handling the language of the field in description of activities and parts of the medieval castle:

tournaments at the village green
inner and outer bailey, keep, gatehouse, court

while the social hierarchy is also described:

the lord and priest who were the big bosses over the villeins, peasants and serfs.

The regularity of the activities is signalled by the adverbials:

often; usually; every Sunday

along with the use of the habitual past, particularly *would be taken.*

There is the hint of a consequence in the use of the conditional clause placed in marked Theme position:

If they didn't, they would be taken before the lord in court.

Our second period study, Text 4.8, was written by a 13/14 year old boy, who, reflecting his greater maturity, is able to provide a more detailed and better organized text, in which aspects of life in his chosen period are selected and marshalled in a more ordered way than in Text 4.7. The complete text was written on *Ancient Roman Times,* where the writer explored *Gladiatorial Games; Education; Art and Architecture;* and *Gods and Religion.* We produce only an extract from the original text of 96 ranking clauses, so that there is no Period Identification here, but only Description.

The opening paragraph provides a clear overall focus for this section of the genre, functioning a little like a *macroTheme* (to be explained more fully in Chapter 5), foreshadowing that the text will deal with two groupings: *high gods* and *lesser gods.* Then, the later sections of the text are introduced using sub-headings which create *hyperThemes* (discussed in detail in Chapter 5) that look back to the opening macroTheme, and also look forward to what is to come in the paragraphs beneath them.

Text 4.8   Ancient Rome: Gods and religion (extract only)

Description

Unlike the Christians with their one god, the Romans had many gods. *These deities were grouped into the high gods and the lesser gods.*

High gods
There were three high gods – Jupiter, Mars, Quirinus. These gods guarded the state or country. Jupiter (the same as the Greek god Zeus) was the supreme god. He dwelt on Capitol Hill in Rome with his two consorts, Minerva [[who was the goddess of wisdom]] and Juno goddess of the moon. The other high gods, Mars and Quirinus were both gods of war. The Roman religion was a savage one which arose from the warring tribes and the need for protection.

The lesser gods
In addition to the three high gods *there were also many lesser gods. Some of the well known ones are Bacchus god of wine and revelry; Vulcan god of fire; Venus goddess of love with Cupid her helper; Neptune god of the seas; Pluto ruler of the underworld and Apollo god of the sun.*

Worship
Every household had an altar or shrine [[at which they would worship // and leave offerings to the gods]]. . . . **On** very special *occasions the Romans would go up the temple and sacrifice an animal such as an ox. . . .*
From their burial rites *we can assume that the Romans believed in the survival of the dead. Many funeral monuments can still be seen in Rome today.*

As with the site studies above, texts such as Text 4.8 rely for their organization on matters other than a chronological framework of the kind found in recounts or even autobiographies, and the writer has had to come up with a different means of arranging the historical content. This in itself is a major challenge, which many learners fail to meet without teacher support. In this case, the writer has drawn heavily on a hierarchical organization, dividing the gods into different classes, creating a taxonomy of 'high gods' and 'lesser gods', foreshadowed in the opening statement and reinforced by the sub-headings.

One measure of the developing maturity of this writer is apparent in his uses of grammatical metaphor, compressing information and creating social phenomena around which the writer develops his description. Some examples are given:

Metaphorical	A congruent version
*the Romans believed in **the survival of the dead***	'The Romans believed **that the dead survived**'
*The Roman religion was a savage one **which arose from the warring tribes and the need for protection**.*	'The Roman religion was a savage one **which arose because the tribes were constantly fighting and people needed to be protected**.'

As with reports, the main Process types are relational of various types, and existential – key resources in description:

*. . . the Romans **had** many gods.*	relational: possessive
*There **were** three high gods . . .*	existential
*Mars and Quirinus **were** both gods of war.*	relational: intensive
*The Roman religion **was** a savage one*	relational: attributive
*. . . there **were** also many lesser gods.*	existential
*Every household **had** an altar or shrine . . .*	relational: possessive

Another measure of the developing maturity of the young writer of Text 4.8 is apparent in his use of various resources of expansion, already referred to above and also in Chapters 2 and 3. In all these cases, the writer uses an element that elaborates on the meaning of another, expressed in a nominal group, by further specifying or describing it:

three high gods – Jupiter, Mars, Quirinus;
Jupiter (the same as the Greek god Zeus);
Minerva who was the goddess of wisdom;
Juno, goddess of the moon;
an animal such as an ox.

Period studies such as Text 4.8 make little use of evaluative language, as their purpose is to describe as completely as possible, and in a reasonably detached manner. One interesting final observation marks the closure of the text, using a marked Theme (expressed in a Circumstance of angle) in which an 'angle' or perspective is given, from which an idea is developed:

> **From their burial rites** *we can assume that the Romans believed in the survival of the dead. Many funeral monuments can still be seen in Rome today.*

Here the writer acknowledges that part of the historian's craft is to marshall evidence from various sources, making 'assumptions' (but by implication, not assertions) about the probable implications. This young writer had displayed a developing sense of the historian's tasks, and the need to be appropriately careful about conclusions reached.

Conclusion

This chapter has sought to review developments in the writing of history from childhood, when history is not a discrete subject, to early adolescence, by which time history has emerged as a separate concern, achieving discrete status in the adolescent years of a secondary education. Two broad groups of history genres were reviewed – chronological and non-chronological – both of which appear in childhood to early adolescence. We have argued that these are foundational to later history studies, in that they introduce children to an interest in the past, developing skills that continue to be used in later historical studies. The chronological genres develop skills of sequencing historical events in time, leading to some capacity to create cause and effect relationships between events. The non-chronological genres develop skills in organizing relevant information and in describing details of sites or periods in history with some care.

The first history texts of early childhood, such as simple recounts of personal experience, show children writing of immediate 'concrete' experience, and dealing with specific entities, often in a limited timeframe. By late childhood, children's language develops so that they can write of events that are distanced from their own experience, displaying an emerging sense of the past and of expanded timeframes, and some capacity for empathetic reflection on historical events. Into adolescence, with all the developing language capacities potentially unleashed in an expanded range of clause interdependencies, developing control of grammatical metaphor, modality and attitudinal lexis, students begin to reveal capacities in evaluation, interpretation and judgement, all of them valued in the senior years. Historical fields gradually become more generalized – the actions of whole populations or groupings over long time spans are dealt with – and there are signs of the abstractions characteristic of history and of other humanities, including English, already discussed especially in Chapter 3. Attitudinally, students move from early expressions of Appreciation of events and phenomena in childhood, towards texts in adolescence that use both Appreciation and some Judgement, as was true for example, in the historical account about the Vietnam War. However, many history texts are free of much evaluative language, as they seek to record and describe historical events dispassionately.

In our next chapter, we shall turn to the history texts of the secondary years, examining how students continue to develop, achieving over time, 'the ability to leap beyond the concrete base of their own experience to reach more abstract principles' in dealing with history (Maton 2007: 17).

Notes

[1] We have not included an historical recount here as the characteristic grammatical features have been sufficiently covered in the discussion of biography and empathetic autobiography.

[2] Coffin (1996) refers to these as 'history reports' and likens them to the descriptive and taxonomic reports of science.

[3] These stage descriptions differ from those of Coffin (2006a) who refers to Orientation ^ Record of events ^ (Evaluation of person).

Chapter 5

Reviewing the Past: Interpreting, Explaining, Arguing and Debating Historical Events

Introduction

While the previous chapter dealt with history texts written by children and young adolescents, this chapter will explore the linguistic resources required in the later years of schooling. What we observe in terms of development in any subject is determined in part by the demands of the educational context in which the learners are operating. Hence, we note that the texts in this study were written primarily within the context of the New South Wales history syllabus, which offers the following rationale for the study of history:

> History provides opportunities for students to explore human actions in a range of historical contexts and encourages them to develop understanding of motivation, causation, consequence and empathy.

> The study of history provides the intellectual skills to enable students to critically analyse and interpret sources of evidence in order to construct reasoned explanations, hypotheses about the past and a rational and informed argument. History also enables students to understand, deconstruct and evaluate differing interpretations of the past. The cognitive skills of analysis, evaluation and synthesis underpin the study of history and equip students with the ability to understand and evaluate the political, cultural and social events and issues that have shaped the world around them. (New South Wales History 7–10 Syllabus (New South Wales Board of Studies (2003a: 8))

These social purposes for writing history reflect the developmental continuum outlined by Coffin (2006a: 47), who suggested that by adolescence students gain the linguistic resources to move beyond simple temporally related genres and basic descriptive genres (of the kind discussed in Chapter 4) towards those in which, by mid- to late adolescence, they must provide explanations of historical events and develop arguments around historical issues.

In Chapter 4 we have already displayed an overview of some representative history genres from the primary to the secondary school years (Table 4.1).

Figure 5.1 provides a more complete view of the topology of genres in history, covering the years of childhood to late adolescence. As the figure suggests, there is a developmental movement across 'families' of genres: the chronologically grouped genres (which emerge in childhood) shift from those of simple temporal sequence, such as personal recounts, towards historical recounts and accounts, involving a move from the specific to the more general, and a corresponding movement to expression of cause and effect in history. The non-chronological genres move from those of simple description of historical site or period in childhood towards interpretation of sites and explanations of causes and consequences in early to mid-adolescence. The rhetorical family of genres belongs to the years of adolescence, and these genres involve taking up a stance, either arguing about history or arguing about historiography, reviewing the values of various sources of evidence, as well as methods of examining them.

In this chapter, we shall consider examples of *site interpretations, factorial and consequential explanations, expositions* and *discussions. Site interpretations* differ

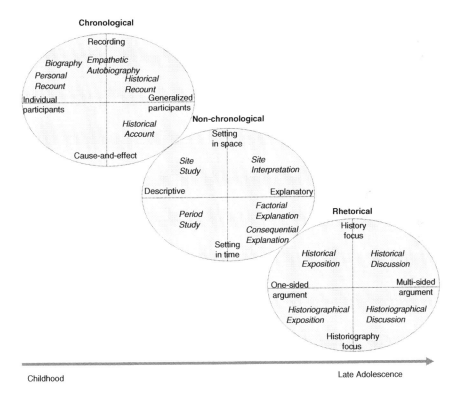

FIGURE 5.1 A topological depiction of some genres of school history along a cline from childhood to late adolescence

from the site studies examined in Chapter 4, in that they offer more than simple description of a site, dwelling instead on some interpretation of aspects of the site. Such texts arise quite frequently in ancient history, when it is necessary to rely heavily on physical evidence in the absence of many written records. *Factorial explanations* identify some significant event in history expressed as an outcome of some kind (e.g. 'the Greek victory in the Second Persian War') and they require an explanation in terms of the factors responsible for it. *Consequential explanations* identify some historical event and then explain its consequences (e.g. 'The impact of World War II on the lives of women'). *Expositions* take up an issue in history and argue a point of view about it (e.g. 'The importance of the ANZAC tradition in Australia'), while *discussions* take an issue and argue positions for and against it, leading to adoption of one of these in the light of the arguments offered (e.g. 'Analyse the historical debates surrounding the British policy of Appeasement in WWII'). The historiographical genres have similar schematic structures to those dealing with historical matters, save that, as we have already noted, they discuss and argue the values of historical research. While the historical expositions and discussions involve 'real world' events and issues, the historiographical genres focus on the more abstract and technical tools of historical enquiry, inducting the more advanced learners into the methodologies of the discipline.

In this chapter we will canvass key developments in the written language of mid- to late adolescence which enable students to engage in interpreting, explaining and arguing. *Textually* writers at this age are having to manage the flow of information in lengthy, complex texts, deploying such strategies as creating metadiscoursal signposts for the reader by foreshadowing at the beginning how the text will unfold (macroTheme) and subsequently predicting the method of development of each stage or paragraph (hyperTheme) right down to the clause in terms of how Themes provide points of departure at the local level (Martin and Rose 2003). Cohesion is now enhanced through the use of 'summarizing nouns' such as *argument* and *evidence* which can function to condense stretches of text. Similarly, grammatical metaphor serves to organize text and compact information, creating high levels of lexical density.

Ideationally, there is increasing interest in what participants say, think and believe, alongside the activities of the material world. We observe a continuing shift into various types of abstraction and the use of the specialist language of the field, such as the naming of particular periods (Martin 2002: 91). Along with the focus on the content of history, there is an equal emphasis on the language needed to discuss the methodologies employed by historians and the issues and problems associated with writing history. In the writing of explanations, we can note the use of a variety of resources for expressing causality, including 'cause within the clause' (Martin 2007: 45) – discussed more fully below.

And *interpersonally*, the resources of Appraisal develop in more subtle ways to evaluate the significance of events and the validity of sources of evidence, to judge the behaviour of historical figures, to engage with members of the discourse community and alternative perspectives and to know when to be circumspect and when to be more direct. The constructedness of historical interpretation is acknowledged, along with an understanding of how language functions to construe different historical meanings. Rather than see historical interpretations as categorical, students recognize that they are provisional, based on evidence that is often 'messy, incomplete and susceptible to different forms of understanding' (Gilderhus 2003: 4), and that writers need to be tentative and allow for various possibilities.

Table 5.1 outlines the texts to be considered in this chapter, providing information about the type of genre, the topic of the writing task, and the age and sex of the writer.

Table 5.1 A selection of interpretive, explanatory and arguing genres in history

Text	Genre	Sex and age of writer
5.1 The Bronze Age Theran Society	Site interpretation	Girl aged 16/17 years
5.2 The Greek victory in the Second Persian War	Factorial explanation	Girl aged 16/17 years
5.3 The impact of WWII	Consequential explanation	Girl aged 14/15 years
5.4 The spirit of a nation	Historical exposition	Girl aged 14/15 years
5.5 The British Policy of Appeasement in WWII	Historiographical discussion	Girl aged 16/17 years

We shall begin by examining an instance of a site interpretation (a genre not identified by Coffin or Martin and Rose) drawing attention first to the skill displayed by the writer in organizing the structure of her genre, so that the text has a strong sense of overall unity.

Interpreting history

Table 5.2 displays the schematic structure of site interpretations, which is similar to those of site studies, save that the second element (the *Assessment of Evidence*) offers some assessment of the historical significance of items examined in the site, and this element is typically recursive since more than one item of evidence is considered. The final element is a *Conclusion*, normally expressed in provisional terms, for by their nature, such genres involve statements about matters that are always inconclusive.

Table 5.2   The schematic structure of site interpretations

Genre	Elements of structure
Site interpretation	Site identification
	Assessment of evidence
	Conclusion

Text 5.1 is a site interpretation, written by a girl aged 16/17 years, which investigates the physical remains of Bronze Age society on the island of Thera and what they tell us about Theran culture. It is a long text of some 157 ranking clauses and we will use only extracts from it.

A major development in later adolescence is the ability to manage the overall organization of lengthy texts. In the more successful texts, the writer often uses the opening element to forecast how the text will be developed. Martin and Rose (2003: 175–205) refer to this as the *macroTheme*. This term is used metaphorically: just as a clause has a Theme, identifying that which is prominent as the point of departure for the clause, so, it is suggested at the level of discourse, there is a 'macroTheme', foregrounding major preoccupations of the passage of discourse. Thus, the term refers to an overarching thematic statement which identifies items of information and/or ideas to be taken up and elaborated upon in later elements of the text. The latter are termed *hyperThemes,* and they function much as do the 'topic sentences' referred to in traditional rhetoric, which normally start new paragraphs. Notions of macroTheme and hyperTheme are useful in that they carry the sense of looking forward and looking back. Successful writing of history, we suggest, involves establishing a strong sense of overall direction using a macroTheme which is then developed more fully through the hyperThemes, looking back on the one hand to the macroTheme and on the other, forward to what is to come within the developing paragraph.

In Text 5.1, the writer offers a macroTheme for the ensuing text, identifying three sources of evidence – *buildings and houses, various artefacts,* and *numerous frescoes* – which she will then draw on to shape the rest of the text. The first hyperTheme links back to the first point in the macroTheme: the evidence provided by *buildings and houses.* It then predicts how this first topic will unfold: palatial mansions, then independent houses, and finally irregular building blocks. These are then elaborated in turn. The second hyperTheme again refers back to the macroTheme, now picking up on the evidence provided by *artefacts.* Again, this is elaborated upon in the rest of the paragraph. The final hyperTheme takes up the third point raised in the macroTheme – the *frescoes* as a source of evidence – dealing in turn with a number of frescoes. Finally, the writer draws on the preceding text to reiterate and strengthen the points announced in the macroTheme.[1]

MACROTHEME
The Cycladic Island of Thera (modern name Santorini) is located in the Aegean Sea to the north of Crete. . . . Because of the absence of written sources, conclusions about the society have been drawn by archaeologists through their interpretations of **buildings and houses**, various **artefacts** and most importantly through the numerous **frescoes** uncovered.

HYPERTHEME 1
Since the site's initial excavation in 1967 approximately one third of the town has been uncovered. . . . The various **buildings** discovered have been used as key evidence in interpreting the social and religious structure of the town as well as an estimation of the town's population (several thousand). There were three obvious types of buildings: large **palatial mansions**, large multi-storeyed **independent houses** and **irregular building blocks**.

ELABORATION
Palatial mansions such as Xeste 2, 3 and 4 (named due to their style of construction) had at least two storeys . . .

ELABORATION
The **independent houses** such as the West House and the House of the Ladies differ as they contained numerous frescoes and shrines. . . .

ELABORATION
Irregular blocks such as Block B and D, are presumed to have been communal housing due to the number of kitchens. . . .

HYPERTHEME 2
As well as the town's layout, archaeologists have used **artefacts** to base their conclusions on.

ELABORATION
The excavation of **pithois** from buildings have revealed information regarding the society's economy. . . .

HYPERTHEME 3
The most spectacular and informative pieces of evidence into Theran society are the **frescoes** which have been uncovered in nearly all of the buildings so far excavated. . . .

ELABORATION
The Young Priestess fresco from room 4 of the West House shows a female wearing a long, heavy garment, holding a vessel. . . .

ELABORATION
The Fisherman Fresco located in room 5 of the West House depicts a naked young man holding bunches of fish. . . .

ELABORATION
The Admiral's Fresco differs from other frescoes because each separate panel illustrates a different event.

MACROTHEME REITERATED
Since initial excavations of Akrotiri in 1967, many archaeologists and historians have been involved in the interpretations of evidence found. Because of these multiple perspectives, the lack of written sources and the damage to other pictorial sources, there are many contradictory conclusions. In depth studies into **buildings and houses**, investigations of various **artefacts** and **frescoes** have revealed a good deal of information. However debate still rages surrounding many of the political, religious, social and economic features of the society. Therefore there is still a great deal to be discovered about Bronze Age Theran society.

FIGURE 5.2   MacroTheme and hyperTheme development in Text 5.1 (based on Coffin 2006a: 73)

Figure 5.2 provides an outline of how the writer skilfully manages the flow of information through the text.

This painstaking attention to the intricate texturing of the argument and the ability to control the flow of information through recurrent patterns of predicting, elaborating and summarizing is not evident in the earlier examples in our corpus. It is a skill, however, required in the senior years of schooling and beyond, where the writer needs to maintain the coherence of lengthy texts and to constantly signal to the reader how the text is developing.

Because site interpretations require students to use the language resources needed for interpreting, in our commentary we will focus primarily on such features. A common interpretive strategy, for example, is the use of 'showing' Processes to identify the meaning or significance of what is revealed:

> *However more recent discoveries . . .* **indicate** *that the vessel may be an incense burner.*

Interpretation also involves thinking and understanding, expressed, for example, in mental Processes:

> *S. Marinatos* **believes** *that it holds a connection between the identity of the owner of the West House and the events and people depicted.*

In justifying their interpretations, historians employ resources such as Circumstances of reason:

> *He states that the fleet is Theran and the warriors are Mycenaean* **due to appearance and weaponry**.

Interpretive work is achieved also through the use of Appraisal resources such as Appreciation, evaluating the significance of the site itself and what it reveals:

> *we can understand that Therans had* **advanced building and architectural skills**

. . . and the validity of the evidence:

> *Often subject matter, appearance and original position of these fresco fragments are* **difficult to determine**.

Interpretations in history are generally conditional, requiring low levels of modality:

> *revealing more about their appearance, clothing,* **possible** *occupations and social class*

And finally, students are required to demonstrate that interpretations vary according to differing perspectives, so the writer needs to manage the interplay of different voices, aligning and disaligning them with each other and with her own views:

> ***Peter Warren agrees*** *that it was an expedition in search of prized items. . .*

The opening element in Text 5.1 – Site Identification – is displayed here, with macroTheme shaded.

Text 5.1 The Bronze Age Theran Society – extracts only

Site identification (macroTheme marked)	*The Cycladic Island of Thera (modern name Santorini) is located in the Aegean Sea to the north of Crete.* *(T)here has been much debate, particularly surrounding the political, religious, social and economic features of the society. Because of the absence of written sources, conclusions about the society have been drawn by archaeologists through their interpretations of buildings and houses, various artefacts and most importantly through the numerous frescoes [[uncovered]].*

The Site Identification establishes the site of interest – the *Cycladic Island of Thera*. Using a Circumstance of reason – *because of the absence of written sources* – it reveals that interpretation is very much at issue.

While the experiential content of the text still employs the language of description found in the earlier site studies, it now must also incorporate the language of interpretation. Detaching herself from the field involved, the writer establishes general and rather abstract bases of interpretation, as in the nominal group:

> *the political, religious, social and economic features of the society*

Interpretation also involves mental Processes of cognition, here realized metaphorically as Participants:

> ***conclusions*** *about the society have been drawn by archaeologists through their* **interpretations** *of buildings . . .*

The text is thus immediately marked as very abstract, dealing with interpretation of matters in the remote past, and while many matters of opinion need to be reviewed in discussing the artefacts involved, and the views of a number of authorities need to be considered, the text is overall reasonably dispassion-ate in its observations. One important aspect of the historical method the student must demonstrate involves the need to base the interpretation on actual evidence.

The second element – the Assessment of Evidence – develops the discussion by taking up, in turn, the evidence from *buildings, artefacts* and *frescoes,* all of which create the hyperThemes around which the three phases of this element unfold. Again only extracts are displayed, and we shall reproduce the first phase of Assessment of Evidence with its hyperTheme establishing directions.

What is of particular interest in this element is the constant use of mental Processes and occasional verbal Processes, which are deployed cleverly through the text, to do with how items have been INTERPRETED, examples of which are indicated. (This development compares with a similar one in the response genres written by older students and discussed in Chapter 3). Their effect is to acknowledge the complexity of observations made, while also demonstrating that the writer engages with the views and interpretations of others, making the text in this sense *heteroglossic* (Martin and White 2005: 99) in that several viewpoints are entertained.

Text 5.1—Cont'd

Assessment of Evidence 1 (hyperTheme marked)	*Since the site's initial excavation in 1967 approximately one third of the town has been uncovered (10 000 square metres). . . . The layout of buildings and the differing architectural design of the buildings HAS BEEN INTERPRETED in different ways. The discovery of bathrooms, <<connected to a sophisticated sewerage system>>, has been an area of debate. N. Marinatos CLAIMS that the rooms were in fact not bathrooms at all, but areas of religious activity and ritual, as she BELIEVES they were a very religious society. (This is reinforced by written records from neighbouring communities like Crete.) From the construction of buildings such as the palatial mansions we CAN UNDERSTAND that Therans had advanced building and architectural skills and due to this as well as the presence of industrial workshops we CAN ASSUME they had an understanding of economic stability.*

Here again we find highly nominalized Circumstances of reason, providing the evidence for the archaeologists' assumptions:

> *From the construction of buildings such as the palatial mansions,* we can understand . . .
> *due to this as well as the presence of industrial workshops* we can assume . . .

Interpersonal resources are also important in interpretation. The writer needs to be able to use, for example, the system of Appreciation in assessing the relative weight and social value of the things being interpreted:

> . . . *bathrooms, connected to a **sophisticated** sewerage system . . .*

The second phase of the Assessment of Evidence now takes up the interpretation of artefacts.

Text 5.1—Cont'd

Assessment of Evidence 2 (hyperTheme marked)	*As well as the town's layout, archaeologists have used artefacts to base their conclusions on. The excavation of pithois from buildings* HAVE REVEALED *information [[regarding the society's economy]]. . . . This* INDICATED *that there was trade [[occurring between the two settlements for some period of time]]. Other artefacts [[uncovered]] include finds such as beds, stools, tables and shelves in the irregular blocks of Akrotiri. The amount of these [[found in a small area]] reinforces the conclusion [[that these buildings were communal dwellings]],* INDICATIVE *of many people [[living in close proximity to each other]]. . . . The fact [[that workshops were found in most houses]]* SUGGESTS *that **despite social hierarchy**, most people had an involvement with the production of goods.*

Here the 'showing' Processes are used to indicate what the artefacts reveal. They are identifying, building connectedness between very abstract entities, and the second participant is often realized in an embedded clause (as discussed in Chapter 3).

> *The excavation of pithois from buildings* HAVE REVEALED *information regarding the society's economy.*
> *This* INDICATED *[[that there was trade occurring between the two settlements]]*
> *The fact [[that workshops were found in most houses]]* SUGGESTS *[[that despite social hierarchy, most people had an involvement with the production goods]].*

At times these Processes are realized metaphorically as Attributes:

> . . . *these buildings were communal dwellings,* INDICATIVE *of many people living in close proximity to each other.*

In addition to the everyday language that we saw in the site studies, here we find a move into field-specific terminology – *archaeologists, artefacts, excavation, pithois, social hierarchy.*

In the final phase of the Assessment of Evidence the writer shifts the discussion to the evidence provided by the frescoes, signalling this with her hyperTheme.

Text 5.1—Cont'd

Assessment of Evidence 3 (hyperTheme marked)	*The most spectacular and informative pieces of EVIDENCE into Theran society are the frescoes [[which have been uncovered in nearly all of the buildings so far excavated]]. . . . The Admiral's Fresco OFFERS AN INSIGHT into Bronze Age Theran society.* It PROVIDES INFORMATION *about the appearance and architecture of coastal towns as well as the countryside and other landscapes and examples of flora, fauna and traditional weaponry.* It SHOWS *the inhabitants of the island,* REVEALING *more about their appearance, clothing, possible occupations and social class. Studies of the Admiral's Fresco, as well as many other frescoes excavated,* PROVIDE CLUES *into the social position and importance of various groups and individuals in Akrotiri, whilst also* SUGGESTING *the possible impacts of religious, military, political and economic features of the Bronze Age society.*

Again we find various resources for indicating what the frescoes reveal, as highlighted in the text.

The uncertain nature of what is said is captured in various ways, for example in the use of modal Epithets and tentative Processes:

*revealing more about their appearance, clothing, **possible** occupations and social class whilst also **suggesting** the **possible** impacts of religious, military, political and economic features of the Bronze Age society*

The historical significance of the frescoes is appraised positively, using high levels of Graduation:

*The **most spectacular and informative** pieces of evidence into Theran society*

The Conclusion brings together all the various elements in the evidence examined, using a hyperTheme that looks back while moving towards summary. Like the opening element, this one is cleverly constructed, the writer reiterating the previous hyperThemes:

*In-depth studies into **buildings and houses**, investigations of various **artefacts** and **frescoes** have revealed a good deal of information.*

and recalling the *debate* alluded to in the introduction as well as the perspectives informing the interpretations:

*debate still rages surrounding many of the **political**, **religious**, **social** and **economic** features of the society.*

Using a highly metaphorical Circumstance in Theme position, the writer summarizes the reasons established for the lack of certainty of the interpretations:

Because of these multiple perspectives, the lack of written sources and the damage to other pictorial sources, *there are . . .*

and cautions that the conclusions reached are necessarily conditional:

Therefore there is **still a great deal to be discovered** *about Bronze Age Theran society.*

Text 5.1—Cont'd

Conclusion (hyperTheme marked)	*Since initial excavations in 1967, many archaeologists and historians have been involved in the interpretations of evidence [[found]].* **Because of these multiple perspectives, the lack of written sources and the damage to other pictorial sources,** *there are many contradictory conclusions. In-depth studies into buildings and houses, investigations of various artefacts and frescoes HAVE REVEALED a good deal of information. However debate still rages surrounding many of the political, religious, social and economic features of the society. Therefore there is still a great deal [[to be discovered about Bronze Age Theran society]].*

Overall, the text is a successful instance of a site interpretation, showing a student historian already skilled in developing interpretation, constructing a coherent schematic structure and providing a strong sense of the competing voices that contribute to the debates over the historical site in question.

Explaining causes and consequences in history

In the previous chapter we saw the first steps towards explanation in the historical accounts of early adolescence. Whereas in historical accounts the chain of causal links unfolds in real time scaffolded by a chronological sequence, the more sophisticated explanations of mid- to later adolescence shift to non-chronological organization in terms of factors and consequences. By mid-adolescence students start to encounter two closely related explanation genres: *factorial explanations*, where multiple factors are seen to result in a particular outcome, and *consequential explanations*, where a specific factor is found to have multiple consequences.

The schematic structures of factorial and consequential explanations are displayed in Table 5.3.

Factorial explanations have an opening element – the *Outcome* – establishing the historical phenomenon to be explained. The second element – *Factors* – is

Table 5.3 The schematic structure of factorial and consequential explanations

Genre	Elements of structure
Factorial explanation	Outcome
	Factors
	(Reinforcement of factors)
Consequential explanation	Input
	Consequences
	(Reinforcement of consequences)

recursive, since several factors are typically responsible. An optional element – the *Reinforcement of Factors* – may conclude the text.

In the case of consequential explanations, the opening element is the *Input*, which identifies the historical phenomenon of interest and it generally indicates the particular 'input' or cause, whose consequences are to be explained. The second element – the *Consequences* – is also recursive since there are normally several consequences of a phenomenon. And again there is an optional concluding element – the *Reinforcement of Consequences*.

Coffin (2006a: 75) sees these explanations as a 'bridge' between the chronologically ordered recording genres and the abstract, conceptually demanding arguing genres, but warns that students can experience difficulties in moving from the chain of cause-and-effect encountered in historical accounts to the 'multiple and simultaneously occurring factors and consequences' of the more complex explanations in later years.

Explaining causes

Text 5.2 is a factorial explanation (60 ranking clauses long), written by a student aged 16/17 years in the final year of secondary school as an examination response outlining the factors involved in the victory of the Greeks in the Second Persian War.

In discussing this text we will look at some key developments in late adolescence in terms of explaining in history: the careful textual management of the factors and how they unfold, the expansion of resources for expressing causality, and the use of Appraisal to evaluate the relative significance of the causal factors.

The first element in the text establishes a macroTheme, organizing the explanation in terms of factors rather than the chronological organization of the earlier historical accounts. The writer lists the various reasons for the Greek victory, foreshadowing the subsequent development of the text which picks up on each factor systematically. This provides a strong textual framework, allowing the writer to marshal the factors in a coherent fashion.

From the outset, the writer demonstrates control over key features of historical explanation. She identifies the outcome – *The victory of the Greeks over the*

Text 5.2 The Greek victory in the Second Persian War
(extracts only)

Outcome	*The victory of the Greeks over the Persians in the Second Persian War*
(macroTheme marked)	*during 480–479 BC came about due to many factors. Three vital factors [[determining the victory of the Greeks]] were leadership, naval strength and unity.*

Persians – and provides three main reasons for the Greek victory – *leadership, naval strength* and *unity,* highlighting their causal role by grouping them under the abstraction *factors.* The factors are evaluated as being *vital.*

Causality is also realized through the use of a causative Process:

> *Three vital factors [[**determining** the victory of the Greeks]] . . .*

as well as a Circumstance of reason:

> *The victory of the Greeks . . . came about **due to many factors.***

Opening directions having been established, the writer of Text 5.2 goes on to develop her explanatory account, elaborating on the first of the nominated factors, leadership. The hyperTheme acts as a pivot, linking backward to the factors announced in the macroTheme and predicting the development of the ensuing element.

We display extracts from the first Factor.

Text 5.2—Cont'd

Factor 1	The leadership of men such as Pausanias, Miltiades and Callimachus
(hyperTheme marked)	greatly assisted in the Greek defeat of the Persians but perhaps the most important man [[in leading the Greeks to victory]] was the Athenian strategist and tactician, Themistocles. Themistocles was described by Plutarch as a man of 'unmistakable genius' and that he was supreme [[at 'doing precisely the right thing at precisely the right moment']].
	Themistocles showed excellent leadership skills as he had the foresight [[to plan for Athens a future as a naval power]]. This ensured **at Artemisium and Salamis in 80 BC and at Mycale in 79 BC**, the Greeks had a chance [[of defeating the Persians]]. . . . The leadership skills of Themistocles played a vital role in the Greek defeat of the Persians.

The role of Themistocles as a causal factor in the victory is appraised using Judgement to evaluate his skills. Also notable, particularly for a text written under examination conditions, is the use of attribution, citing from a primary source (and thereby distancing the writer from the judgements by attributing them elsewhere):

> *Themistocles was described by Plutarch* **as a man of 'unmistakable genius'** *and that* **he was supreme** *[[at 'doing precisely the right thing at precisely the right moment']]. . . . Themistocles showed* **excellent leadership skills***.*

Extracts only will be given from the second and third Factors, sufficient to reveal how the student developed her text.

Text 5.2—Cont'd

Factor 2 (hyperTheme marked)	Another factor [[contributing to the Greek defeat of the Persians during the Second Persian War]] was the Greeks' naval strength. The Greek naval powers were clearly demonstrated at Artemisium and Salamis. . . . The naval strength of Greece led to the Greek defeat of the Persians during the naval battles in 480–479 BC. . . . .
Factor 3 (hyperTheme marked)	A further reason for the Greek defeat of the Persians is Greek unity. **In the battle of Plataea**, it was seen that Greek unity was a <u>vital</u> factor in their victory over the Persians.

The Themes of each of the elements contain causal nominalizations, reminding the reader that the social purpose of the text is to explain:

> *Another **factor** [[contributing to the Greek defeat of the Persians during the Second Persian War]] was the Greeks' naval strength.*
> *A further **reason** for the Greek defeat of the Persians is Greek unity.*

The writer displays a mature ability to reason using the resources of grammatical metaphor. Whereas in science, causal reasoning is deliberately explicit, often realized congruently by clauses joined by causal conjunctions (see Chapter 7), in history there is a tendency towards 'cause within the clause' (Martin 2007: 45). In the following example a causal relationship is set up between a nominalized factor (*the naval strength of Greece*) and a nominalized outcome (*the Greek defeat of the Persians*) linked by a causative Process (*led to*):

Nominalized factor	Causative Process	Nominalized outcome
The naval strength of Greece	*led to*	*the Greek defeat of the Persians*

A more congruent version, such as that which a younger writer might have produced, would have been realized as two clauses:

Independent clause	Dependent clause of reason
The Greeks defeated the Persians	because the Greek navy was strong.

Finally, the concluding element reiterates the factors that have been canvassed, again evaluating them as *important and essential*:

Text 5.2—Cont'd

Reinforcement of factors	*From studying the battles between the Greeks and the Persians it is evident [[that leadership, naval strength and unity were three important and essential factors [[in leading the Greeks to victory in the second Persian War during 480–479 BC]]]].*

Our analysis reveals a confident mastery of the key resources needed for historical explanation in later adolescence:

- organization of the text in terms of a number of causal factors;
- the use of a range of grammatical structures for expressing causality (clauses and Circumstances of reason and result; causative Processes; nominalizations of cause including abstractions such as 'factor' and 'reason');
- evaluation of the relative significance of causal factors and judgement of the capacity of those affecting the course of history.

Explaining consequences

Text 5.3 is a consequential explanation (58 ranking clauses) written by a girl of 14/15 years. The student had been asked to assess the impact of World War II on women's lives and roles. The text begins by identifying World War II as the factor – the Input – that changed women's lives. This is followed by a series of outcomes – the Consequences: liberation and equality; women entering the workforce and taking on traditionally male roles; the hostility encountered by the women; and the involvement of women in the armed forces. The text concludes not with a Reinforcement of Consequences but with a further Consequence – the eventual withdrawal of women's independence – commenting on the short-lived nature of this impact.

Though the expression is at times awkward, the text does, nevertheless, display some significant signs of development. As with the previous text, we see causality expressed indirectly through a range of resources, including causative Processes, Circumstances of reason and abstract Participants (see also Coffin 2004). Grammatical metaphor features in various ways, including the compacting of clauses into 'things' that can then function as causal agents or outcomes. Appraisal resources are drawn on to assess the impact of the war on women and the writer attempts to employ rudimentary citation practices.

Text 5.3   The impact of World War II on women's lives and roles

Input	Women's lives and roles in Australian society were <u>irreversibly changed and impacted upon</u> by WWII. **As is said by Darlington**, many women demanded to be more directly involved in the War effort than they had been allowed in previous Wars.

In contrast with Texts 5.1 and 5.2, written by older students, the text lacks a strong macroTheme. The opening element does, nevertheless, reveal in very general terms the overall preoccupations of the text and establishes the general direction.

Attitudinally, there is a very forceful evaluation of the War's impact on women, whose lives are said to have been *irreversibly changed and impacted upon*.

It is also immediately apparent that this young writer recognizes the need to demonstrate that she has consulted sources in constructing her text, for as we have noted earlier, this is a requirement of the historian's task. From the outset, with the somewhat clumsy *As is said by Darlington*, she foregrounds engagement with the views of other, more authoritative, voices.

The writer goes on to explain the consequences of the War's impact. In the interests of space, a paragraph has been omitted.

Text 5.3—Cont'd

Consequence 1 (hyperTheme marked)	ANZAC Day.org STATES one of the main issues [[involved in the changes [[wrought by the events of WWII]]]] as women's liberation from traditional gender roles and, more importantly, the previously unheard of equality [[it gave them]]. Women not only took on the male role of breadwinner and financial head of households, but played an active role in the War at home.

Consequence 2 (hyperTheme marked)	*The use of propaganda [[utilizing women's new-found freedom and equality in society]] encouraged them to join the War effort in different roles and capacities.* The site GOES ON TO SAY that **during the War** more women entered the workforce in traditionally female jobs. Many also took on jobs previously open to men only. They also gained all or nearly all the male pay rate for these. The pre-War rate for women was typically 54% of men's in most jobs, and **by the end of the War** was closer to 70%. Darlington's Australian History AGREES, saying that increasingly women were needed in traditionally male jobs because of increased Wartime production of munitions and other war materials, and to replace men [[who had enlisted]]. **Contradictory to ANZAC Day.org**, he SAYS that women were paid little more than half the wages [[paid to men]] [[for doing the same jobs]].
Consequence 3 (hyperTheme marked)	*Possibly the greatest factor in women's fight for equality IS EXPLAINED by Darlington, through the portrayal of the various War organizations [[which were created]].* . . . 'RetroActive 2' STATES 1941 as the year [[when Australian women would be allowed to enrol in the armed forces]], although only nurses would serve overseas and in battle zones. ANZAC Day.org SAYS that the service experience had a profoundly liberating effect on many women, and EXPLAINS how some sought jobs after the War [[that would continue their independence and liberation]]. Many had problems [[giving up the responsibility [[the War had given them]]]]. Others, however, were happy [[to return to the 'normality' of domestic life]] when the War ended.

Causality is again realized indirectly through the use of such resources as: causative Processes:

*the changes **wrought** by the events of WWII*
*the use of propaganda . . . **encouraged** them to join the War effort*

Circumstances of reason:

because of increased wartime production of munitions

and abstract Participants:

*the greatest **factor** in women's fight for equality*
*a profoundly liberating **effect***

As with the previous two texts, the writer goes beyond explanation to introduce an element of interpretation. Appraisal resources are used to evaluate the significance of the impact of the war, the writer appraising the events as having high social value, particularly for women. This is boosted through the use of strong Graduation (slightly mitigated in the second example through the use of the modal 'possibly'):

> *the previously **unheard of** equality it gave them*
> *Possibly the **greatest** factor in women's fight for equality*
> *the service experience had a **profoundly** liberating effect*

The writer also uses comment adjuncts to intrude an evaluation of an event's importance:

> *and, **more importantly**, the previously unheard of equality it gave them*

These represent significant developments as the student moves further into taking a stance and arguing for a position.

As noted above, the text displays a sustained use of attribution – an essential skill in historical argumentation that is not so apparent in the texts of younger writers. In Appraisal theory, this is referred to under Engagement, where the writer of a text engages with other members of the discourse community, including the reader and other authors. While we could be critical of the writer's reliance on a handful of popular, secondary sources and neglect of citation conventions, there are signs of growing maturity. The fact, for example, that the writer does not simply quote passages directly from the source text enables her to interpret and evaluate the source and integrate its message into her own argument. She also shows an emergent ability to orchestrate other voices, aligning them to strengthen her point:

> *Darlington's Australian History **agrees**, saying that increasingly women were needed in traditionally male jobs*

and pitting them against each other, introducing an element of critique:

> ***Contradictory to ANZAC Day.org**, he says that women were paid little more than half the wages paid to men.*

The final stage of the text shifts to a negative outcome – that ultimately social attitudes didn't appear to have undergone enduring change.

This text reveals developmental advances on the history texts we examined in Chapter 4, particularly in terms of its use of grammatical metaphor, a range of resources for realizing causality, and its deployment of sources. It does not yet, however, display the high level of abstraction, the subtle integration of

---

Text 5.3—Cont'd

Consequence 4 (hyperTheme marked)	*Finally, Darlington* EXPLAINS *how women's independence was taken away from them by the Government, Catholic Church and media as the War drew to a close. He* SAYS *that it is clear [[that women were expected // to return to their <u>traditional gender and family</u> roles, // whether they wished to or not]]. It seems that << even after all [[women had done in aid of the war effort and their liberation from tradition]],>> there would be no change in social attitudes.*

---

source material and the confident textual crafting observed in the texts by older students.

Arguing in history

As we noted above, in history two important arguing genres are those that require the writer to adopt a position and argue for it, either endeavouring to persuade the reader to accept the proposition (*expositions*) or debating two (or more) sides of an issue before reaching a conclusion (*discussions*). We have some evidence in our corpus for the writing of expositions and discussions by early adolescence in history, though they gain greater importance as adolescents move up the years of secondary school.

Table 5.4 displays the schematic structures of arguments and discussions, drawing on Coffin (2006a: 68–70).

Table 5.4   Schematic structure of arguing genres

Genre	Elements of structure
Exposition	(Background)
	Thesis
	Arguments
	Reinforcement of thesis
Discussion	(Background)
	Issue
	Perspectives
	Position

Expositions often begin with an optional element – the *Background* – providing contextual information about the relevant historical period and/or some key figures. The second element – the *Thesis* – states the general proposition to be argued. The third element – the *Argument* – is recursive, since more than one argument in support of the Thesis is provided. The final element – the *Reinforcement of Thesis* – reasserts the Thesis in the light of the arguments that have been provided.

Discussions offer a more balanced view of matters than expositions because they aim to consider alternative positions and perspectives on some matter before arriving at a conclusion. A discussion also often has an optional *Background* element which provides relevant contextual information. The second element – the *Issue* – briefly states the issue to be considered, normally summarizing the competing views about it. The third element – the *Perspectives* – offers a series of arguments from different perspectives so that different views are foregrounded, and by its nature this is recursive. The final element – the *Position* – involves the writer in adopting a position about the Issue in the light of the various perspectives reviewed.

We can recognize finer distinctions within these genres in terms of whether the argumentation is dealing primarily with *historical* events and figures or with issues of *historiographical* methods (the analysis and evaluation of source materials). The schematic structure, however, remains as above.

In order to argue successfully, students need to have a confident understanding of the historical facts and their location in time and place. They need to be able to recognize the problematic nature of such knowledge – that interpretations are contingent and that people have differing perspectives. In adopting a position, they must locate various types of evidence and evaluate its usefulness. Such a demanding task requires sophisticated use of language, particularly in terms of gaining control over the organization of lengthy texts, dealing with the increasingly abstract nature of historical discourse, and persuading the reader through detached reasoning rather than emotional appeals. The instance of historical exposition we shall consider is well organized, though whether its reasoning might always be considered 'detached' is doubtful, as we shall see.

Historical exposition

Text 5.4 (116 ranking clauses) is a history assessment task written by a girl of 14/15 years. The task required the students to argue that certain elements of the ANZAC tradition and spirit have remained constant in Australian society. (The acronym 'ANZAC', incidentally, stands for 'Australian and New Zealand Army Corps', and it was coined in World War I).

As with Texts 5.1 and 5.2, the macroTheme foreshadows how the text will unfold. In this case, the writer has selected certain ANZAC qualities that have endured: courage and determination, suffering and survival, comradeship and initiative. Each of these is taken up systematically in the following stages and elaborated upon. The final stage then threads back through the arguments and pulls together the points made.

We shall reproduce the Thesis, looking in addition below at only a couple of the Arguments proposed as well as the Reinforcement of Thesis.

Text 5.4   The spirit of a nation (extract only)

Thesis (macroTheme marked)	*In the year 2005, << when Australians all over the world will be commemorating the 90th anniversary of the Gallipoli campaign and the forging of the ANZAC tradition,>> they will be remembering a group of courageous and determined young people [[who knew the meanings of suffering and survival and the value of knowing true comradeship]]. A group of people [[who possessed the gifts of initiative // and who passed these onto following generations of Australians]].*

The opening marked Theme cleverly captures a broad sweep of history, with its references, on the one hand, to contemporary *Australians all over the world*, in *the year 2005*, and on the other hand, to *the Gallipoli campaign* (of the past) they will be *commemorating*. Successful history writing displays such a capacity to deal with extended stretches of history using dense nominal groups, while also revealing the significance attaching to the event involved.

The value position adopted is expressed using positive Judgement involving very general and abstract referents:

> *a group of courageous and determined people;*
> *the meanings of suffering and survival;*
> *the value of knowing true comradeship*

and it remains for the subsequent text is to provide evidence for the Judgement made, by reference to people and events, developed in such a way that the writer looks back to the opening, reaffirming its values, elaborating on them, while also moving forward. The effect is to create recurrent patterns of predicting, elaborating and moving to some concluding observation before a new Argument is introduced.

We shall demonstrate the point by reproducing the first Argument in full, displaying its hyperTheme and the manner in which this is elaborated.

The hyperTheme offers a generalization about the ANZAC tradition, and the claim that its most recognizable aspects are *courage, resourcefulness and adaptability*. The writer then proceeds to detail how Simpson's character embodied these attributes.

We observe how the writer deals with the interpersonal demands of argumentation as she attempts to persuade the reader to her point of view. The dominant

---

Text 5.4—Cont'd

Argument 1
(hyperTheme
marked)

The most recognizable aspects of the ANZAC tradition [[that remain constant in Australian society today]] are courage, resourcefulness and adaptability. John Simpson Kirkpatrick, <<more commonly known as Simpson, the man with the donkey>> embodied this spirit. He was the *'typical' Australian soldier. Described by Bush as 'witty, always cracking jokes, happily lazy at times, careless of dress', popular with his peers but a handful to his sergeant. Still he showed courage to the point of recklessness.* **After being reported missing on the first day in Gallipoli** *it was found that he had recovered a tame donkey from the steep cliffs on the area, and had begun work as a lone, unarmed unit, transporting wounded soldiers from Monash valley to ANZAC cove. Simpson always left his donkey in a safe position as he dashed out into the open to retrieve a wounded man.* **Unconcerned with his personal safety** *he would then take the soldier to receive medical attention.* **When warned of the perilous nature of his daily activities** *he would reply 'my troubles'.* **Known to all as 'Simpson the brave'** *he showed a spirit [[which became synonymous with ANZAC]]. He was killed by a machine gun bullet through the heart, less than four weeks after his arrival.*

---

interpersonal motif in the text is that determined by the task – evaluation of the qualities of the World War I soldiers which have persisted in Australian culture. The judgements are all very positive, reflecting a high degree of social esteem, for example:

> *popular with his peers*
> *resourcefulness and adaptability*
> *witty, always cracking jokes*
> *he showed courage to the point of recklessness*
> *he dashed out into the open*
> *unconcerned with his personal safety*
> *'Simpson the brave'*
> *happily lazy at times, careless of dress*
> *a handful to his sergeant*

In the interests of space, we will select only one other Argument to examine in detail before turning to the final element in the text. Another hyperTheme signals the start of a new Argument, this time with regard to the conditions that the soldiers endured.

It is not only at the broad text level that this writer is striving for increased coherence. A notable developmental shift throughout the text is the use of abstract terms with a summarizing function:

Text 5.4—Cont'd

Argument 2
(hyperTheme
marked)

*The conditions in Gallipoli tested the endurance of all [[involved]].
Winters were <u>freezing cold and muddy</u> but by mid year the weather had
become <u>extremely hot</u> and soldiers had to suffer <u>plagues of disease-carrying
flies and fleas</u>. There was <u>never enough water</u> and <u>food was hardly
consumable</u>. One soldier, Ion Idriess, recalls 'I wrapped my overcoat over
the tin and gouged out the flies, then spread the biscuit, held my hand
over it and drew the biscuit out of the coat. But a lot of flies flew into my
mouth and beat about inside. I nearly howled with rage'. <u>Worse than
this, the hygiene conditions were abominable, toilets were open pits and
corpses lay rotting in no-mans-land</u>. The wounded and many of the
able-bodied men quickly contracted dysentery, diarrhoea, gastroenteritis
and infections. Despite the conditions, the soldiers kept their spirits up
by swimming, and playing carelessly on the beach amidst occasional
enemy fire.*

---

the Gallipoli **campaign**
the ANZAC **tradition**
his daily **activities**
terrible **conditions**
the **situation**

Such terms play a cohesive role and function in a similar way to grammatical metaphor inasmuch as they collapse meaning sequences into a single lexical item. The
term 'campaign', for example, represents a series of events in the real world.

In some cases, the events, practices and beliefs are left implicit, referring
outside the text to a phenomenon which can be taken for granted. The ANZAC
'campaign', for example, could be referred to without providing the details
within the text, assuming that the reader is familiar with the events that took
place. Sometimes, however, these 'summarizing nouns' refer explicitly to a
sequence of processes in the text itself, creating an endophoric ('within the
text') cohesive tie. In the following example (Figure 5.3), the word *conditions*
foreshadows the ensuing text which then spells out what the conditions are.
The term is used again at the end to summarize what the soldiers endured.
While such abstractions appear in mid-adolescence, by later adolescence a
more extensive range is employed, as we shall observe in Text 5.5.

We now turn to the final element of structure – the Reinforcement of
Thesis – which also reiterates the macroTheme. The text again deals in very
abstract generalizations, evident in the opening nominal group: *the spirit [[that
made the ANZACs [[who they were]]]]* – and abstraction is sustained throughout.
It is apparent that the element looks back to the generalizations with which
the text opened, while it also brings it to a closure.

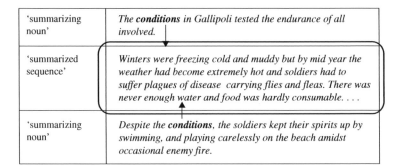

'summarizing noun'	*The **conditions** in Gallipoli tested the endurance of all involved.*
'summarized sequence'	*Winters were freezing cold and muddy but by mid year the weather had become extremely hot and soldiers had to suffer plagues of disease carrying flies and fleas. There was never enough water and food was hardly consumable. . . .*
'summarizing noun'	*Despite the **conditions**, the soldiers kept their spirits up by swimming, and playing carelessly on the beach amidst occasional enemy fire.*

FIGURE 5.3   Abstract noun foreshadowing and summarizing a sequence

---

Text 5.4—Cont'd

Reinforcement of Thesis (Reiteration of macroTheme marked)

The spirit [[that made the ANZACs [[who they were]]]] was there well before the Gallipoli campaign. It had been born of necessity in two developing nations where resilience, resourcefulness and mateship meant survival. The sacrifice at Gallipoli was enormous for such young countries and touched everyone in some way, guaranteeing the tradition a place in the hearts and minds of all generations. The spirit [[that defined [[who Australians were]]]] now had a name, ANZAC.

Lest we forget.

There are at this point no references to specific persons such as Simpson nor to the specific conditions at Gallipoli. Instead, the writer abstracts away from persons and events to offer a sweeping, unqualified generalization that builds Appreciation: *the spirit that defined who Australians were now had a name, ANZAC.* In writing as she does, the writer reveals she has been inducted into some of the values of the culture, using institutionalized criteria to make judgements about the spirit of ANZAC and the behaviour of soldiers in war, as well as that of civilians in peace. The overall evaluation is made in terms of a public social, ethical and moral framework widely known and endorsed in Australia. Acquiring the ability to express such evaluation in historical argumentation in such a manner is important. However young writers need to learn to distance themselves from morally charged positions and adopt a more measured tone if they want to convince the reader of their point of view (Martin 2002: 103). Again, while this text of mid-adolescence shows features not evident in the texts by younger writers, there is still room for development in terms of the adoption of a more dispassionate stance and a willingness to critique and problematize the issue.

Historiographical discussion

Whereas Text 5.4 is an exposition presenting arguments dealing with events and key figures in history, Text 5.5 is a discussion, weighing up divergent perspectives on an historical issue. In this case, however, the writer goes beyond considering different views on the historical matters to evaluating the soundness of the historians' interpretations. The emphasis is therefore on issues around historiography, not simply issues of history.

Developmentally, historiographical discussions are the most demanding of the history genres. Students are being asked not simply to 'do' history, but to critically reflect on the nature of history. They need to know how to detect omissions, bias and stereotyping, to discern fact from opinion, and to evaluate interpretations of historical data in terms of who made the interpretation and the historical and cultural context in which the interpretation was made. They consider the provenance, completeness and significance of evidence-based accounts of events and people in the past.

Text 5.5 critiques the different perspectives taken by historians with regard to the issue of the appeasement policy adopted by the British Government in World War II. Although written under examination conditions, this is a well-developed text (despite some inelegant sentence structures). Following a brief sketch of the policy – the *Background* – the writer outlines the area of debate – the *Issue*. In this case, two issues are identified: the origin of the policy and the extent to which the policy was a success or failure. The text then deals with each issue in turn, presenting the views of various historians – the *Perspectives* stage. Crucially, however, as each perspective is canvassed, the writer shifts to a critique – or *Historiographical Analysis* – of the validity of the position. (In this text, the historiographical analysis forms a distinct stage in the text, though in other texts it is often found interspersed throughout the discussion.) The text concludes with the writer's stance – the *Position* statement – though not with regard to the historical debate but to the historiographical issues. Because this is a very long text (185 ranking clauses), only extracts will be referred to.

Here we will focus on only two features that are fundamental to historiographical discussion at this advanced level: the use of various types of abstraction and of the language of evaluation.

From the outset, this text is highly abstract. In the Issue stage, the writer is establishing the social purpose of the text by using abstractions relating to the nature of the discussion genre, for example:

> *This **controversial topic** has had historians **in debate** over many years*
> *two **areas of debate** have been **contested***
> *they include the **debates** on the origin of appeasement*
> *When examining **debates** and the **different attitudes and approaches***

The Issue element provides the macroTheme, signalling the development of the text in terms of the two major issues identified by the writer. It also emphasizes the fact that the purpose of the discussion is not simply to debate the historical issues but to explain the positions taken in terms of the historiographical factors.

Text 5.5   The British Policy of Appeasement in World War II (extracts only)

Background	*Appeasement was a foreign policy [[employed by the British Government]].* **In particular,** *the policy came into prominence with the appeasement of Adolf Hitler prior to the outbreak of the Second World War.*
Issue/s (macroTheme marked)	*This controversial topic has had historians in debate over many years as to the actual policy of appeasement as it was employed by the British Government, especially by the Prime Minister, Neville Chamberlain, and the outcomes [[adopting such a policy]] made.* **In particular,** *two areas of debate have been contested by a number of historians and they include the debates on the origin of appeasement and its relationship to earlier policies, and the extent [[to which appeasement was a success or failure]].* **When examining debates and the different attitudes and approaches [[historians make towards them]],** *it is essential [[to identify the historiographical issues [[that influenced their writing]]]]. Amongst other ideas, these issues included the context of the historians such as their education, bias, use of evidence, purpose for writing and their historical and political backgrounds.*

We can start to distinguish two types of abstraction in this extract. The writer is bringing together two fields – one concerned with the domain of the historical content and the other concerned with argumentation around that content. Each of these fields has its own abstractions, for example:

Historical content domain	**Historical argumentation domain**
- *appeasement*	- *controversial topic*
- *a foreign policy*	- *debate*
- *the outbreak of the Second World War*	- *contested*
- *the origin of appeasement*	- *historiographical issues*
- *its relationship to earlier policies*	- *ideas*
	- *attitudes*
	- *approaches*
	- *bias*
	- *use of evidence*
	- *purpose for writing*

The abstractions of the historical content domain tend to reflect events and phenomena located in a particular setting in the material world of the past, whereas the abstractions of the domain of historical argumentation tend to reflect the world of mental and verbal activity (such as ideas and arguments) at a more general level.

There is very little evaluative language at this stage, apart from **controversial topic**, as the writer is not adopting a position but simply framing the issues.

After a reiteration of the first issue, the Perspectives stage introduces one of the historians with a view about this issue, Paul Kennedy. The reiteration of the issue functions as a hyperTheme for the ensuing element.

Text 5.5—Cont'd

Issue 1 (hyperTheme marked)	*The first debate [[that can be examined in terms of these issues]] is that of the origins of appeasement.*
Perspective A	*Paul Kennedy is a revisionist historian [[who wrote Tradition of Appeasement as a British Foreign Policy 1865–1939]]. **In his chapter, 'Strategy and Diplomacy'**, he* SUGGESTS *that appeasement had been a foreign policy of Britain and had been a working model since 1865. He* SUGGESTS *that the policy was introduced based on a number of factors including [[it being a <u>pragmatic, conciliatory, reasonable</u> approach]] and other factors such as morality and Britain's domestic national situation, economy and global position. Kennedy also* SUGGESTS *that Britain used it to avoid confrontation, eliminate antagonism and reduce commitment. Thus he is* ALLUDING *that Chamberlain only continued with appeasement as a matter of political tradition. He* BELIEVED *Chamberlain pursued it as <u>he dominated his cabinet, was unable to admit his faults [[in choosing it]], was intolerant of criticism and had a genuine loathing of war</u>. He also* THINKS *the policy was <u>reasonable</u> in that the Government was <u>cautious</u> after World War I, <u>had no allies</u> and <u>could only fight a war if their dominions supported it</u>.*

Here the focus is not so much on historical matters as on Kennedy's interpretation of those matters – a step away in abstraction from the events themselves. As indicated in the extract, every sentence begins with a verbal or mental Process projecting his words and thoughts.

Kennedy's interpretation involves evaluation of the issues, both in terms of Appreciation of the policy:

a pragmatic, conciliatory, reasonable approach

and Judgement of Chamberlain's behaviour:

he dominated his cabinet, was unable to admit his faults in choosing it, was intolerant of criticism and had a genuine loathing of war

Having reported Kennedy's position, the text shifts to an analysis of the extent to which we can rely on his views to be reasonable and accurate. There is a minimal hyperTheme to introduce the analysis.

Text 5.5—Cont'd

Historiographical analysis (hyperTheme marked)

The historiographical issues arise in that Kennedy is a revisionist historian. He is also a trained historian with a PhD from Oxford and a Professorship at Yale University. [[Being a trained historian]] is therefore going to influence his work and make it attempt to be more accurate. In terms of training, Kennedy is also an expert on diplomacy, international relations and military strategy. As such his opinions and perspectives on the policy of appeasement and its origins will differ from a colleague [[who does not have this training or background]]. [[Writing in 1984]] enabled Kennedy to have time [[to reflect on history]] and he was therefore not influenced by time or contemporary feeling. He also had access to the Public Records of the time period following their release in 1967. This enabled Kennedy to gain a more balanced attitude and perspective to his account.

The abstractions are now those of historical argumentation:

*historiographical **issues***
*his **opinions** and **perspectives***
*a more balanced **attitude** and **perspective***

Kennedy is identified as a 'revisionist' and the trustworthiness of his views is evaluated positively through Judgement of his capacity:

He is also a trained historian with a PhD from Oxford and a Professorship at Yale University.

which would render his work *more accurate*. He is also judged as having expertise in related fields such as *diplomacy, international relations and military strategy*. The fact that he is writing at a distance from the time and has access to Public Records is also regarded positively, enabling *a more balanced attitude and perspective*.

The matters raised in this paragraph are then compressed in the ensuing stage as 'these historiographical issues', an abstraction functioning textually to summarize the preceding text and to provide a point of departure for the following text. The hyperTheme – Gilbert's perspective on the debate – is slightly delayed as the writer reminds the reader of the historiographical issues at stake.

Text 5.5—Cont'd

Perspective B (hyperTheme marked)	*These historiographical issues need to be addressed in order to understand why historians differ in opinions and accounts despite researching the same topic. For example, Martin Gilbert also examined the origins of appeasement in his 1963 book, The Appeasers, reinterpreted in The Roots of Appeasement, 1966. His views differ to Kennedy's as he believes that the British Government followed J.M. Keynes' approach to appeasement, that is to appease Hitler which would ease the guilt of the British from the harsh treatment of the Germans in the Treaty of Versailles. . . .*

In reporting the views of another historian, Martin Gilbert, the writer of the text again draws on the kinds of abstractions characteristic of historical interpretation:

*why historians differ in **opinions** and **accounts***
*despite researching the same **topic***
*His **views** differ to Kennedy's*
*J.M. Keynes' **approach** to appeasement*

. . . as well as the kinds of processes involved in the field of historical inquiry:

*in order to **understand** why historians differ*
*despite **researching** the same topic*
*Gilbert also **examined** the origins of appeasement*
***reinterpreted** in The Roots of Appeasement*

The text then proceeds to explain the differences in the views of the two historians by providing an historiographical analysis of the contexts in which they were writing.

Text 5.5—Cont'd

Historiographical analysis (hyperTheme marked)	*Gilbert believes appeasement began in 1914 following the outbreak of World War I where people began to adopt pacifist attitudes and began to avoid war at any cost. This view obviously differs greatly from Kennedy who believes the origins of the policy were established almost three quarters of a century earlier. Therefore in order to understand why the accounts differ it is essential [[to examine historiographical issues such as context]] to gain an increased knowledge of the historian and their context. Gilbert was a Jew and expert on the holocaust who is therefore likely [[to have formed his own opinion on the appeasement of Hitler]]. In terms of training, he is a distinguished historian who was a Fellow at Merton College, Oxford. As such, his account could be considered to be reliable. His purpose [[for writing]] however demonstrates his bias in that he claims to be encouraged by men [[who dealt with this sign of 'British weakness']]. . . . By studying the historiographical issues, the reader is able [[to appreciate how and why the accounts of the two historians vary // despite writing on the same topic]].*

Again we find the kinds of abstractions typical of historiographical inquiry:

*This **view** obviously differs greatly from Kennedy*
*why the **accounts** differ*
*it is essential to examine **historiographical issues** such as **context***
*his own **opinion** on the appeasement of Hitler*
*his **account** could be considered to be reliable*
*His **purpose** for writing*

In terms of Appraisal, the writer again draws on Judgement of the historian's capacity and Appreciation of contextual factors in evaluating the reliability of the propositions proferred. Gilbert is judged positively as having great expertise:

he is a distinguished historian who was a Fellow at Merton College, Oxford

Because of his training in historical investigation, his views can be considered *reliable*. However, as *a Jew* and an *expert on the holocaust* his account could be regarded as biased.

After considering the second issue – the extent to which the policy could be regarded as a success or failure – the text concludes with the writer's Position, in this case an affirmation of the need for attention to historiographical procedures in interpreting historical issues. As above, we find abstractions pertaining to historiography such as *debates, topic, historiographical issues, purpose for writing, specific contexts, accuracy, validity* and *influences on their argument.*

Text 5.5—Cont'd

Position (reiteration of macroTheme marked)	*These two debates and their relevant historians all demonstrate that in* **order to successfully use and understand a <u>controversial</u> topic such as appeasement,** *relevant historiographical issues such as the historian's purpose [[for writing]] and their specific contexts must be examined to determine the accuracy, validity and influences on their argument.*

In recognizing the linguistic complexity of this text, we can identify a number of different types of abstraction associated with historiographical argumentation. As noted previously, the first distinction is between those abstractions associated with the domain of historical matters:

> **the origins of the policy** *were established almost three quarters of a century earlier;* this **sign of 'British weakness'**

and certain abstractions associated with historiographical argumentation referred to by Halliday and Matthiessen (2004: 469) as *projection nouns.* These can be further subdivided into verbal Process nouns representing locutions and mental Process nouns representing ideas.

Projection nouns	
Verbal Process nouns	**Mental Process nouns**
e.g. statement, report, news, rumour, claim, assertion, argument, insistence, proposition, assurance, intimation, question, dispute	e.g. thought, belief, knowledge, feeling, notion, suspicion, sense, idea, expectation, view, opinion, prediction, assumption, conviction, discovery, doubt, question

Halliday and Matthiessen (2004: 469) also identify *fact nouns* (fact, case, point, rule, principle, grounds, chance, possibility, likelihood, certainty, proof, indication, implication, evidence, issue, problem, requirement) where there is no explicit projection.

In Text 5.5 we find the following examples of projection nouns and fact nouns:

Projection nouns		Fact nouns
Locutions	*debate*	*issue*
	criticism	*purpose*
	accounts	*evidence*
	argument	*factor*
Ideas	*ideas*	*point*
	strategy	*topic*
	opinions	*approach*
	knowledge	*perspectives*
	thesis	
	views	

As with Text 5.4, the abstract nouns discussed above often play a textual role in summarizing a stretch of text:

Gilbert believes appeasement began in 1914 following the outbreak of World War I where people began to adopt pacifist attitudes and began to avoid war at any cost.

This view obviously differs greatly from Kennedy . . .

Gilbert also says he used sources 'which cannot be named'.

This point suggests that the reliability of Gilbert's argument needs to be questioned

In these examples, 'this view' and 'this point' refer back to locutions articulated in the preceding text, condensing a sequence of processes into an abstract 'thing'.

With regard to evaluation, the judicious use of Appraisal resources is integral to historiographical analysis. These operate at two levels: first in reporting the historian's interpretation (based on Judgement of the behaviour of historical figures and Appreciation of historical factors) and second in evaluating these interpretations, expressing Judgement of the expertise of the historian and Appreciation of the adequacy of evidence, the influence of contextual factors, and the reliability of conclusions. Such work is preparing the students not only to be discerning consumers of historical information but also, for those pursuing tertiary study, to participate in the kind of critical analysis required of the discipline.

Lexical density in the genres of history

Figure 5.4 displays the details of lexical density in our two broad families of history genres – those that record and describe, and those that explain and argue. The figures for the former family reveal that the density starts around 3 to 4 in childhood and rises to about 5 by early adolescence. The figures for the latter family (with one exception) reveal a movement from over 5 to between 6 and 7. The general movement accords with those found in subject English, though it is in fact closer to the movement for response genres than that for stories.

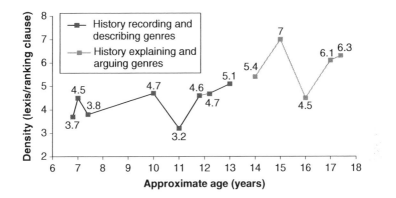

FIGURE 5.4   Lexical density in history generes

Conclusion

The language demands in writing history experienced by mid-adolescents include a move away from the recounting and explaining of events within a chronological timeframe (though this continues in various guises) to the interpreting and explaining genres. In explaining the reasons for, and results of, the historical events and changes, students use a variety of linguistic resources for reasoning about causes, influences, outcomes and consequences. Their texts are carefully crafted in terms of the flow of information and have higher levels of lexical density than those of younger writers. Topics tend to focus on historical periods in a variety of geographical and cultural contexts, now dominated by the specialist vocabulary of history denoting generalized participants in settings of time and place. Students start to reflect on the significance of events and why certain people, periods or innovations are regarded as

School Discourse

having social value to varying degrees. In late adolescence, students argue about historical propositions and discuss historical issues. There is an emphasis on matters of historiography and the lexis of historical inquiry becomes more prominent. A major development is the recognition of alternative viewpoints and conflicting accounts.

Note

[1] In fact, Martin (Martin and Rose 2003: 179) refers to this final element as 'macroNews', a term used to suggest what comes towards the end of a sequence of discourse, distilling crucial information, while also achieving some closure. Like Coffin (2006b) we have not used the notion of macroNews, since we judge the notions of macroTheme and hyperTheme as sufficient for the discussions involved in this book.

Chapter 6

Observing and Writing about the Natural World

Introduction

School science seeks to initiate the young into an understanding of scientific knowledge and scientific methods, and this has consequences for the scientific discourses that students learn to write, for it involves learning a technical language and a set of written text types or genres which encode scientific principles and procedures. In the latter half of the 20th century various progressivist and/or constructivist pedagogies had considerable influence on the teaching and learning of science (and other subjects) in the English speaking world, with often deleterious consequences (also alluded to in Chapter 2 with respect to English). That is because they frequently failed to develop an appropriate knowledge of science, its methods or its writing practices, leaving students unskilled. The impact of such pedagogies was still apparent in some Australian curricula at the time of writing this book, though it had also become clear that some reassessment had commenced, and that science education was being promoted in a more ordered way, at least in some states. The two New South Science school syllabus statements for school years *Kindergarten to Year 6* (New South Wales Board of Studies 1991)[1] and *Years 7–10* (New South Wales Board of Studies 2003c), for example, provide evidence of a more systematic approach to the teaching of scientific knowledge, including some of its history, while they aim to develop skills said to be distinctive to the discipline. Thus, the rationale statement for the 7–10 Syllabus reads in part:

Science provides a distinctive view and way of thinking about the world. The study of science has led to an evolving body of knowledge organized as an interrelated set of models, theories, laws, systems, structures and interactions. It is through this body of knowledge that science provides explanations for a variety of phenomena and enables sense to be made of the biological, physical and technological world. An understanding of science and its social and cultural contexts provides a basis for future choices and ethical decisions about local and global applications and implications of science. *Years 7–10 Science Syllabus* (New South Wales Board of Studies 2003c: 8).

Science deals with the phenomena of the natural world, involving careful observations of the phenomena concerned, and documentation of the methods used to make the observations, as well as conclusions reached. An important feature of science is that it builds on its traditions, so that various theories, methods and practices that have informed the emergence of science in the past are part of the knowledge that is taught and learned in its name in schools. In this sense, its knowledge structures are 'hierarchical' (Bernstein 2000: 155–74), meaning that they expand by subsuming various theories and principles, integrating these into a coherent body of knowledge having a logic and internal unity. While physics is typically cited as the paradigm case with such a knowledge structure, the other branches of science – biology and chemistry for example – function similarly. This is not to suggest that scientists all agree, or that that there are not significant issues always up for debate. However, it is to suggest that science functions with reasonably stable knowledge bases, that these are understood by members of the scientific community, and that even where scientists disagree – indeed, particularly where they disagree – they do so in the light of considerable consensus about what constitute established ideas and principles for working scientifically and for building scientific argument. Bazerman (1988) has offered an account of the history of scientific English from the 17th century on, tracing the evolution of the 'experimental article' in particular. Relatedly, Halliday and Martin (1993) discuss the emergence of scientific language in the English speaking tradition, using systemic functional linguistic theory to draw attention, among other matters, to its particular discourse features and the challenges these can pose for children learning science. O'Halloran (2007) offers a recent discussion of knowledge in science and mathematics, tracing aspects of the emergence of hierarchical knowledge structures in science.

Veel (1997),[2] reporting the findings of a genre-based study in secondary science classrooms in Sydney, argued that school science, while intimately related to science in the wider community, nonetheless differs from it. In wider contexts, including universities and and/or industrial and technological sites, science is practised, but also often challenged, as part of the process of building and applying scientific knowledge. In schools, Veel suggested, challenge is less common, and children spend a great deal of time reproducing science in their various activities, including writing. Science education is sometimes criticized for such a tendency, just as it is sometimes criticized for its apparently arcane uses of language, which can alienate, leaving students unable to access the discourses of science. While acknowledging the potential sources of difficulty, Veel (1997: 169) also noted, however, that a function of school science is that it necessarily simplifies and reduces the knowledge of science, in the interests of making it learnable by children: hence some of the genres of school science often do involve reproducing scientific knowledge and principles. Indeed, the very repetition of experimental procedures is in any case part of learning that they are replicable, and hence capable of validation, so that anyone following the same steps will get the same results, and hence reach the same conclusions. As for scientific terminology, a function of science will be that children learn to manipulate often unfamiliar technical language, as a necessary part of mastering the subject. These things are part of the process of recontextualization of knowledge that Bernstein (1990, 2000) argued is a feature of all school teaching and learning.

Veel (1997), Unsworth (2000) and Martin and Rose (2008) have all offered discussions of science genres, providing both typological and topological perspectives, and while we shall not consider all types, nor discuss those we select with the detail they employ, we shall draw on their descriptions in examining the texts we have collected, while also proposing at least two genres they do not propose. Our discussions are also informed by consultation with practising scientists, referred to below. As in earlier chapters, the genres discussed are selected for their relevance in tracing the developmental trajectory involved when children learn to write science, and no attempt is made to consider all those potentially found in schools. What is constant to all the genres we shall identify in this chapter and in Chapter 7 is careful attention to the study of natural phenomena, whether these are observed and recorded, experimented with, classified, described, explained or discussed.

In this chapter we shall consider *procedural recounts, demonstration genres, research articles* and *field studies,* all to do with observing, experimenting with, and documenting natural phenomena, where such phenomena are investigated either in the laboratory, or in the field. In Chapter 7, we shall turn to *reports,* to do with classifying and describing natural phenomena, and *explanations,* to do with explaining how or why natural phenomena occur, while we shall also consider *discussion* genres, sometimes found in school science, at least by the mid-adolescent years.

The developmental processes in learning to write science are similar to those discussed in earlier chapters, though there are differences, many to do with attitudinal expression. The movement is from the congruent to the non-congruent and from the immediate and 'concrete' to the increasingly abstract. As we have noted in earlier chapters, modality emerges in late childhood to early adolescence, and modal verbs in particular occur in school science texts, involved in writing statements about the likelihood/probability of some phenomenon occurring. Many science texts, however, offer no overt attitudinal expression, and this is a principal source of difference compared with either English or history. Scientific methods and procedures require that matters be reported in a disinterested fashion, where it is the phenomenon itself that requires consideration, and the object – ideally – is to arrive at some truth in a dispassionate way. Of course, it would be false to argue that attitude and evaluative stance have no role in science writing. The decision to select one phenomenon over another for investigation in itself has some attitudinal significance, though evaluative language is nonetheless restrained. Feelings in particular are rarely expressed, even among novice writers, as children learn quite early that these are irrelevant to the meanings of science.

A topology of experimental research genres

Like Bazerman, Halliday (2004a: 145) sees 'the birth of scientific English' in the work of Isaac Newton, for example in his *Treatise on Opticks* (1704). Many of the discourse features in Newton that Halliday identifies remain evident in contemporary science writing, including the procedural recounts children learn to write. For that reason, they are worth mentioning here. Thus, Halliday notes, departing from the earlier practices of writing science found in Chaucer for example, Newton used material Processes to tell what he did (e.g. *I held/ stopped/removed the Prism*), while he used Processes of projection to tell what he found or 'observed' (*I observed the length of its refracted image to be many time greater than its breadth* . . .). Further, Newton used the passive voice at those points where 'the balance of the information' required that an item be placed in Theme position (*the Sun's beam which was propagated into the Room* . . .). Halliday suggests that the contemporary use of the passive voice favoured by science writers (in practice often not observed), is historically recent, and it was not found in Newton, for he often thematized himself (Bazerman makes a similar observation.) Tense choices varied, involving the past, to create what Newton *did,* the future to tell what he said *will appear,* and some present tense choices to record what he said *appears* to be so. Apart from these matters, Newton used technical language, much of it built using grammatical metaphor, and while that is not a feature of the writing of young children writing science, it does emerge by late childhood to adolescence, as we have noted above. Clause complexes were 'intricate', employed in building steps taken in the experiment, reasons for these, and observations made as a result. As we have suggested in looking at developments in our previous chapters – in the cases of stories and response genres, for example – clause complexes that are 'intricate' emerge after about the age of 8/9, becoming more varied, as children master the various clauses of expansion, as well as those of projection. They thus become a feature of children's science writing, especially from late childhood and throughout the years of adolescence, though the extent to which intricate clause relations are deployed depends on the field and the genre.

Figure 6.1 sets out a model of the topology of these genres.

Procedural recounts, outlining an aim, a record of events observed and some conclusion, are prototypical science genres, learned in childhood and henceforth endlessly recycled by science students and scientists alike. However, by

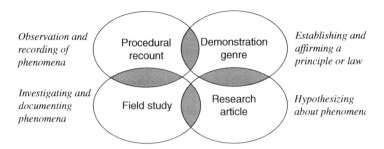

Observation and
recording of
phenomena

Procedural
recount

Demonstration
genre

Establishing and
affirming a
principle or law

Investigating and
documenting
phenomena

Field study

Research
article

Hypothesizing
about phenomena

FIGURE 6.1   A topology of experimental/investigative genres in school science

mid- to late adolescence, while procedural recounts are still employed, they are also often overtaken by developments in at least two directions. One such direction involves the appearance of *demonstration genres,* not found in Veel (1997), Unsworth (2000) or Martin and Rose (2008), which involve pursuing an experimental procedure in order to affirm a scientific principle, or even a law. No originality is claimed or sought in such a text; on the contrary, the intention is to validate, yet again, an established principle. These also outline an aim, a record of the demonstration and a discussion, where the latter affirms the principle or law. The other direction taken involves the appearance of larger genres, normally called r*esearch articles,* which investigate by outlining background information for the study, providing an aim, a hypothesis, and discussions of results and conclusions reached (though other elements are often found).

Field studies, also not found in the genre discussions of Veel (1997), Unsworth (2000) and Martin and Rose (2008), are related to research articles, though their purposes and method are different. They are associated with several kinds of scientific studies – ecological, biological and earth sciences, to name a few – and they emerged in the 19th century in areas such as biology or geology, where investigative work in some site was required. Many of Darwin's original investigations were field studies, investigating for example the behaviour of birds and other creatures in their natural environments. Field studies involve an aim and statement of the site or context to be investigated, and an account of the procedures undertaken as part of their investigations, some of which may be experimental (e.g. testing the quality of the water in a particular location). Their object is to understand the site and its phenomena. The conclusion may recommend changes and it may also identify further problems and/or hypotheses to be explored.

While the four genres differ, they all involve some kind of problem to do with natural phenomena, and observational methods and carefully conducted procedure(s) to investigate the phenomena. Hence Figure 6.1 shows areas of overlap.

Table 6.1 A sample of experimental and investigative genres: procedural recounts, demonstrations, research articles and field studies

Text	Genre	Sex and age of writer
6.1 'Plants need air'	Procedural recount	Boy aged 7/8 years
6.2 'Distillation'	Procedural recount	Girl aged 12/13 years
6.3 'AC Induction Motor'	Demonstration	Boy aged 17/18 years
6.4 'First to live, last to die'	Research article	Girl aged 15/16 years
6.5 'A study of the local street'	Field study	Boy aged 8/9 years
6.6 'Mullet Creek catchment'	Field study	Boy aged 15/16 years

Table 6.1 sets out the procedural recounts, demonstration, research articles and field study to be considered in this chapter.

Procedural recounts

Table 6.2 Schematic structure of procedural recounts

Genre	Elements of structure
Procedural recount	Aim
	Record of events
	Conclusion

Table 6.2 displays the schematic structure of procedural recounts. The *Aim* states as clearly as possible what the purpose of the scientific experiment is to be, and it normally includes advice about materials or equipment to be used; the *Record of Events* reveals what was done in an accurate ordered way; and the *Conclusion* reveals what was established.

Texts 6.1 and 6.2, both procedural recounts, were written, respectively, by a student in early childhood, and in early adolescence. Like most genres written in school science, these texts make use of images. Traditionally, the images in science were diagrammatic, though today many types of images and diagrams are found in children's science textbooks, and they encounter various examples in websites, CDROMs and DVDs. While such images or diagrams are not necessarily the same as those in the professional publications of science, they nonetheless initiate children into many of the multimedia practices of science (Lemke 2002: 24). Images then, are very much part of the mode of communication learned and employed in writing science from the earliest years. They have an essential role in building meaning, though they are not addressed in this discussion, since our focus is on the verbal text.

Text 6.1 offers a Record and a Conclusion, revealing what has been learned or 'shown'. No aim is provided, though the title reveals the general interest. The first element identifies *materials* required, and is so labelled.

Text 6.1   Plants need air

Materials required	*Material: 2 pill bottles (one with a cap)*
	Beans
	Water
Record	*What we did*
	First we soaked 50 beans. Then we filled both bottles with the soaked beans and put a little water in the bottom of each.
	Next we put the cap tight on one of the bottles and left the other open.
	Finally we shook the water over the beans.
	What we observed
	The seeds [in the bottle with the cap off] started to sprout.
Conclusion	*Conclusion*
	Plants need air to grow.

In terms of overall textual organization, we can note firstly the series of headings (all underlined by the child), pointing directions to be taken. Under the heading *What we did,* there is a series of unmarked topical Themes, identifying class members (*we*). The pattern changes with the latter two headings, for it is the phenomena being studied that are thematized. Thus, under the heading *What we observed,* specific reference is used to identify the seeds, where an interesting early use of two embedded phrases extends the meaning:

> *the seeds [in the bottle with the cap off].*

Then, under the last heading *Conclusion,* the young writer uses generic reference to write of *plants* in Theme position:

> *plants need air to grow,*

showing he is aware he now generalizes about plants from the specific experimental activity recorded. Apart from these matters, the ordered sequence of steps in the Record is marked by a series of conjunctive relations (*first, then, next, finally*). Experientially the text uses mainly material Processes, for example:

> *we soaked; we filled; we shook,*

and one mental Process of cognition:

> *we observed,*

deployed much as Newton used such a process.

The same basic structure appears in Text 6.2 (whose writer was 12/13) though there are grammatical changes characteristic of a writer in early adolescence. For example, four marked Themes appear, realizing the directions taken in the experiment, and hence in the Record, while one also starts the Conclusion. Some other grammatical matters are noted below.

Where the grammar in Text 6.1 is entirely congruent, that in Text 6.2 shows non-congruent realizations. Note for example the nominal group structure:

> *many times of repeating this process.*

The writer could have written 'After we had repeated this process many times', though the nominalization achieves a desirable outcome, in that it removes human agency, foregrounding instead the *many times* involved, making this a phenomenon of relevance to the experiment.

Text 6.2   Experiment: Distillation

Element of structure	Text
Aim	*Aim: To extract oil from leaves i.e. eucalyptus oil or lemon scented tea tree oil.*
Record	*Observations:* ***After heating the contents of the flask*** *it started to rise and bubble (boil). We were aiming to prevent boiling, so <<**as soon as bubbles appeared**>> the Bunsen would be moved away, and so on.* ***After many times of repeating this process***, *milky liquid started to drip out of the end of the condensor tube. This liquid was the lemon-scented tea tree oil, which was a milky colour. The tea tree oil had a strong scent, as it was 'lemon scented tea tree oil'.*
Conclusion	*After* ***the condensing*** *the leaves must evaporate, as the end result was free of leaves.*

The Conclusion also involves two instances of nominalization, though the grammatical expression is rather awkward:

*After **the condensing** the leaves must evaporate, as **the end result** was free of leaves*

The meaning is a little obscured here, since more congruently (and accurately) the writer actually meant: 'After the liquid had been condensed // the leaves must have evaporated // because there were no more leaves left in the condensor tube'.

Acknowledging the clumsiness of the expression, we can note that the use of *the condensing* compresses, removing human agency, while creating a phenomenon which is foregrounded. The nominalization in the last clause creates another phenomenon, *the end result*, having both temporal and causal significance.

Finally, we can note that the text is generally free of attitudinal expression.

Demonstration genres

We shall now turn to Text 6.3, an example of a demonstration, by a boy aged 17/18 and in his last year of schooling, though these can occur earlier. The text is included next because it reveals how similar many of its features are to those of a procedural recount, while it provides evidence of the developmental changes apparent in the writing of a much older student writing such a genre.

Table 6.3 displays the schematic structure of demonstrations.

Table 6.3 Schematic structure of demonstrations

Genre	Elements of structure
Demonstration	Introduction
	Demonstration record
	Discussion

The *Introduction* states the purpose of the experiment, in particular revealing the scientific principle or law which is to be demonstrated, while it also indicates any materials or equipment needed; such information is typically clarified by use of a figure. In addition, it indicates the steps to be taken in pursuit of the demonstration involved. The *Demonstration Record* reveals the results obtained. The *Discussion* element discusses the result, reaffirming the principle or law that has been demonstrated.

Text 6.3 outlines an experiment demonstrating *Lenz's Law* in physics, which states that the magnetic field of any induced current opposes the changes that induced it. While the experiment is in itself simple to execute, it leads to enunciation of an abstraction: *the principle of an AC induction motor.* Such an abstraction is created using grammatical metaphor, for it depends on observing a number of events in the physical world – detailed in the text – and abstracting away from these to create a broad generalization. The language in Text 6.3 is remarkable for the absence of attitudinal expression, while there is no overt reference to the person involved in the study, a matter to which the use of the passive voice at times contributes. The effect is to foreground the phenomenon of interest. Theme choices are unmarked, and the text contains some highly abstract nominal groups.

The Introduction details the aim and the steps to be taken, while a figure is used to illustrate what is to be done. The set of steps – the *procedure* – is detailed

as a series of points, using the imperative mood, and employing simple material Processes, reminiscent of the processes Halliday observed in Newton.
Abstraction is introduced when reference is made to the *variables*. Things
which are 'variable' are subject to change and it is important to be able to
quantify the kinds of variables that may impact on a scientific experiment and
its results. The very notion of a variable in this sense depends on previously
established knowledge concerning what might constitute such a phenomenon.
The writer of Text 6.3 thus exhibits familiarity with some reasonably abstract

---

Text 6.3   Experiment: AC Induction Motor

Introduction   *Aim: To demonstrate the principle of an AC induction motor.*
Method:
Apparatus:

- *Horseshoe magnet*
- *Swinging plate*
- *Wooden frame for plate*

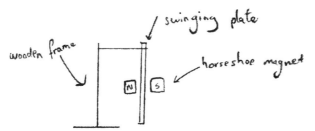

FIGURE 1   The experimental set-up

1) *Set up the equipment as shown in Figure.*
2) *Move the magnet quickly away from the plate, and observe and record the
   motion of the plate.*
3) *Move the magnet from a position away from the plate quickly towards it,
   to the starting position around the plate as shown in Figure 1. Observe
   and record the motion of the plate.*

INDEPENDENT VARIABLE: The direction of the magnet.
DEPENDENT VARIABLE: The direction of movement of the plate.
*CONDITIONED VARIABLES: The plate used, the magnet used, the wooden
frame used.*

Demonstration   *Risk assessment: The magnet was heavy, and could be dropped on a toe.*
record   *Covered footwear was used, and care was taken to reduce this risk. Also, the
wooden frame consisted of a sharp, nail like object [[on which to hang the
plate]]. This could cause injury, especially to the eye. To reduce this risk, care
was taken.*

(Continued)

Text 6.3—Cont'd

Results:

DIRECTION OF MOVEMENT OF MAGNET	DIRECTION OF MOVEMENT OF PLATE
towards *away*	*towards* *away*

Discussion

Discussion: The experiment demonstrated Lenz's Law. The eddy current [[produced]] must have been produced in such a way [[as to oppose the motion of the magnet]].
The movement [[produced in the plate]] was minimal, though movement was still visible. The experiment could be improved by increasing the strength of the magnet, or the speed [[with which it is moved]] in order to produce more movement in the plate. The experiment could also be improved by repetition.
The principle of an AC generator was evident through the movement produced in the plate. It shows that a magnetic field can produce movement.

---

principles and methods, when he identifies his three variables. Effectively he defines them, for there are three implicit identifying Processes involved:

> *The independent variable is the direction of the magnet.*
> *The dependent variable is the direction of movement of the plate.*
> *The conditioned variables are the plate used, the magnet used, the wooden frame used.*

The Demonstration Record uses the past tense, signalling that matters are recorded after the event, and there is further compression of meaning in the nominal groups, using grammatical metaphor:

> *direction of movement of magnet*

and

> *direction of movement of plate.*

The notion of *risk assessment* is another abstraction. Incidentally, one practising scientist we consulted observed that a statement of risks and how they are addressed has become more commonly a feature of such genres than in the past, suggesting that it may become a recognized element of structure in the future.

Apart from these matters, there is some grammatical metaphor expressed in one Circumstance of manner, for it expresses a causal connection between events:

*The eddy current [[produced]] must have been produced **in such a way [[as to oppose the motion of the magnet]]**.*

More congruently this might read:

'The magnet did not move // because the eddy current opposed it.'

Finally, the Discussion uses two relational identifying Processes, among other things, to reveal what has been 'shown', and again this is reminiscent of Newton:

*The experiment **demonstrated** Lenz's Law*

and, in the last clause:

*(the movement produced in the plate) **shows** [[that a magnetic field can produce movement]].*

This is a very abstract text, marked by a level of abstraction not found in the writing of younger students, either in childhood or in early adolescence.

Research articles

Our data suggest that procedural recounts, while found in childhood, are not as common as reports, to be considered in our next chapter, but they are the commonest of the scientific text types written in early adolescence, and they continue to be used throughout the years of adolescence. Demonstrations, such as Text 6.3, and research articles, tend to emerge by mid-adolescence. Research articles incorporate some of the elements found in procedural recounts (and indeed in demonstration genres), but they embrace a number of other elements, and they pursue those principles for mounting scientific argument, which, Bazerman (1988: 79) suggests, have been fundamental in the emergence of experimental reports or articles. Such principles constrain the manner in which the argument is constructed, so that it is a different kind of argument, for example, from that found in the expositions of history (Chapter 5) or the thematic interpretations of English (Chapter 3). In fact the language capacities needed to write a research article, like those for writing field studies, are those that typically emerge in adolescence. They are apparent, as we noted above, both in the expansion of all resources found within clauses, and in the expanded range of clause interdependencies that develop by late childhood to mid-adolescence, contributing to the shaping of the arguments of written scientific discourse in a number of ways. There are variations in the overall structures of research or experimental articles, though some reasonably constant features emerge. The schematic structure offered here draws on the work of a group of practising scientists at the University of Technology, Sydney (personal communication), and on discussions in Martin and Rose (in press), though differing a little from that proposed by the latter. Table 6.4 displays the schematic structure we have identified.

Table 6.4   Schematic structure of research articles

Genre	Elements of structure
Research article	(Abstract)
	Introduction
	Aim
	Method
	Results
	Discussion
	Conclusion
	(References)

The *Abstract* – which is optional – summarizes what is in the article. The *Introduction* explains the background to the investigation, establishing a context and the significance of the study. It normally alludes to other relevant papers, indicates why the problem is important, and outlines the aim of the particular experimental investigation, specifying the hypothesis that is to be tested by the experiment. The *Method* element details how the investigation was/is to be conducted, identifying equipment used and procedures followed, as well as any risks involved. It also identifies the observations that were to be made and how they were measured. The *Results* element identifies what was found, typically using tables, graphs, diagrams or photographs as well as the verbal text. The *Discussion* considers what inferences can be made from the data obtained, and what information can be derived from the results. It also considers new (or further) questions that emerge from the results and possible explanations. The *Conclusion* presents a summary of the outcomes of the study and their significance. The *References* element – also optional, though generally present – lists other related studies consulted.

Text 6.4, by a girl aged 15/16, is a research article, whose structure accords closely with that displayed in Table 6.3, though it shows some variations. The text is a long one (230 ranking clauses), and it was presented on a series of

12 large boards mounted in the classroom, in the manner of poster displays at the conferences professional scientists attend. The student had been asked to design and implement a research investigation, following procedures taught by her teacher, a fact made evident by the fact that all her fellow students followed similar procedures for designing and writing up their investigations, though there was considerable variation in their choices of problems examined (others included, for example, a test for measuring hearing loss in people of different ages, and a test of the water-holding properties of a number of brands of balls used in playing softball).

We shall make selective use of the text, commencing with the opening element, the *Aim*. Headings and sub-headings function as part of the textual metafunction, shaping and giving directions to the discourse. Topical Themes, with one exception, are unmarked, and their function is to facilitate the unfolding of the text and, in the first paragraphs at least, they identify algae or some features of them. The opening paragraphs are in one sense grammatically simple, in that they are built using a number of simple clauses, a number not conjunctively related: their complexity resides in the dense nominal groups in which participants are expressed. By contrast, the latter part of this element shows grammatical intricacy, in that it uses a number of interdependent clause complexes.

We should note, before displaying the text, that the student was wrong when she said that an alga is a 'single celled' plant. There are, in fact, many single-celled algal species, though many others are multicellular and therefore macroscopic, for example, the giant kelps. Furthermore, the 'black algae' she refers to may have been moulds, and therefore fungi, rather than algae. It is probable that the teacher corrected these errors, though we have no information about that.

Of the large nominal groups deployed, some identify, as in the opening clause with its relational identifying Process:

> *The aim is [[to determine //which household or pool products affect //and kill black-spot algae // and to determine // if the pool product [[we are currently using]] is the most effective and efficient // to kill all the algae.]]]]*

while others describe:

> *This form of Algae is very slow growing but very hardy.*

Other Processes are existential, whose function is also to identify, though in a different sense:

> *there are 30,000 different varieties of algae [[all containing chlorophyll]]*

Text 6.4 First to live, last to die

Introduction/ **Aim**	*INTRODUCTION* *Aim: The aim of my Science Experiment is [[to determine //which household or pool products affect //and kill black-spot algae // and to determine // if the pool product [[we are currently using]] is the most effective and efficient // to kill all the algae.]]]]* *Black-Spot Algae:* *An alga is a microscopic single celled form of plant life which may be introduced into the water by wind and rain from the atmosphere. There are 30,000 different varieties of algae [[all containing chlorophyll]]. They are one of the hardiest and most widespread living organisms on this planet.* *Black-Spot Algae is a formation of 1 to 3cm sized black (or dark blue-green) spots, which attach and adhere to pool surfaces. Black-Spot Algae form a layered structure, where the first layer (which chlorine may kill) protects under layers from further destruction. Black-Spot Algae are similar to the black Algae [[that is found on bathroom shower tiles and in silicone seams near the bath]]. It is also found in aquariums as dark blotching on the glass sides. This form of Algae is very slow growing but very hardy. It is extremely chlorine resistant.* *HYPOTHESIS* <u>*My hypothesis may be biased*</u> *as I already know the effectiveness of the pool products from past use in the pool, so they would already appear to be the most efficient. However, I believe that bleach would be more effective and I'm not completely convinced the pool products are the most successful.* *I believe either Pool Clear Acid or Bleach will have the most effective impact on the algae's growth.* *I believe these two products will be the most effective as acid creates such an uninhabitable environment for algae, and bleach is proven to kill algae and grime in bathrooms and laundries.* *OUTLINE* **In order to determine what kills blackspot algae the best and to verify my hypothesis** *I chose 5 different chemicals. These products included three pool chemicals and two household chemicals.* *I also decided to check four environmental factors [[which may impact the growth and life of Algae]]. I thought I would test these environmental factors in an effort [[to understand //why our Spa does not have Blackspot algae //and the Pool does, //even when the chlorine level in both is the same.]] The only obvious difference is [[that the Spa is much hotter //and has a cover on most of the time.]]*

CHEMICALS

Salt Water Boost
Salt water boost is granular chlorine used to 'shock dose' and boost the pools normal chlorine levels. It is normally added weekly.
Active Ingredient: Sodium Dichloro Isocyanurate (630 g/Kg available chlorine)

White King
A common household bleach used in bathrooms and kitchens.
Active Ingredient: Sodium Hypochlorite (42 g/l – available chlorine 4.0% m/v)

Morning Fresh
Morning Fresh is a common household dishwashing detergent used for cleaning kitchenware and crockery.
Active Ingredient:

Pool Clear pool acid
Pool acid used to maintain correct Ph level of pool water.
Active Ingredient: Hydrochloric acid 32% (345 g/l)

Blackspot treatment – concentrated granular algaecide
Granular chlorine spread directly onto blackspot algae to eliminate it.
Active Ingredient: Trichloroisocyannuric acid (900 g/Kg available chlorine)

Text 6.4—Cont'd

EXAMPLE OF PROCEDURES

Equipment required
- ➤ calibrated eye dropper (1 ml and 2 ml markings)
- ➤ calibrated measuring spoon (1 ml and 2 ml markings)
- ➤ measuring jug
- ➤ sample jars with labels
- ➤ ink pen
- ➤ chemicals to be used in experiment
- ➤ safety equipment for handling chemicals

Procedures

Step 1.
Clearly label the sample jar with the chemical and amount of chemical to be added.

Step 2.
Add 50 ml of de-chlorinated water to the sample jar.

Step 3.
Add ½ teaspoon to black spot algae to the sample jar.

Step 4.
While wearing the correct safety equipment, add the required amount of chemical, either 1 ml or 2 ml.

For the following liquid chemicals.
<u>Morning Fresh</u> – safety equipment required is safety glasses only as this product is classified non-hazardous
- Place a small amount of Morning Fresh on a table spoon.
- Obtain the required amount of chemical using the eye dropper.
- Place the chemical into the sample jar and attach the lid
- Place the jar on the storage tray.
- Clean the eye dropper by flushing with clean water several times.

<u>White King Bleach/Pool Clear Acid</u> – **These chemicals are extremely hazardous.** Safety equipment required is safety glasses, dust mask, rubber gloves and apron.
- Obtain the required amount of chemical directly from the chemical's container using the eye dropper.
- Place the chemical into the sample jar and attach the lid
- Place the jar on the storage tray.
- Clean the eye dropper by flushing with clean water several times.

Grammatical metaphor is frequently used to create the nominal groups building phenomena of various kinds, some expressed as the technical language of science. Possible congruent realizations are also displayed.

In all such cases the nominalized expressions, when realized more congruently, lead to clause complexes in which actions are expressed in verbal

Non-congruent expression	Congruent realization
*They are **one of the hardiest and most widespread living organisms on this planet.***	*Algae are very hardy //and they live very widely on this planet.*
*Black-Spot Algae is **a formation of 1 to 3cm sized black (or dark blue-green) spots, which attach and adhere to pool surfaces.***	*Black-Spot Algae consist of black or dark blue-green spots that are 1 to 3 cm long, // and they attach and adhere to the surfaces of pools.*
*It is also found in aquariums as **dark blotching on the glass sides.***	*It also appears in aquariums// where it grows in blotches on the glass sides.*

groups, while conjunctive relations between clauses are rendered explicit. Grammatical metaphor has a particular role in creating the technical language characteristic of scientific English (Halliday and Martin 1993). The writer of Text 6.4 shows herself well in control of many of the features of scientific English in building the technical language and/or the abstractions in which it is expressed. But there are other ways in which the writer displays a control of the written language, found particularly in the clusters of clause interdependencies used.

Thus, echoing some of the features of Newton's language, the section devoted to the *Hypothesis* uses mental processes and various dependent clauses of enhancement, involving reason, result, purpose and time, all of them involved in building meanings relevant to the hypothesis involved. An opening clause is followed by two dependent clauses as shown:

My hypothesis may be biased
as I already know the effectiveness of the pool products from past use in the pool (clause of reason)
so they would appear to be the most efficient. (clause of result)

Then the writer proceeds, using projecting mental Processes and another one of reason:

However, I believe //that bleach would be more effective
and I'm not completely convinced //the pool products are the most successful . . .
I believe // either pool Clear Acid or Bleach will have the most effective impact . . ..
I believe // these two products will be the most effective
as acid creates such an uninhabitable environment for algae (clause of reason)

The *Outline* of the method is then introduced, using a clause of purpose in marked Theme position:

> **In order to determine** // **what kills blackspot algae the best** // **and to verify my hypothesis** // *I chose 5 different chemicals,*

while later clauses include two more of projection, the first of which reads:

> **I also decided** //*to check four environmental factors [[which may impact the growth and life of Algae]],*

and the second involves quite an intricate example of grammatical metaphor expressed in a Circumstance of purpose, in which several clauses are embedded:

> **I thought** *I would test these environmental factors* **in an effort [[to understand** //*why our spa does not have blackspot algae //* **and the pool does** // *even when the chlorine level in both is the same.]]*

Congruently this would read:

> 'I thought
> I would test these environmental factors
> because I wanted to understand
> why our spa does not have blackspot algae
> and why the pool does,
> even when the chlorine level in both is the same.'

The metaphor is useful because human agency is removed in the wording of the Circumstance.

In Appraisal terms, the hypothesis section is of interest as well. Where the opening of the element is largely free of attitudinal expression (though expressions like *very slow growing* or *extremely chlorine resistant* show intensity, building emphasis, hence high Graduation), this section offers some Appreciation of the writer's own action in hypothesizing, where a reservation is openly acknowledged:

> *My hypothesis may be biased as I already know . . .,*

and a degree of negative Appreciation of the effectiveness of the pool products:

> *I'm not completely convinced the pool products are the most successful.*

Later elements show a table detailing observations made at intervals in the experimental phase, displayed here, and other matters not displayed. One small section from the Results element is displayed for its interest in terms of how the observations made are recorded. Here the grammatical intricacy noted by Halliday in Newton's work is again evident. The opening clause (using a causative Process) establishes 'what was observed', while the subsequent sets of interdependent clauses build their meanings by weaving various equal and dependent clauses.

SAMPLE OF DATA

Experiment observations
Chemicals - Variable 1 ml
NOTE: Algae appearance before chemicals added was dark green

Time period	Salt Boost	Black spot treatment	Pool Clear pool acid	White King bleach	Morning Fresh
1 minute	algae yellow to white, granules dissolved	Granules not dissolved, algae sitting on top of granules	Algae went light brown instantly	Light fading of algae	No colour change
4 hours	All algae white	All algae white, granules not dissolved	Algae light brown	Algae white, larger pieces green in centre	Algae light green
Day 2	All algae white	All algae white, granules not dissolved	Algae light brown	Algae white, larger pieces green in centre	Algae light green
Day 4	All algae white, algae breaking down	All algae white, algae breaking down, granules dissolved	Algae light brown	Algae white, flaky Only a little green in centres	Algae light green
Day 6	Algae white, flaky	Algae white, flaky	Algae brown, larger pieces olive green in centre	Algae white, flaky Only a little green in centres	Algae olive green
Day 8	Algae white, flaky	Algae white, flaky	Algae brown, larger pieces olive green in centre	Algae white, flaky Only a little green in centres	Algae olive green
Day 10	Algae white, flaky	Algae white, flaky	Algae light green	Algae white, flaky Only a little green in centres	Algae olive green
Day 12	Algae white, flaky, some clear flakes	Algae white, less flakes	Algae green, some dark green	Algae white, flaky Only a little green in centres	Algae light brown
Day 14	Algae white, flaky, some clear flakes	Algae white, less flakes	Algae mostly dark green, looks like its recovering	Algae white, flaky Only a little green in centres	Algae light brown

After outlining the results the student provides a Conclusion. In fact, the Conclusion is quite cleverly shaped, drawing on all the resources of Theme (some marked, and realized in dependent clauses), modality, several dense nominal groups (some metaphorical) realizing phenomena discussed, and a range of transitivity choices, and clause types, alluded to below. The writer offers some Appreciation of her findings, for though her hypothesis was *incorrect*, she had established *the most important thing [[I learnt from my experiment]]*.

Text 6.4—Cont'd

Results
(extracts only)

The Black-Spot Algaecide:
The algaecide [[used for this condition]] caused a gradual but consistent deteriorating effect on the algae]]. **Once the chemical reacted with the algae** // *it lost all colour,* // *broke down,* // *and died,* // *which left sediment at the base of the container.* **At the end of the observation period** *the algae had died off* // *and didn't make a recovery.*

Conclusion
(extracts only)

After reviewing the results of my observations *it would appear [[that the Salt-Boost Chlorine and the Black-Spot Treatment Algaecide are the most effective products //to kill Black-Spot Algae // and ensure // they don't re-grow.]]*

. . . .

Hypothesis Review:
Despite the fact [[I could have based my hypothesis on previous information and past experience with the pool products]], *I believed other chemicals may have been more effective. My hypothesis [[that Pool Clear Acid or White King Bleach would have the most effective impact on the algae's appearance and growth]] was incorrect.* **As it turns out,** *the two chlorine based pool products were the most effective although the other products [[used]] still impacted the algae's health to some degree.*

. . . .

The most important thing [[I learnt from my experiment]] is [[Blackspot Algae is tough stuff to kill]]. The acid had a pH of less than 0.5, a concentration of between 8 and 17 grams/litre. Most life cannot survive in this environment but the algae re-generated. The cold, dark or heat did not kill it in the periods [[tested]]. It survived the bleach and dishwashing liquid as well.
This showed me why the alga was one of the first life forms on the planet Earth. It also proves to me that algae will also survive long after most species of life are long extinct.

Three topical Themes are significant in shaping the directions of the argument here, the first realized in a dependent clause of time, alluding in summary way to what has been observed:

After reviewing the results of my observations *it would appear [[that the Salt-Boost Chlorine and the Black-Spot Treatment Algaecide are the most effective products //to kill Black-Spot Algae // and ensure // it doesn't re-grow.]],*

the second expressed in a Circumstance of concession, alluding to the hypothesis, now disproved:

Despite the fact [[I could have based my hypothesis on previous information and past experience with the pool products]]*, I believed other chemicals may have been more effective,*

while the third, realized in a clause of manner, alludes to what has been achieved:

as it turns out*, the two chlorine based pool products were the most effective although the other products [[used]] still impacted the algae's health to some degree.*

Most transitivity choices are relational in this element, realizing statements of what is the case, though two verbal Processes project:

*This **showed** me //why algae was one of the first life forms . . .*
*It also **proves** to me // that algae will survive . . ..*

Various dense nominal groups identify phenomena, some used in relational Processes that appraise the qualities of phenomena, expressing some Appreciation:

The two chlorine based pool products *were the most effective,*
the most important thing [[I learnt from my experiment]] *is [[Blackspot Algae is tough stuff* [[to kill]]].

Text 6.4 has many of the characteristics of a successful student in mid-adolescence in writing science, though the errors about algae we have alluded to were unfortunate.

Field studies

Table 6.5 reveals the schematic structure of field studies, though like research articles, these can vary. In the school science program, field studies are typically undertaken in ecological endeavours of some kind, tracing the relationships between biological and environmental factors. They are found in environmental science and geography. The *Introduction* provides background information about the field, as well as sources of concern or problems. It reveals what is to be investigated and why this is important. The *Field Features* element provides information about the field site, for example, natural environmental factors, or the impact of human activity, recording what is observed. The *Results* discusses

Table 6.5 Schematic structure of field studies

Genre	Elements of structure
Field Study	(Abstract)
	Introduction
	Field features
	Results
	Conclusion
	(References)

the matters observed and recorded while the *Conclusion* rounds things off, normally making recommendations for action. The *References* element indicates sources of information used to inform the study. Like the research article, a field study seeks to investigate and record scientific phenomena, and while some implicit hypothesis may be involved, the object is not primarily to test any hypothesis, but to amass information that might provide a basis for future actions, including proposing hypotheses for further testing.

We shall briefly examine Text 6.5, a simple field study undertaken by a boy aged 8, included here as early evidence of the emergence of field studies. The boy had been asked by his teacher to investigate his own community, identifying and observing sources of environmental pollution, and any items that could be recycled. Text 6.5 was set out as a series of steps in a power point presentation. Extracts only are displayed. The text records observation of data, the making of some predictions over what is observed and some discussion. While the child offers occasional Judgement about people:

people shouldn't leave the autumn leaves,

The text is largely free of attitudinal expression, while the recording of observations, predictions, results and explanations all reveal an attempt to record matters in an objective fashion.

While the language is reasonably simple, characteristic of a child of 8, it is interesting that he makes use of several dependent clauses, employing them to weave together steps in the way he reasons about phenomena:

*Everything was left by people even the natural things// **because people should get their droppings in bags** (clause of reason) // **to throw away** (clause of purpose)*
*They should put them on the garden //**to save water**. (clause of purpose)*
*The tissue is gone //**because they fall apart easily**. (clause of reason)*
*It hasn't rained yet // **so the river is still okay**. (clause of result)*
*Car oil spills. Still there // **because it didn't rain**. (clause of reason)*
*I think a chain would be good [[to have]] // **so I don't know** //why nobody took it. (clause of result)*

Text 6.5—Cont'd

Field features	***Investigation***

First I checked my street for pollution and drew a map in a notebook
Next I listed natural pollution and pollution left by people

NATURAL   LEFT BY PEOPLE
Autumn leaves   Tissues
                 Petrol caps
                 Car oil spills
                 Plastic bag
                 Concrete lump
                 Apple core
                 Scraps of foam
                 Metal chain
                 Bottle tops
                 Drink bottle
                 Lollipop stick

Everything was left by people even the natural things because people
should get their droppings in bags to throw away. Another thing is
[[*people shouldn't leave the autumn leaves*]]. *They should put them*
on the garden to save water. That is called mulch.
Next I made predictions about [[*what will happen to the rubbish*]].

- *Tissue. This will rot away when it rains.*
- *Petrol cap. I will keep it I think for a souvenir.*
- *Car oil spills. Rain will wash the oil to the river and hurt pneumatophores.*
- *Plastic bag. The bag says biodegradable but it doesn't work. It is supposed to go back to nature.*
- *Concrete block. Maybe the garbage men will take it.*
- *Apple core. Birds and ants will eat it.*
- *Metal chain. Maybe it could lock up a motorbike.*
- *Bottle tops. Maybe someone will put it in the bin.*
- *Drink bottle. Same.*
- *Lollipop stick. Same.*

Results   ***Testing Predictions***
After two weeks I looked all round the street again. These things had changed.

- *Tissue. Gone.*
- *Car oil spills. It hasn't rained yet so the river is still okay.*
- *Plastic bag. The biodegradable bag is still there*
- *Concrete block. Gone.*
- *Apple core. Gone. I think the birds and ants liked it.*
- *Metal chain. Still there.*
- *Bottle tops. Gone.*
- *Drink bottle. Gone.*
- *Lollipop stick. Gone.*

Conclusion   ***Explaining what occurred***

- *The tissue is gone because they fall apart easily.*
- *I took the petrol cap.*

(Continued)

Text 6.5—Cont'd

- *Car oil spills. Still there because it didn't rain.*
- *Plastic bag. I think it doesn't work.*
- *Concrete block. Taken by garbage truck.*
- *Apple core. Gone. I think the birds and ants enjoyed it.*
- *Metal chain. I think a chain would be good to have so I don't know why nobody took it.*
- *Bottle tops. People tidied up.*
- *Drink bottle. People tidied up.*
- *Lollipop stick. People tidied up.*

Text 6.6, written by a boy aged 16, is a more mature instance of a field study. It is quite long (1527 ranking clauses) and was written in geography. It records a field study of the *Mullet Creek Catchment*. The creek involved, incidentally, is to be found near the Australian city of Wollongong, where some of the texts used in this book were collected. We shall examine the opening element, in which the writer provides some background information about the physical site and a statement of the aim of the investigation. Several quite dense nominal groups (some involving grammatical metaphor) are used to identify phenomena and/or entities of interest, and while several clauses are relatively simple, such as the first, which creates a single sentence, others are deployed in clause complexes relevant to building aspects of the problem or of the aim.

One marked Theme (expressed in a grammatical metaphor) establishes reference to previous events, realized in a Circumstance of time:

Before human invasion, *this ecosystem was unspoiled,*

while another, realized in two dependent clauses of concession, acknowledges previous useful activity:

while some problems have been recognized (clause of concession)
and (while) some improvements have been made by Wollongong City Council (clause of concession)
more needs to be done.

The third marked Theme introduces a clause complex in which two dependent clauses of purpose and a clause of result express the aims:

During a fieldtrip on Thursday 2nd June, tests were carried out
in order to describe current conditions at Mullet Creek, (clause of purpose)
and (in order to) identify the impacts of human activities (clause of purpose)

Text 6.6   Mullet Creek Catchment (extract only)

Introduction	**Introduction**
	Mullet Creek Catchment is the heart of the water flow of the Illawarra region. Spread across the catchment is a diverse environment, where many natural processes occur. **Before human invasion,** *this ecosystem was* <u>unspoiled.</u> *Human activities have had some* <u>very negative</u> *impacts on the catchment and its natural processes.* **While some problems have been recognised, and some improvements have been made by Wollongong City Council,** <u>more needs to be done.</u>

During a fieldtrip on Thursday 2nd June, tests were carried out in order to describe current conditions at Mullet Creek, and identify the impacts of human activities so that extra management strategies could be formulated and recommended.

Location *(see Figure 2)**
The Mullet Creek Catchment is located on the south coast of NSW in the Illawarra district. It spreads through the entire Illawarra area. The site [[where the tests were carried out]] was at the Canoe Club, William Beach Park, in Brownsville, near Dapto.

The Catchment
The Mullet Creek catchment covers an area of 73 square kilometres and spreads from sea level on the shores of Lake Illawarra, all the way up to over 570 metres high onto the Illawarra Range. The upper reaches of the catchment are subject to very intense rainfall.

* Not reproduced.

---

so that extra management strategies could be formulated and recommended. (clause of result)

The writer shows skill in creating an Introduction that establishes aims and purposes for the field study, where these include establishing problems needing attention and some value positions about the propriety of addressing these. The directions to be taken in later elements are thus clarified. The directions are then pursued in the Field Features element (the longest in the text), in which the student outlines information about the *Natural environment* (*habitat survey, water quality* and *soil quality*) *Human impacts* (*erosion, recreational activity, agriculture, residential impacts* and *vegetation*). An extract shows how the writer shapes the directions taken.

Three marked Themes are used, the first of which is realized in a dependent clause of concession:

Although the right side (north side) of the creek scored well in all the sections, with good, dense vegetation cover, *the left side (south side) of the creek was shocking,* the second in a dependent clause of manner:

> **As shown in the field sketch** *(see Figure) there is a huge man-made rock*
> *retaining wall on the left bank, ensuring that the bank remains stable,*

and the third in a Circumstance of manner:

> **Instead of the natural vegetation,** *there is only a field of kikiyu grass*
> *which borders onto a road, making both Bank Vegetation and Verge*
> *Vegetation, as well as Bank Erosion and Stability, poor.*

Table 6.6 giving the *Habitat Survey Text Results,* is one of three such tables in the text, the others to do with recording measures of water and soil quality. These involve use of scientific methods to arrive at the data, so that the student reveals familiarity with established procedures, learned at some earlier point, and utilized here in the field study. A developing maturity in understanding scientific procedures and the language in which to construct them is thus evident in this writer.

Two further extracts from the Field Features element will be displayed, the first of which is selected because it provides a *factorial explanation* outlining causes of a phenomenon (similar to the factorial explanation genres to be discussed more fully in Chapter 7, where we shall in fact discuss this explanation in more detail). Its presence provides further evidence that by mid- to late adolescence young people often show considerable facility in deploying a range of grammatical resources to control written English for subject science, including embracing more than one genre type within their written texts. Thus, the first paragraph reveals the phenomenon involved:

> *Agriculture is one of the major land uses,*

and it is said to *have a significant impact on the creek and its ecosystem.* Subsequent paragraphs go on to explain the nature of the impacts – or factors involved. These are signalled very clearly using textual Themes (*firstly, secondly, thirdly,* and *fourthly*).

As already noted, this extract will be examined in Chapter 7.

The final extract we shall display from this element, addresses *Management Strategies* and a *Conclusion* follows this. The discussion of *Management Strategies* begins with a claim that there are several ways that *negative human impacts* can be addressed, while the writer goes on to itemize possible steps for *Rehabilitation.* Here negative Appreciation of the impacts of human settlement is indicated, while Judgement is expressed about what has been done in terms that state that *more will be needed.* These sections of the text are indeed the most opinionated and judgemental.

Text 6.6—Cont'd

Field features
(extracts only)

Natural Environment

The natural environment of William Park Beach and the Mullet Creek Catchment is unique. There are many segments of the environment which contribute to the delicate biodiversity of the area.

Habitat Survey

Table 6.6 Habitat survey test results

Test	Left Bank Score	Right Bank Score	Overall Score
Bank Vegetation	2 (poor)	6 (fair)	4 (poor)
Verge Vegetation	2 (poor)	6 (fair)	4 (poor)
In-stream Cover	2 (poor)	8 (good)	5 (fair)
Bank Erosion and Stability	1 (poor)	8 (good)	2.5 (poor)
Riffle, Pools and Bends	3 (fair)	3 (fair)	3 (fair)
TOTAL SCORE	10 (very poor)	31 (good)	18.5 (poor)

The Habitat Survey was carried out on the bridge, looking down at the creek, facing west toward the weir and the golf course. **Although the right side (north side) of the creek** scored well **in all the sections, with** good, dense vegetation cover, *the left side (south side) of the creek was* shocking.
As shown in the field sketch *(see Figure)*, there is a huge man-made rock retaining wall on the left bank, ensuring that the bank remains stable. This structure had to be constructed as the ground on the left bank is* bare *of natural vegetation, making it* vulnerable to erosion.
Instead of the natural vegetation, *there is only a field of kikiyu grass which borders onto a road, making both Bank Vegetation and Verge Vegetation, as well as Bank Erosion and Stability,* poor.
The In-steam Cover and Riffles, Pools and Bends both rated fairly. *The right side of the stream had good In-Stream Cover, making up for the lack of it on the left side. There were some small bends and riffles along the creek also, ensuring a* fair rating *for that section.*

* Not reproduced.

It is apparent that modality, attitudinally coloured lexis and other resources help build the overall values to do with environmental conservation. Thus, after identifying possible *Management Strategies*, the writer moves to establishing

---

Text 6.6—Cont'd

Field features
(extract only)

Agriculture

Agriculture is one of the major land uses of the land in and around the catchment area. **As mentioned above,** the weir and irrigation have had a large impact, let alone the paddocks surrounding the area. **Near the Canoe Club,** there were several paddocks to harbour introduced species (mainly cows and horses) These paddocks and their occupants have a significant impact on the creek and its ecosystem.

Firstly, a great amount of native vegetation has had to have been cleared to make space for the paddocks. The removal of native flora would destroy the homes and food source of some of the smaller organisms in the area. **With fewer plants and trees in the area around the creek,** the soil would suffer dreadfully, and this lack of plants may be one of the sources of the lack of stability in the creek bank and the large amount of erosion.

Secondly, the introduced animals themselves could do great harm to the natural environment. The creatures would not only graze and interfere with the native plants, but at the same time be competitors for native fauna for food.

Thirdly, fertilizers used for agriculture could cause problems. As the fertilizer is placed directly onto the soil, it is quite easy for it to infiltrate the ground or become run off during the next rainfall. Fertilizer could make its way into the creek, and pollute it even more.

Fourthly, pesticides used for agricultural benefits will have negative effects. Pesticides kill not only pests, but native organisms as well. They can also easily intoxicate the creek, wreaking havoc on the ecosystem.

---

what should be done, using modality to express Judgement about desirable behaviours people should pursue:

> A number of strategies **must** be used to improve the quality of the Mullet Creek Catchment and its environment

As the element unfolds, strategies such as *weed removal* are outlined, and the writer draws his account of these matters to a close by again expressing Judgement:

> but more is needed to make a significant difference.

He then goes on to outline several possible steps for education, using modality and introducing Judgements about the values of these:

> Firstly signs **could** be erected around the creek. . . . .
> Secondly, public meetings **could** be conducted, where environmental officers **could** educate the people of the uniqueness of the area and [[how they can care for it]]. . . . .

Text 6.6—Cont'd

Field features
(extract only)

Management strategies

There are a number of ways in which some of the <u>negative</u> human impacts mentioned above can be reduced. <u>A number of strategies must be used to improve</u> the quality of the Mullet Creek Catchment and its environment. Wollongong City Council have already started some programs, <u>but more will be needed.</u> These will benefit both the flora and fauna, as well as local residents.

Rehabilitation

Rehabilitation is <u>essential</u> for improving conditions at Mullet Creek. Firstly, <<**as the Bank and Verge Vegetations scored <u>badly</u> in the Habitat Survey (see Figure 3**)>> <u>something must be done to improve native vegetation. Weeds must be eradicated from the area so that new, native vegetation can be planted. The weeds should be removed carefully, preferably manually, as chemicals would harm the native flora that is already in the area.</u>
After weed removal, <u>the original plant species must be planted back into the area, in the correct numbers. The plant locations should be as close to [[how they were originally]] as possible.</u> **As the plants grow**, they will encourage native creatures back into the area. The roots will also improve soil and bank stability, lowering erosion. Deep rooted plants will also keep the water table down. There is already some revegetation happening around the area, near the large meander, <u>but more is needed to make a significant difference.</u>
. . . .

Education

It is <u>essential</u> that the local community is aware of Mullet Creek and its unique ecosystem. Many residents are already <u>harming the creek unintentionally</u> through activities such as car washing. The education could take various forms.
<u>Firstly, signs could be erected around the creek. These signs could both encourage people not to litter and to mind where they step, as well as informing them of the natural beauty and complex ecosystems in the area.</u>
<u>Secondly, public meetings could be conducted, where environmental officers could educate the people of the uniqueness of the area, and [[how they can care for it]].</u>
<u>These strategies would raise the much needed awareness [[that Mullet Creek requires]] so both local and visiting people can appreciate the Catchment without harming it.</u>

Conclusion

The Mullet Creek Catchment is a complex ecosystem [[consisting of many types of plants and animals]]. <u>There are many human activities which occur in and around the catchment which have negative effects on it.</u> However, management strategies are being devised, so that the creek can become a <u>cleaner and healthier</u> place, benefiting both the local ecosystems and the local community.

The Conclusion opens with a relational clause of attribution which establishes an important characteristic of Mullet Creek Catchment:

Mullet Creek Catchment is a complex ecosystem [[consisting of many types of plants and animals]]

while an existential clause then introduces a clause complex elaborating on this, using two dependent (non-defining relative) clauses:

There are many human activities // which occur in and around the catchment // which have negative effects on it.

Finally, a further series of interdependent clauses constructs the writer's last observation, indicating grounds for optimism:

However, management strategies are being devised,
so that the creek can become a cleaner and healthier place (clause of result)
benefiting both the local ecosystems and the local community. (clause of result)

A very short bibliography is attached to the field study, not reproduced here.

An overall strong value position about the importance of conserving environmentally sensitive areas is established in Text 6.6, making it rather different from the other texts reviewed in this chapter. Such attitudinal expression is more common in texts of environmental science than in the others discussed.

Lexical density in the experimental/investigative genres

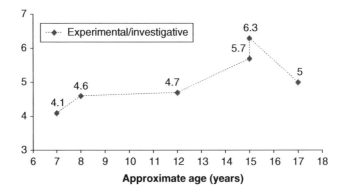

FIGURE 6.2 Lexical density in a sample of experimental/investigative science genres

Figure 6.2 displays the lexical density for the texts we have discussed in this chapter, arranged with respect to age. The three texts of childhood to late childhood (Texts 6.1, 6.2 and 6.5) all have densities of 4 or more, so that they show greater densities than do the stories and response genres by children of comparable ages considered in Chapters 2 and 3. Beyond about the age of 11 or 12, so our texts suggest, the density increases, hovering between 5 (as in Text 6.3) by a student aged 17/18, and 6.3 (as in Text 6.4) by a 15/16 year old. Science texts, on this sample, are reasonably dense, even in the earliest years.

Conclusion

Experimental and investigative science genres are important text types for children in childhood and adolescence, for they encode fundamental scientific principles that shape a great deal of scientific knowledge and activity. The procedural recount represents the prototypical experimental genre, learned in childhood and early adolescence, and remaining important throughout adolescence, though by mid- to late adolescence it is often subsumed into the research article and/or the demonstration genre. The field study, more common in adolescence than childhood (though we did consider an early instance) has elements similar to the other genres, and its principal characteristic is that it amasses significant information about some scientific phenomenon so that it can be used to inform possible future scientific endeavour. In general, experimental/investigative genres have restrained attitudinal expression, though field studies sometimes express values. In terms of language development, the first science texts are expressed congruently, shifting towards greater abstraction after early adolescence, when the resources of grammatical metaphor and an expanded range of clause interdependencies in particular open up new areas of meaning making for apprentice scientists.

Notes

[1] At the time of writing this book, this syllabus was undergoing review: http://news. boardofstudies.nsw.edu.au/index.cfm/2007/3/15/K6-Science-and-Technology-syllabus-review-set-to-commence (accessed 15 November 2007).

[2] The results of the study discussed by Veel are also reported in Korner, McInnes and Rose 2007.

Chapter 7

Interpreting Phenomena of the Natural World

Introduction

Where Chapter 6 considered children's writing of experimental or related investigative genres, in which information is derived from laboratory investigation or practical field work, this chapter will consider development in writing genres mainly devoted to *interpretation*, whether that involves classification, description and explanation of, or discussion about, natural phenomena. In these cases, the information will have been derived from classroom discussion and/or students' individual researches of the relevant literature.

The genres we are terming *interpretative* are reports, explanations and discussions, though of these, it seems discussions are the least common in school science, at least in Australia. While all scientific genres may be said to involve some interpretation, we have grouped these as interpretative in contrast with the experimental genres, whose focus is more immediately on 'finding things out' about phenomena than on elucidating broader principles or ideas. In practice, in the broader community of scientists outside schools, the experimental genres and their findings often provide the data with which, later on, they construct reports that classify and describe phenomena, or explanations that tell how or why something occurs, or that provide the data around which argumentative discussions of the science itself and/or its applications may be developed. This is because experimental/investigative procedures, once their findings have been properly validated, can lead to generalizations about phenomena, which in turn create various scientific principles and explanations, and sometimes even the 'laws' recognized in various branches of science, such as Lenz's law, alluded to in Chapter 6. However, many scientific genres are built upon scientific evidence amassed without experimental procedures, for many scientific phenomena are not amenable to experimental activity. One thinks for example, of the activity of astronomers studying the solar system, or of much biological work – that of Darwin is a famous

example – where the data are built using careful observation and documentation of phenomena. In such instances, the data amassed over time lead to
hypotheses that are tested in the light of evidence, and thence to generalizations that will be used in writing various reports, explanations and discussions,
though such generalizations are always in principle subject to challenge and/
or modification in the light of other research, while genres other than those
mentioned are written as well.

For the purposes of school science, as we noted in Chapter 6, many of the
genres found, though related to those of adult scientists, are text types used
for the apprenticeship of young learners. Reports and explanations represent
two important such text types. Where reports describe natural entities and
other phenomena, explanations tell how or why phenomena occur. Reports
are typically written as 'stand alone' texts in childhood, when they are produced as reasonably short texts, and when they are within the capacity of
even very young children learning to handle written discourse. In the years of
adolescence they are longer and they are often found in larger texts incorporating explanations, though other genres may be found. Explanations, though
sometimes written in childhood, are not common, while in adolescence they
are more common, when they are sometimes found as part of larger texts, as
in the field study we examined in Chapter 6. As for discussion genres, also
considered in Chapter 5, these address some significant issue, reviewing arguments in favour of, and against, a course of action, an idea or a position, and
they arrive at some conclusion or recommendation. We have some evidence
that these are found among young science writers by mid-adolescence, though
they are not common. From childhood to adolescence, science students seem
to write mainly procedural recounts, research articles, demonstrations, field
studies, reports and explanations. They are also sometimes asked to research
and write biographical recounts on the lives of famous scientists, not very different from those considered in Chapter 4. They are also often asked to write
short answers to questions, though we shall not consider these, because they
do not provide the more sustained passages of written discourse that interest
us in tracing the ontogenesis of writing ability.

We shall consider reports first, since they emerge very early in the writing of
young children, remaining relevant among older writers.

Table 7.1 displays the texts to be examined in this chapter, mostly reports
and explanations, though there is one discussion genre included.

Of the reports we shall examine, the first three, written from early to late
childhood, are instances of 'stand alone' texts, while the fourth, written in
mid-adolescence, incorporates an explanation within its overall structure. We
shall outline the schematic structures of both types of scientific genres, before
proceeding to discuss them.

Table 7.1   A sample of reports, explanations and discussion genres

Text	Genre	Sex and age of the writer
7.1 'Venus'	Report	Boy aged 7/8 years
7.2 'Bats'	Report	Girl aged 7/8 years
7.3 'Antarctic Food Chain'	Report	Girl aged 10/11 years
7.4 Down Syndrome'	Report	Girl aged 15/16 years
7.5 'Non-destructive testing and destructive'	Report	Boy aged 17/18 years
7.6 'How the fruit gets in the can'	Explanation	Girl aged 7/8 years
7.7 'Lunar eclipse'	Explanation	Boy aged 11/12
7.8 'Plant fertilization'	Explanation	Girl aged 12/13 years
7.9 'The impact of agriculture on Mullet Creek'	Explanation	Boy aged 15/16 years
7.10 'Electronic radiation from mobile phones is a health risk'	Discussion	Boy aged 15/16 years

The schematic structures of reports and explanations

Table 7.2   Schematic structure of descriptive and classifying reports

Genre	Elements of structure
Report	General statement
	Description
	(References)

Table 7.2 displays the schematic structure of descriptive and classifying reports.

We shall recognize two types of report, found in the school data we have collected: *descriptive* and *classifying*. The first two are drawn from Veel (1997) and Unsworth (2000), while the third is drawn from Martin and Rose (in press). Reports start with a *General Statement*, which in a descriptive report establishes the thing or entity involved, often using technical language to identify the class to which this belongs:

Bats are mammals. They are the only mammals [[that can fly]].

A classifying report establishes a phenomenon, and then classifies sub-phenomena according to some criteria. Thus a text establishes a *food web* in the Antarctic, whose elements are to be described in terms of how the creatures in the chain eat, or are eaten by, others in the chain:

Almost all life in Antarctica is in the sea and in the deep blue there is a food web.

The *Description* element provides a description of the entity or phenomenon, and this element varies, depending on the field of knowledge being constructed. Developmentally, learning to handle description seems to emerge quite slowly, and children in early childhood experience some difficulty in determining how to sequence the matters described. Text 7.1, to be examined below, reveals difficulties of this kind, while Text 7.2 manages rather better.

Table 7.3 Schematic structure of sequential, factorial and causal explanation genres

Genre	Elements of structure
Explanation	Phenomenon identification
	Explanation

Table 7.3 displays the schematic structure of scientific explanations, and again this description draws on the work of Veel (1997), Unsworth (2000) and Martin and Rose (in press) though we shall not recognize all the scientific explanations they identify, selecting those which have emerged in our collection of texts. The various science genres described by Veel, Unsworth and Martin and Rose are drawn for the most part from textbooks, most of them school textbooks in the case of Veel and Unsworth, though those discussed by Martin and Rose appear to be both school and university textbooks. These are legitimate sources from which to derive descriptions of the various science genres. However, it does not follow that all the genres identified are actually written by students in schools, and it would probably be surprising if they were. Schooling is about apprenticeship, and in practice, while several genres emerge as commonly found in school writing, others do not. Our description accords with the instances we have collected, though we are aware that others may well be found. Our selection is sufficiently representative to allow us to trace the ontogenesis of writing capacity. Scientific explanations, though closely related to those of history considered in Chapter 5, are nonetheless labelled differently, reflecting the impact of the different fields and purposes found in science from those of history.

Schematic structures of three kinds of explanation genres are discussed here: *sequential, factorial* and *causal*.

All explanation genres commence with a *Phenomenon Identification*, stating the phenomenon of interest as in:

> *There are two different eclipses and scientists discovered a long time ago how*
> *eclipses occur. An eclipse is [[when the earth or Moon blocks out the light*
> *of the Sun.]]*

The *Explanation* element varies depending on the type of explanation. A sequential explanation explains some phenomenon by establishing the sequence or order in which things occur, involving several phases; our example below, not devoted to a natural phenomenon, explains the process of picking and canning fruit. A factorial explanation explains a set of factors responsible – often interconnected – for the phenomenon, and these too involve several phases, for example, factors responsible for Down Syndrome. A causal explanation explains how or why some abstract phenomenon – typically one that is not readily observable – occurs, and it outlines causes for it, such as a lunar eclipse.

Reports

Text 7.1 was written by a boy aged 7/8 years, and it emerges from class work on the solar system. It was accompanied by a drawing of Venus.

Text 7.1   Venus

General statement	*Venus is a planet in our solar system*
Description	*Venus is the same size as Earth. It is a sphere. It is yellowish orange with some black. Venus is the second planet from the Sun between Mercury and Earth. Venus orbits the Sun in 235 Earth days. It spins once in every 244 Earth days. Venus is very old and rocky. The sky is orange with flashes of lightning.*

The General Statement successfully classifies the planet Venus:

Venus is a planet in our solar system,

while the rest of the text makes good use of other lexis (some of it technical), using relational Processes to describe, such as:

It is a sphere
Venus is very old and rocky,

and some material Processes to build actions:

Venus orbits the Sun in 235 Earth days.

However, the matters described are not well sequenced, so that the information moves rather indiscriminately from size to colour, to orbiting practices and the nature of the sky on Venus.

Text 7.2, by a girl of much the same age as the writer of Text 7.1, is rather longer, and its descriptive information is better organized. The descriptive elements are labelled to reveal how the organization works. No image was provided with this text.

Text 7.2 Bats

General statement	*Bats are mammals. They are the only mammals [[that can fly]]. There are more than 1000 kinds of bats like vampire bats, long-eared bats, three-tail bats and fruit bats.*
Description:	
Appearance	*Bats look like a rat and bird together they look like a flying rat.*
Feeding habits	*Some bats eat blood, fruit, fish and cactus too.*
Capacities	*A bat can hear from a kilometre away. They are nocturnal. Bats see by their pupils because they open them up wide to see.*
Breeding	*Bats have live babies. Bats drink milk from their mothers they can have three babies a year.*

In a manner characteristic of such text types, the first element establishes the entity involved, using relational Processes to classify:

Bats are mammals
they are the only mammals [[that can fly]],

and an existential Process, compressing a great deal of information into the nominal groups that realize the Existent:

There are more than 1000 kinds of bats like vampire bats, long-eared bats, three-tail bats and fruit bats.

Like Text 7.1 the text uses a series of unmarked Themes, and that is in fact a feature of reports, since their function is to establish an entity and then to describe it. For these reasons it is the entity itself that is primarily thematized. The organizational sequencing of the information depends on the experiential information constructed and the manner in which this is ordered: here there is a movement from appearance, to feeding habits, and thence to capacities.

Reference is handled a little awkwardly at times in the Description. For example, in the element devoted to 'Capacities', the child moves from *a bat* to *they* and thence to *bats* in as many clauses. However, her choices all reveal that she is aware she is writing of a species, not an individual bat. In other ways, the text is grammatically more complex than Text 7.1, for though it builds its information using mainly simple clauses, it has at least one sentence which uses two dependent clauses to build its meanings:

Bats see by their pupils
because they open them up wide (clause of reason)
to see. (clause of purpose)

Text 7.3, by a girl aged 10/11, is a classifying report, detailing the sub-groups of living creatures in the *food web* found in Antarctica, mainly in terms of how each type of creature eats, and/or is eaten by, others in the chain. It does this by describing the *primary* and *secondary consumers*, as well as the *top predators*, each group of which represents another 'type' in the food chain. The text shows evidence of emergent development, compared with the earlier texts, in terms of length, lexis and grammatical organization. Theme choices, with two exceptions, are unmarked, for this is a genre that essentially describes.

Text 7.3   The Antarctic Food Chain

General statement	*Almost all life in Antarctica is in the sea and* **in the deep blue** *there is a food web.*
Description:	
Type 1	*First off, there is plankton, phyto-plankton, (two types of small, microscopic life forms) and diatoms at the bottom of the food chain. These small life forms are part of the class 'Primary Producers'. They are eaten by larger primary consumers such as Krill, shrimp and small fishes.*
Type 2	*Krill is a fish-like creature with ten legs. Shrimp is like a prawn. These creatures feed on the smaller primary consumers and are fed to the secondary consumers.*
Type 3	*The secondary consumers consist of whales (preferably the blue whale) seals, larger fishes and penguins. The blue whale can weigh up to one hundred and seventy four tonnes and is the largest whale in existence. All of these secondary consumers are pretty high in the*

Type 4	*food chain, but not high enough [[to not have a predator]].* *The top predators in Antarctica have only one member-the killer whale, a carnivorous 27-foot long killing machine.* **With powerful teeth**, *they are the top of the food chain.*

No images accompanied this text.

Process types are either relational and to do with describing creatures:

Krill **is** *a fish-like creature with ten legs,*

or material, involving the actions of the creatures:

They **are eaten** *by larger primary consumers such as Krill, shrimp and small fishes.*

Text 7.3 functions well, in that it is well organized and it deploys its technical language successfully. It displays many of the characteristics of a young writer in late childhood, well in control of the resources necessary to enter a secondary schooling. These include, for example, capacity to deploy dense nominal groups:

*Krill is a **fish-like creature with ten legs**,*

some of which build their information using apposition to elaborate upon the meaning involved:

*The top predators in Antarctica have **only one member-the killer whale**, a **carnivorous 27-foot long killing machine**.*

The clauses are reasonably simple, as befits a text whose primary purpose is that of description. Where there are clause interconnections, they mainly involve simple additive relationships, linking clauses of equal status as in:

Almost all life in Antarctica is in the sea // and in the deep blue there is a food web,

though there is a contrastive relationship, also linking equal clauses:

All of these secondary consumers are pretty high in the food chain//
but (they are) not high enough [[to not have a predator]].

Text 7.4, a report written by a girl aged 15/16, represents further developmental growth, both because the grammatical organization is more intricate than the earlier texts, and relatedly, because this text incorporates explanation as one element of the structure. In the latter sense, it is a more complex text than the earlier ones, incorporating classification, description and some causal explanation.

The text emerged from a class project in which students were asked to research some human genetic condition causing disease or abnormalities. The text concerns *Down Syndrome*, and students were told they must name the disease and go on to describe its symptoms, diagnosis, cause, incidence, treatment and control. Sources consulted were also to be listed. The General Statement defines the condition, while the Description element primarily describes, though one phase within this element, devoted to *Causes*, provides a factorial explanation of factors responsible for Down Syndrome. It will be observed that all Theme choices are unmarked until the phase devoted to *Causes*, when some marked Themes occur, relevant to foregrounding aspects of the factorial explanation. Up to that point, the primary purpose of the text is to amass descriptive information. The text is lexically dense, partly because of the use of technical language to do with the knowledge involved, and partly because, at least when describing symptoms of the disease, the writer simply lists a set of points expressed as nominal groups. These matters are discussed below.

Text 7.4   Down Syndrome

General statement	***What is Down Syndrome?***
	Down Syndrome is a chromosomal disorder [[that affects the genetic make up of a human beings]]. Its cause is directly related to a mutation or abnormality of chromosome 21.
Description:	
Symptoms of the disease	***Symptoms of the disease***
	People with Down Syndrome suffer from a range of physical and mental symptoms. Most of the physical symptoms are apparent from birth but the level of mental incapacitation, which affects the person's ability to learn and interact, needs to be assessed when the child is older.
	The main symptoms [[associated with Down Syndrome]] are:

✓ *A smaller than average skull*
✓ *Low muscle tone throughout the body*
✓ *A large tongue*
✓ *Extra folds of skin under the eyes*
✓ *A flattened nose bridge*
✓ *Some level of learning disabilities*

There are also some other health conditions that can affect people with Down Syndrome. These are:

   ✓ *An over active or under active thyroid gland*
   ✓ *Heart abnormalities*
   ✓ *A higher risk of acute leukemia*

All of the above conditions can be effectively treated with proper diagnosis and the appropriate treatment.

Diagnosis

Diagnosis of the disease
Diagnosis of the disease usually occurs before birth. Ultra sounds can pick up abnormalities in the foetus, but further testing needs to be done to confirm Down Syndrome. There is also a blood test [[that can be performed]], this tests the mother's blood for abnormal levels of 3 chemicals, which indicates the risk of the baby [[developing Down Syndrome]]. The only definite way [[to diagnose Down Syndrome for sure]] is [[to perform an amniocentesis]]. This involves removing a small amount of amniotic fluid, that surrounds the foetus, which is then tested to confirm that the baby has Down Syndrome. Some patients however, still go undiagnosed till birth.

Causes

Exact causes of the disease
Down Syndrome is caused by an abnormality in the human chromosome 21. The reasons [[why these abnormalities occur]] are unknown. There are three different ways [[in which this chromosome can be abnormal //and cause Down Syndrome.]]

Factor 1

1. *The baby is born with an extra copy (a third copy) of chromosome 21 in every cell. This is referred to as Trisomy 21 and it is the cause of about 95% of all cases of Down Syndrome. The risks of Trisomy 21 increase as the age of the mother increases. This is shown in the image.*

Factor 2

2. **In the second type**, *a piece of chromosome 21 attaches itself to some of the other chromosomes. This is called translocation.* **If the baby also has two normal 21st chromosome** *it will show the traits of Down Syndrome.*

Factor 3

3. *The third type is much the same as the second; a piece of chromosome 21 attaches itself to some of the other chromosomes.* **In this case** *however, only 1 normal chromosome 21 is present.* **If this occurs** *the baby will not show the traits of Down Syndrome but their children could.*

Incidence

Incidence of the disease
About 1 in 800 babies are born with Down Syndrome. **With a population of about 20 000 000** *this works out to 25000 people who have Down Syndrome or 0.125% of the population.* *

*This figure relates to Australia.

Text 7.4—Cont'd

Treatment and control

Treatment and control of the disease

*There is no cure for Down Syndrome. There is not much need of treatment for the physical side of the disease but **due to the learning and behavioural disorders [[caused by Down Syndrome]]** people [[who have it]] usually need special care. The mental side can be severe or mild depending on the person. Those with mild symptoms can sometimes get jobs and live independent lives, or in group homes. This is not the case for all. Some patients need to be cared for, for the rest of their lives. This task is often left up to the parents or they are put into nursing homes. **As for the control side of things,** there is no definite way [[to predict Down Syndrome]] therefore it is hard to stop it occurring. **With the advances in prenatal tests** it can be detected very early in the pregnancy. This then gives the parents a choice of [[whether or not they want to continue with the pregnancy.]]*

(A set of references is provided, not reproduced here.)

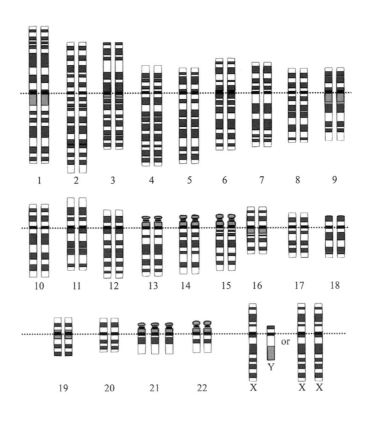

The text shows a high level of abstraction about the phenomena, some involving use of grammatical metaphor. We shall select examples only to demonstrate the point, while also commenting on other grammatical features. The General Statement uses a relational attributive Process to define the phenomenon, where the nominal group is expanded with embedding:

Down Syndrome is a chromosomal disorder [[that affects the genetic make up of human beings]],

while the *cause* of the condition is introduced, using grammatical metaphor:

Its cause is directly related to a mutation or abnormality of chromosome 21.

More congruently, such an expression might read, where the relationship between events is made explicit with a clause of result:

'Chromosome 21 *mutates so that it becomes abnormal* (clause of result)
and (so that) this produces a person with Down Syndrome'. (clause
of result)

Grammatical metaphor in such instances captures and compresses a great deal of information, establishing the focus for subsequent discussion.

The phases of the Description devoted to *Symptoms* and *Diagnosis* of the disease largely build description. A very large relational identifying Process is involved when the writer identifies the *main symptoms [[associated with Down Syndrome*), itemizing them in turn, using only nominal groups to name them and all creating abstractions. Examples include:

a smaller than average skull
some level of learning disabilities.

The phase devoted to *Diagnosis* achieves some density because of its tendency to use embedded clauses in several nominal group structures, all of them creating abstract expressions:

*There is also a blood test [[that can be performed]], this tests the mother's blood
for abnormal levels of 3 chemicals, which indicates the risk of the baby
[[developing Down Syndrome]].
The only definite way [[to diagnose Down Syndrome for sure]] is [[to perform
an amniocentesis]].*

The phase devoted to *Exact causes of the disease* marks a shift linguistically, for it is here that the resources of explanation are needed. A statement about cause is established:

> *Down Syndrome is caused by an abnormality in the human chromosome 21.*
> *The reasons [[why these abnormalities occur]] are unknown,*

while factors responsible are introduced:

> *There are three different ways [[in which this chromosome can be*
> *abnormal //and cause Down Syndrome.]]*

These are then explained in three listed points. The first introduces a technical term to name the phenomenon of interest:

> *The baby is born with an extra copy (a third copy) of chromosome 21 in every*
> *cell. This is referred to as **Trisomy 2** and it is the cause of about 95% of all cases*
> *of Down Syndrome,*

while the second also involves a technical term:

> *In the second type, a piece of chromosome 21 attaches itself to some of the other*
> *chromosomes. This is called **translocation**,*

and here a conditional clause in marked Theme position expands the explanation of this phenomenon:

> ***If the baby also has two normal 21ˢᵗ chromosomes** it will show the traits of Down*
> *Syndrome.*

The third type is said to be similar to the first, though here, as in the case of the second type, two marked Themes – the first expressed in a Circumstance of condition, the other in another conditional clause – help shape the explanatory detail:

> *The third type is much the same as the second; a piece of chromosome 21*
> *attaches itself to some of the other chromosomes. **In this case** however,*
> *only 1 normal chromosome 21 is present. **If this occurs** the baby will*
> *not show the traits of Down Syndrome but their children could.*

A pattern emerges, different from that of the earlier elements and phases, in which explanatory information about causes is constructed, interwoven with conditional information regarding the occurrences of Down Syndrome.

The phase devoted to *Incidence* (which is brief) returns to building description, while the final phase is longer and grammatically a little more intricate, since it deals with *Treatment and control of the disease.* One marked Theme, built using grammatical metaphor, occurs early in the phase:

due to the learning and behavioural disorders [[caused by Down Syndrome]]
people [[who have it]] usually need special care.

More congruently such an expression, might read, revealing that the causal connection is expressed differently:

'People with Down Syndrome do not learn well and they also often behave in such a way [[that they have to be taken care of]].'

Another marked Theme occurs in the following clause complex, which also has a dependent clause of result:

As for the control side of things, *there is no definite way [[to predict Down Syndrome]] //therefore it is hard to stop it occurring* (clause of result)

A further marked Theme begins another clause

With the advances in prenatal tests *it can be detected very early in the pregnancy,*

where this is immediately followed by another clause of result (captured in the use of the conjunction *then* which means 'therefore'):

This then gives the parents a choice of [[whether or not they want to continue with the pregnancy.]] (clause of result)

We shall briefly examine one more report – an instance of a *descriptive report* – included here to round out the discussion of the types of reports included in our review. We shall reproduce only part of Text 7.5, (which has 130 ranking clauses) written by a boy in his last year of schooling, and aged 17/18. Two phenomena (*destructive and non-destructive testing*) are being described, and a General Statement followed by Description is provided for the first, while no General Statement is provided for the second (no doubt because it seemed obvious, in view of the heading the student wrote), though Description of the second phenomenon is provided. We have thus identified two elements. With one exception the Themes are unmarked, normally identifying one of the two phenomena under discussion.

Text 7.5   Non-destructive testing and destructive

Phenomenon 1:
General statement/   *Non-destructive testing is a method of analyzing a material in such*
  Description   *a way [[that the material is still safe for further use]]. That is, non-*
                              destructive testing does not damage the material in any way. This
                              test will usually be carried out just after production or while the
                              product is in place.
                              Different types of non-destructive testing include visual inspection,
                              a dye penetrant test, magnetic particle testing, acoustic monitoring,
                              x-ray testing and ultrasonic testing.

Phenomenon 2:
Description   *Destructive testing is often used when a non-destructive test would*
                              not obtain the results [[required (i.e. a metals yield point, failure
                              point, hardness, ductility, and its modus of elasticity)]].
                              By testing these properties, *a material can be assessed and*
                              improved upon. Destructive tests can be an easier method of
                              identifying problems in a material, and can yield more accurate
                              results and information.

Dense nominal groups are evident, building the abstractions that mark this text, apparent even in the two phenomena under discussion but also in such expressions as*:*

> *magnetic particle testing, acoustic monitoring, x-ray testing and ultrasonic testing.*

Such density is one important measure of an older student writing science.

We shall now turn to explanation genres in order to explore further aspects of writing development in science.

Explanations

When we introduced the schematic structure of explanations above, we noted that such text types are not as common in the years of childhood as are reports, though they appear by late childhood to early adolescence, after which they are quite common, often in longer texts that incorporate other genres. We have few explanations by young writers in early childhood, and that seems to be because the nature of an explanation is difficult for young children. Text 7.6, drawn from research by Sandiford (1997), and written by a girl aged 7/8, does not explain a natural phenomenon, like other texts discussed in this chapter. It is included because it is a successful instance of a sequential explanation, and it would seem that sequential explanations are the earliest types of explanations learned by children. The text emerged from class work in the

---

Text 7.6 How the fruit gets into the can

Phenomenon identification *Lots of fruit is picked from orchards and put into cans.*

Explanation sequence *People pick the fruit in cherry pickers. <u>After that</u> the fruit gets put into big crates. <u>Then</u> it is taken to the cannery. <u>Next</u> it is tipped into a big bin at the cannery. **At the cannery** the fruit is washed and checked and cleaned. **<u>After</u> it is washed** it is cut into bits. The smaller bits are removed and may be processed into jam or juice. <u>After that</u> the stones are removed. <u>Then</u> the fruit is weighed and put into the filling cans, with a light syrup or juice. Any steam is forced out. <u>Then</u> the cans are sealed. The sealed cans are lightly cooked and heated and <u>then</u> they are cooled down. The filled cans are ready for labeling. **<u>After</u> they have been labeled** they are taken to the supermarket.*

---

integrated science/social science, in which the children were learning about how fruit is picked and processed in a cannery. The Phenomenon Identification establishes the phenomenon to be explained, while the Explanation Sequence makes extensive use of temporal sequence, created using either temporal conjunctive relations (shown with an underline) or marked Themes of time. The latter are realized either in Circumstances of time, or dependent clauses of time.

The grammar of the text is entirely congruent, and the text depends considerably for its success on the various temporal resources that build the sequence. It is an impressive achievement for a child of 7 or 8.

Text 7.7, also drawn from Sandiford's work, was written by another girl, aged 11/12, and on the brink of passing into a secondary education. Both elements of the text use unmarked Theme choices, and their effect is to thematize either the phenomenon itself or some aspect of it. In this sense, the text is reasonably simple. However, its most striking characteristic, compared with Text 7.6, is its grammatical intricacy, apparent in the various clause interdependencies employed to build the text. In this sense, the text marks considerable developmental advance on the earlier text. The phenomenon involved is in fact harder to deal with, for while temporal sequence of event is important, as in Text 7.6, the natural cycles of events addressed in this text make other demands on the language. This is a phenomenon whose explanation depends on more information than that which is available to the naked eye, as would be all the steps in Text 7.6. The point here is not that the information involved needs researching – the canning of fruit did as well – but rather that the natural phenomenon is quite abstract and difficult to explain. This is a causal explanation.

Text 7.7 Eclipses

Phenomenon identification	*There are two different eclipses and scientists discovered a long time ago how eclipses occur. An eclipse is [[when the earth or Moon blocks out the light of the Sun.]]*
Explanation sequence	***Solar Eclipse*** *A solar eclipse occurs when the moon moves in front of the Earth and blocks the Sun, but the Sun is not completely blocked because the outer atmosphere of the sun flashes and can still be seen and that is called the Corona. This can only be seen in some parts of the earth and happens for a few minutes.* ***Lunar Eclipse*** *A lunar eclipse occurs when the Earth is between the Sun and the Moon. The Earth blocks the light to the Moon and the Earth's shadow falls on the Moon and this is called the Umbra. The Moon doesn't disappear completely when there is a lunar eclipse but grows darker.*

The Phenomenon Identification involves two clause complexes, the first of which has three clauses, the second only one. The first clause complex is quite cleverly positioned and constructed, for it establishes what is known, using an opening clause whose existential Process classifies:

There are two different eclipses,

while the next, equal, clause uses a mental Process of projection, telling what was done on the past:

and scientists discovered a long time ago

and the third, projected clause establishes what was found:

how eclipses occur.

The way is thus cleared to define eclipses using a relational Process:

An eclipse is [[when the earth or Moon blocks out the light of the Sun.]]

Note the quite intricate clauses involved in the commencement of the Explanation Sequence, involving several dependent clauses, some of whose conjunctions are elliptical, which expand the information:

A solar eclipse occurs
when the moon moves in front of the Earth (clause of time)
and (when it) blocks the Sun, (clause of time)
but the Sun is not completely blocked
because the outer atmosphere of the sun flashes (clause of reason)
and (because it) can still be seen (clause of reason),

while the last clause, introduced using an additive conjunction, involves a referential item *that* to refer back to what has been explained and to introduce the technical term that defines:

*and **that** is called the Corona.*

The second phase of the Explanation Sequence is grammatically less intricate, though two dependent clauses of time and one of result are interwoven with others to build the sequence involved, and to introduce a second technical term:

A lunar eclipse occurs
when the Earth is between the Sun and the Moon. (clause of time)
The Earth blocks the light to the Moon
and (therefore) the Earth's shadow falls on the Moon (clause of result)
*and this is called the **Umbra.***
The Moon doesn't disappear completely
when there is a lunar eclipse (clause of time)
but grows darker.

We have earlier noted that children in their writing seem to master temporal clauses, followed normally quite rapidly by causal clauses (where these include reason and result clauses). The writer of Text 7.7 revealed facility with both dependent clause types, employing them to expand and enhance the experiential information involved to build an account of lunar eclipses. She was thus demonstrating a good control of important language resources in a manner consistent with that of a successful writer in late childhood to early adolescence.

Text 7.8 is by a girl who was a little older than the writer of Text 7.7, and unlike the latter, it uses grammatical metaphor. This is another instance of a causal explanation, in which both temporal and causal connections between events are involved, some of them expressed in overt clause interdependencies, others in grammatically different ways, to be discussed below.

We note, before displaying the text, that one awkward expression occurs in the second sentence, which reads: *The male parts are the stamens and the anthers.*

This does not clearly establish the relative positions of the two parts, and might more accurately have been stated thus:

'The male parts are the stamens and the anthers. The anther (which contains the pollen sacs) is held on the stalk of the stamen.'

Text 7.8   How do plants fertilize?

Phenomenon identification	The reproductive female part of a flower consists of a stigma. The male parts are the stamens and the anthers. These are the parts [[that make fertilization possible]].
Explanation sequence	*The first step in fertilization is pollination.* **When the pollen sacs [[that are contained in the anthers]] are ripe** *the anther breaks open and sets the pollen free. Then, birds, insects or wind carry the pollen to another flower of the same species. This is called cross pollination.* **When the pollen is carried to the stigma of the same flower** *it is called self-pollination. Cross pollinated plants are usually healthier than self pollinated ones. Many plants do not self pollinate because of this.* **Once the pollen reaches the stigma of the same species of flower** *it begins to grow. It does not stop growing until it reaches the ovary.* **When it arrives** *it pierces the ovary wall and then it goes through the ovule. This is [[how plants fertilize]].* **When the plant fertilization is finished** *nearly all the lower parts (of the flower) die and fall off because their work is done.*

The Phenomenon Identification uses grammatical metaphor to establish the issue to be explained, introducing technical language to do so. Like the comparable element in Text 7.7, this is cleverly constructed, though the resources used are different. Expressed more congruently the element would read:

'A flower has a female part // and it has two male parts. The female part of the flower is the stigma //and the male parts are the stamens and anthers. A flower reproduces // if the male parts fertilize the stigma.'

The first two sentences in the congruent version both have two equal clauses linked by simple additive conjunctions. However the third sentence involves two clauses, the second of which is a dependent clause of condition. We say this is conditional (rather than temporal, though that might be suggested) because the relationship suggested best captures the meaning otherwise expressed in the notion of *possibility* evident when the writer says:

These are the parts [[that make fertilization possible]].

In other words, fertilization is possible if the parts work together.

By deconstructing the grammatical metaphor in this manner we thus reveal some of the reasoning involved in building this explanation. Like other causal explanations discussed by Veel (1997: 179) for example, this one deals with quite abstract experience, requiring a careful account of the causes.

The Explanation, using more technical language, commences by defining the *first step*:

The first step in fertilization is pollination,

while the subsequent clauses develop the account of fertilization using temporal connectedness

When the pollen sacs [[that are contained in the anthers]] are ripe (clause of time)
the anther breaks open
*and **(then) sets the pollen free**.* (clause of time)
Then, birds, insects or wind carry the pollen to another flower of the same species. (clause of time)

The final sentence uses a strategy also used in Text 7.6 to introduce a technical term. That is, it employs the referential item *this* to refer back to the previous sequence of events and writes of it:

this is called cross pollination.

The next phase in the Explanation is commenced using a marked Theme expressed in a dependent clause of condition (though it may appear to be temporal), which establishes a process that occurs:

When the pollen is carried to the stigma of the same flower

and then names it:

it is called self-pollination.

The text goes on to provide further information:

Cross pollinated plants are usually healthier than self pollinated ones,

and the final clause uses a Circumstance of reason in which *this* refers back to what has just been written, making clear that cause here is the primary issue:

*Many plants do not self – pollinate **because of this**.*

A similar pattern emerges in the next phase, for though temporal connections between events are certainly established, because their sequence is important, the overall meaning primarily concerns *how* the process occurs, rather than *when* it occurs. The writer states:

> *Once the pollen reaches the stigma of the same species of flower// it begins to grow. It does not stop growing // until it reaches the ovary. When it arrives // it pierces the ovary wall // and then it goes through the ovule.*

Then, in the next clause another referential item – *this* – is used to refer back to what has been written, while the other participant in the clause is realized in an embedded clause:

> *This is [[how plants fertilize]].*

The final phase, again started with a Theme realized in a temporal clause, nonetheless has a causal intent, made evident in the final clause, which is one of reason:

> *When the plant fertilization is finished // nearly all the lower parts (of the flower) die // and fall off // **because their work is done**.*

Text 7.8 provides useful evidence of what a student in early adolescence can achieve by way of establishing causal explanation, despite it occasional errors in expression.

We shall now turn to our last instance of an explanation, already introduced in Chapter 6 (see page 179). It emerged, it will be recalled, as one element in a field study we examined in that chapter and it dealt with the influence of agriculture on the ecology of *Mullet Creek*. It is a factorial explanation, outlining several interconnected factors or impacts associated with agriculture. As they are clearly listed, the organization of the text is easily identified. To avoid confusion, this text is here referred to as Text 7.8, though it did appear in the earlier chapter with another name. The Phenomenon Identification element establishes what is effectively a macroTheme, or overarching theme, for the explanation, discussed in Chapter 5.

The various impacts or factors are introduced and explained using several resources, apart from the obvious textual Themes (*firstly, secondly, thirdly* and *fourthly*). Each factorial element commences with a hyperTheme, while the rest of the element expands upon this. As each hyperTheme is elaborated upon, modal verbs are often used, suggesting probable consequences of agriculture, while marked Themes also contribute:

Text 7.9   The impact of agriculture on Mullet Creek

Phenomenon identification (macroTheme marked)	*Agriculture is one of the major land uses of the land in and around the catchment area.* **As mentioned above,** *the weir and irrigation have had a large impact, let alone the paddocks surrounding the area.* **Near the Canoe Club,** *there were several paddocks to harbour introduced species (mainly cows and horses) These paddocks and their occupants have a significant impact on the creek and its ecosystem.*
Explanation Factor1 (hyperTheme marked)	*Firstly, a great amount of native vegetation has had to have been cleared to make space for the paddocks. The removal of native flora <u>would destroy</u> the homes and food source of some of the smaller organisms in the area.* **With fewer plants and trees in the area around the creek,** *the soil <u>would suffer dreadfully</u>, and this lack of plants <u>may be one of the sources of the lack of stability</u> in the creek bank and <u>the large amount of erosion.</u>*
Factor 2 (hyperTheme marked)	*Secondly, the introduced animals themselves <u>could do great harm</u> to the natural environment. The creatures <u>would not only graze and interfere</u> with the native plants, <u>but</u> **at the same time** <u>be competitors for native fauna for food</u>.*
Factor 3 (hyperTheme marked)	*Thirdly, fertilizers used for agriculture <u>could cause problems.</u> As the* **fertilizer is placed directly onto the soil,** *it is quite <u>easy</u> for it to infiltrate the ground or become run off during the next rainfall. Fertilizer could make its way into the creek, and <u>pollute it even more.</u>*
Factor 4 (hyperTheme marked)	*Fourthly, pesticides used for agricultural benefits will have <u>negative</u>. Pesticides kill not only pests, but native organisms as well. They can also easily intoxicate the creek, <u>wreaking havoc</u> on the ecosystem*

The removal of native flora would destroy the homes and food source of some of the smaller organisms in the area.
   With fewer plants and trees in the area around the creek, *the soil*
    would suffer dreadfully, and this lack of plants may be one of the sources
     of the lack of stability in the creek bank and the large amount of erosion.
Secondly, the introduced animals themselves could do great harm to the
natural environment . . . .
The creatures would not only graze and interfere with the native plants,
Thirdly, fertilizers . . . could cause problems
As the fertilizer is placed directly onto the soil, *it is quite easy for it to infiltrate*
the ground or become run off. . . .
Pesticides . . . will have <u>negative</u> effects. . .

The writer of Text 7.9 shows facility in deploying a range of resources both to provide overall organization for his text and to build the particular qualities

of factorial causes that concern him. His general attitudinal values about the
negative effects of agriculture are made clear.

We shall now turn to discussion genres, which, while they can occur in science by mid-adolescence, are not common. First, however, we shall return to
some of the issues to do with argument and challenge in science education to
which we alluded in Chapter 6, for these should be reviewed for the light they
throw on arguments in science education, and the relative absence of texts
that challenge.

Argument in science

In Chapter 6 we made reference to the fact that science education has been
sometimes criticized on the grounds that it does not sufficiently involve
students in writing texts that challenge aspects of scientific knowledge. The
argument can be misleading, for it tends to obscure the fact that in learning to
research and write science genres, children are learning some fundamental
principles for proposing and shaping scientific argument. Of course, such
argument does not typically involve challenge, if by that is meant seeking to
critique or overturn some kind of scientific orthodoxy. About that we shall
have more to say below, first saying a little more about the nature of scientific
argument as it is traditionally expressed.

The various reports and explanations discussed in this chapter, though
not experimental, certainly involve children in researching and locating the
necessary scientific information with which to develop scientific accounts of
various kinds. Though they are not overtly argumentative, their observations
may lead to arguments. However, as we suggested in Chapter 6, the various
experimental genres require children to learn principles for designing experiments, proposing hypotheses, observing phenomena, amassing evidence and
considering the results obtained, where these matters all involve argument. It
will be recalled that in their discussions of the emergence of experimental articles, both Bazerman (1988) and Halliday (2004) whom we cited in Chapter 6,
demonstrated that these involve marshalling various language resources in
order to construct argument. They were of course writing of scientific endeavour among adults, though the research articles children write are certainly
related to those that Bazerman and Halliday discussed. For reasonably recent
evidence of the continuing power of the experimental or research article
among practising scientists, we need look no further than the remarkable
research article devoted to *A structure for deoxyribose nucleic acid* (or DNA), published by Watson and Crick in 1953 that literally changed for all time the manner in which the basic building blocks of life are understood. Indeed, in the
scientific world the identification of DNA is spoken of as representing a 'paradigm shift' in our understanding of the laws of inheritance. There can be no

doubt that research articles have been, and continue to be, very commonly sites for expression of vigorous scientific challenge and argument.

School science is of course different from the science of professional scientists, for as we have noted more than once, school science is for apprenticeship. The demonstration genres we considered in Chapter 6 are evidence of a pedagogical interest in having even senior school students undertake experimental procedures that replicate, but also (re)validate, some fundamental scientific principles. The research articles and field studies we considered potentially involve students in arriving at more independent conclusions, albeit by employing some traditional principles of scientific argument to do so. For all students, an apprenticeship into science involves mastering the principles of science and the language in which they are encoded. Competent students of science can develop skill and facility in marshalling scientific arguments, and some even go on to win awards for their achievements in undertaking scientific studies.[1] At least some students will go on, in time, to write genres in the tradition of Watson and Crick. They may even, indeed, write to challenge Watson and Crick. But it is a safe bet that if and when they do this, they will write experimental articles whose overall structure and method of marshalling the argument is similar to that of Watson and Crick. If that were not the case, what they wrote would very likely not be recognized as scientific challenge at all, at least not in a form to be taken seriously. There are real constraints on the manner by which, even in the world of practising scientists, arguments of various kinds can be proposed, though such constraints should also be recognized as facilitative, in that they enable the construction of scientific arguments.

When criticisms are sometimes offered of the failure of science education to encourage the writing of genres that challenge, there seem to be two possible avenues to pursue in order to address such criticisms. One avenue would propose that children should be encouraged to examine and discuss ethically sensitive issues that emerge in science, such as genetic modification of crops, or the cloning of animals, to mention only two. These are often taught about in science, but written discussion of the ethical implications of such topics are not necessarily pursued. Where such ethical discussion were sought, it would not be within the terms of one or other of the genres we have so far discussed, for these are not amenable to such discussion. Rather, it could be within the terms of an argumentative or expository text, whose structure would be similar to that of the expositions in history considered in Chapter 5, where a particular value position was adopted and argued; or it could be within the terms of a discussion genre, reviewing arguments for and against the proposition, before reaching a conclusion. Such a discussion genre will be considered below.

The other avenue that might be pursued in the name of teaching science for challenge would involve children in taking up environmental issues and topics, such as global warming or environmental depredation. The field studies we discussed in Chapter 6 were exercises in environmental or ecological science. The only cautionary comment we would make, following Veel (1997) is that at least some of the science produced in the name of environmental science, fails to distinguish that which is reliably established and authenticated scientific observation from personal opinion.

It is no part of our plan to pursue these matters further, since they are beyond the scope of this book. We have raised them because they help explain the relative absence of what are termed genres that 'challenge' or critique. Our general conclusion is that while a case should be made for more frequent writing of texts that take up and argue sensitive ethical issues in science, especially among students in adolescence, the fact that they are not so common is not evidence in itself for a claim that students do not receive an education in argument about science. They receive an education in the principles of argument traditionally held most dear in science. When these principles are badly taught, they no doubt become dull, even pointless, not calculated to invite any interest in the issues – ethical or otherwise – that are a feature of science. But that is a matter of bad pedagogy.

A discussion genre in science

Discussion genres have been already introduced in Chapter 5 when considering historical argument, and though not common in school science, they are sometimes written by older students. A discussion genre in science involves identifying an issue, and then developing arguments for and against, normally reviewing evidence, before offering a conclusion or a recommendation. Such a genre is, by its nature, opinionated, though certain conventions apply by which the opinion is developed. Evidence is to be offered with respect to each argument, and the writer, while expected to express an opinion, should show that he or she does this in the light of the evidence. The schematic structure we shall display for discussions in science is labelled differently from that displayed for historical discussions, though the overall purpose is very similar.

Text 7.9 (with 130 ranking clauses) addresses the issue 'Electromagnetic radiation from mobile phones is a health risk'. The opening element identifies the Issue, drawing attention immediately to the fact that opinion differs over it:

Table 7.4   Schematic structure of science discussion genres

Genre	Elements of structure
Discussion	Issue
	Arguments
	Recommendation

'Electromagnetic radiation from mobile phones is a health risk'. The scientific world is divided by this statement. Some believe that mobile phones can cause great illness, while others believe that the phones are completely harmless.

Here the writer detaches himself from the issue by referring to *the scientific world* and the fact that *some people believe . . . while others believe* otherwise. The two mental Processes with their non-specific Participants, reveal that this is a different kind of genre in construction, with different meanings at issue. We can trace some of the ways the Arguments in favour of the statement are developed in the next element, and we will comment on these below. Some attitudinal expression is evident in the way research evidence is appraised. Thus, it is said to be *difficult* to get reliable evidence about human brains. However, in general the element seeks to record dispassionately what is known from research.

Text 7.10   Electromagnetic radiation from mobile phones is a health risk

Issue (macroTheme marked)	*'Electromagnetic radiation from mobile phones is a health risk' The scientific world is divided by this statement. Some believe that mobile phones can cause great illness, while others believe that the phones are completely harmless.*
Arguments in favour (hyperTheme marked)	*Considerable amounts of research are done each year into the issue. However, it is* <u>*difficult*</u> *to get accurate results from human brains as a subject must be dead to study the brain in detail. Hence, the results from this research area always vary from scientist to scientist, but many researchers draw similar conclusions from their data.* **According to most,** *mobile phones' electromagnetic radiation can have negative effects on humans, such as Alzheimer's disease, brain tumours, leukaemia and cell damage. It has been discovered [[that 30% of brain tumours of mobile phone users develop on the side of the head on which they hold their mobile]]. Are these two facts related or merely coincidental? Other symptoms have been discovered that relate to excessive mobile usage. These include nausea, fatigue, headaches, and burning sensations to the skin.* **Since humans are so hard to test on,** *numerous animals have been tested on. Furthermore, it has been found [[that some species react//when exposed to the radiation of the mobile phones]].* **When a rat is subjected to intense exposure of the radiation from the phone,** *some of its brain cells are destroyed. The cells [[destroyed]] are essential to the rat's memory, movement and learning, and this is thought to be a premature onset for illnesses including Alzheimer's disease. It has also been discovered by Nottingham University, UK, [[that female nematode worms are also affected by mobile phone radiation]].* **When exposed,** *they produce more stress hormones, grow 10% larger, and produce more eggs. Are these results usable? Can we take the results found in these experiments and apply them to humans? Or do the brain structures of these creatures cause them to react differently and there is nothing to fear?*

The first paragraph pursues the matters referred to in the Issue, offering a statement in one clause:

Considerable amounts of research are done each year into the issue,

whose meaning is then developed in a clause complex that involves a causal clause:

However, it is difficult to get accurate results from human brains
as a subject must be dead to study the brain in detail. (clause of reason)

The arguments vary depending on the scientist the writer uses, and he again detaches himself from the issues by attributing the authority to others, displaying capacity for Engagement with others' points of view:

According to most, *mobile phones' electromagnetic radiation can have negative effects on humans . . .*

or by alluding to the discoveries of others, not identified:

It has been discovered [[that 30% of brain tumours of mobile phone users develop on the side of the head on which they hold their mobile]].

A second paragraph goes on:

Since humans are so hard to test on, numerous animals have been tested on,

and this is turn is developed further.

The element draws to a closed with a series of rhetorical questions, not a feature of the other science genres we have been discussing:

Are these results usable? Can we take the results found in these experiments and apply them to humans? Or do the brain structures of these creatures cause them to react differently and there is nothing to fear?

In the subsequent element outlining Arguments against the proposition, the writer starts to personalize the discussion, though giving some authority to his claims by referring to:

many people, like myself, [[who believe //that the radiation emitted by mobile phones is perfectly harmless]]

This is further elaborated, and some Appreciation of the dangers of radiation is expressed, though it is qualified:

> *The electromagnet radiation may be dangerous in large amounts*

The grammar gets a little more intricate as the writer introduces one causal clause and one conditional clause to develop his case, now suggesting some Judgement about the value of research:

> *In my opinion,<<**as no solid evidence has been found to prove that mobile phones actually are a health risk**>>*, (clause of reason)
> *there is no reason to stress and worry about it.*
> ***Even if mobile phones do emit harmful radiation***, (clause of condition)
> *there are so many more appliances that would emit radiation, like computers and televisions.*

Another rhetorical question concludes the element:

> *Why worry about phones?*

Text 7.10—Cont'd

Arguments against (hyperTheme marked)	*On the other hand, there are many people, like myself, [[who believe //that the radiation emitted by mobile phones is perfectly harmless]]. The electromagnetic radiation may be dangerous in large amounts, and phones do not discharge enough to make them dangerous. In my opinion,<<**as no solid evidence has been found to prove that mobile phones actually are a health risk**>>, there is no reason to stress and worry about it. **Even if mobile phones do emit harmful radiation**, there are so many more appliances that would emit radiation, like computers and televisions. Why worry about phones?*
Conclusion	*In conclusion, there is much speculation about the safety and health risks concerning mobile phones. **While there are many concerns for public safety**, the case against the mobile phone is yet to be proven. Already, some manufacturers produce radiation shields to protect the more nervous of the public. However, <<**until something concrete can be proven**>>, I see the mobile phone as a harmless tool of communication.*

A short bibliography follows, not reproduced.

The Conclusion reiterates a point made at the beginning, re-establishing the issue, but detaching the writer's own identity from the statement, hence making it more authoritative:

> *In conclusion, there is much speculation about the safety and health risks concerning mobile phones.*

Two dependent clauses create marked Themes to help unfold the argument, the first being one of concession:

> **While there are many concerns for public safety,** *the case against the mobile phone is yet to be proven*

while the second is one of time and it appears in a clause complex in which in the final clause the writer's identity is asserted again:

> *However,* <<***until something concrete can be proven***>>, *I see the mobile phone as a harmless tool of communication.*

Text 7.9 has been revealed as different from the earlier text types reviewed in this chapter, since its purposes are different. This is a genre whose primary purpose is to review evidence and to offer opinion, and while in our view the writer is probably too dismissive of the results he cites from admittedly conflicting sources of information, he makes clear that he is offering personal Judgement.

Lexical density in the interpretative genres

Figure 7.1 shows that in the case of reports, the texts of early childhood (7.1 and 7.2) have similar lexical densities (3.9 and 3.7), while the other three, (7.3, 7.4 and 7.5), written in late childhood to adolescence, have densities of 6.1, 5.7 and 5.4, so that the general movement in achieving greater lexical density holds here, as in other subjects and genres. As for the explanations, these similarly start with a relatively low lexical density, thence moving up to

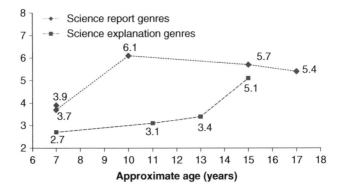

FIGURE 7.1 Lexical density in a sample of science interpretative genres

counts of 3 or more, though the last (Text 7.9) has a density of 5.1. The discussion genre, not displayed on the graph, has a density of 4.9. While there are variations, when compared with the sample in Chapter 6, the overall trend is clear. The density of texts tends to increase past late childhood to adolescence, hovering between 3 and 6.

Conclusion

This concludes our second chapter on writing development in science. The developmental processes by which children achieve mastery of writing in science have been revealed to be similar to those found for other subjects, in that the developmental shift is from the congruent to the non-congruent and from the immediate to the abstract. Yet the meanings of science are not those of either English or history, for science involves the study of natural phenomena, whether observing, recording, experimenting with, describing or explaining these. Consequently, the grammar is deployed rather differently in writing science from the ways it is used in the other subjects. Even where children write genres found in other subjects – such as recounts or reports – they do not mean in the same ways. The meaning-making processes of science have a long history, embracing established traditions for constructing the hierarchical knowledge structures of the subject. While these traditions are most immediately obvious in the range of experimental/investigative genres reviewed in Chapter 6, they are also realized in the reporting and explanatory texts discussed in this chapter.

Note

[1] The *Young Scientist of the Year Awards*, for example, sponsored by the Science Teachers' Association of New South Wales, is an annual event, though there are other similar awards.

Chapter 8

The Developmental Trajectory in Writing

Introduction

As we noted in Chapter 1, previous research on writing development, while often very useful, has not normally provided an overview of the ontogenesis of writing from early childhood to late adolescence, and this study has sought to repair the omission. In bringing this volume to a close, we argue that educational policy and practice need a theoretically motivated model of writing development from early childhood to late adolescence. Such a model should be based on a functional linguistic theory, and one, moreover, that allows us to address, among other things, what have been some enduring questions about the significance of the teacher's role in fostering writing development. Is writing development a matter of 'what comes naturally' over time, or is it a matter of teacher intervention and guidance?

In this chapter, we commence by briefly reviewing some of the arguments over 'nature versus nurture' in writing development, concluding that such arguments can be put to rest in the light of recent research over human development, including development in oral language and literacy. We then go on to outline some recent policy initiatives on writing curriculum and assessment in different parts of the English-speaking world, providing some sense of the official contexts in which writing and its values are understood. At times writing has received less official attention than has reading, though there are signs of change. We shall go on to summarize what we have proposed of the developmental trajectory in learning to write in English, history and science, and conclude by outlining ways such research can inform policy and practice.

The nature/nurture debate

More than one colleague has asked the question: to what extent is what children produce in writing a result of their socioeconomic background, mediated by teacher expectations, or of their own inborn capacities? How do we know that what appears to be developmental progress in writing is no more than what emerges, given a child with a favourable family background and a teacher who supports the child in learning? Is it possible to separate environmental influence from the influence of biological inheritance? At least one person even suggested that we could never know what constitutes 'true' writing development because the teacher (who in some cases could be the parent) is always present: the implication was that the teacher 'gets in the way' of an otherwise 'natural' process, as if such a thing were possible without human interaction! All this is a version of the 'nature/nurture' debate, which throughout much of the 20th century often featured in educational discussions, including discussions about language learning and more specifically, about the learning of literacy. From time to time it has been argued, on the one hand, that children's school performance depends primarily on what nature gave them, so that the teacher's contribution, while important, is relatively negligible in the overall scheme of things; on the other hand, it has been argued that it is the impact of the educational processes that is essential to performance, and that whatever is inborn or 'innate' is crucially shaped by the work of teachers.

While acknowledging the issue has been important, we suggest that the 'nature/nurture' debate rests on a false opposition, for in truth there is only 'nature *via* nurture', in the words of Ridley (2003) writing in the light of late 20th and early-21st-century research on the human genome. Indeed, an overwhelming body of research on the human brain, from more than one discipline, now confirms the very intimate association of genetic capacity and environmental and/or sociocultural impact in shaping the nature of persons, including their language capacity (e.g. Edelman 1992; Halliday 1993, 2004b; Deacon 1997; Tomasello 1999; Edelman and Tononi 2000; Matthiessen 2004; Tronick 2007). Humans are born with the genetic capacity to develop language but it is the complex social processes in which children are nurtured that facilitate and indeed make possible the emergence of language. Writing of the emergence of language and the human brain, Halliday (2004b) writes:

> We know that the brain has evolved in the context of the
> increasing complexity of our relationship with our
> environment; this has to mean both the natural and the social
> environment, without privilege to either one of the two.
>
> (Halliday 2004b, 34–5)

Language evolved very early in the history of the human species – probably about 2.5 million years ago (Oppenheimer 2003: 25) – and it facilitates the emergence of a 'higher order consciousness' (Edelman and Tononi 2000: 198), allowing individuals to shape a sense of identity, negotiate relationship, and construct and organize experience, information and knowledge of the world. Literacy, on the other hand, appeared very late indeed in the history of the human species, and though there is some debate about the origins of writing systems (see, for example, Halliday 1985; Coulmas 1989; DeFrancis 1989;

Schmandt-Besserat 1996), writing appears to have emerged, in Mesopotamia and the Nile delta, at least, by about 4000 BC, later in China and Mexico (Halliday 1985: 16). While oral language is the primary symbolic system available to humans, learned in family and community, writing is the 'second order symbolic system' (Halliday 1993: 109). The invention of literacy (and of numeracy too) led to the institution of schooling, for literacy is learned differently from speech, though capacity to learn it at all depends on the learning of speech first, during the years prior to the start of schooling.

The teaching of writing, like that of reading, is a fundamental responsibility of schooling, and what teachers do is very important in ensuring that children learn to write, as well as read. Hence we need skilled, well educated teachers, possessed of considerable knowledge of oral language and literacy, who can devise clear goals for teaching and learning, guiding and directing the various learning activities in which children engage across the years of schooling from kindergarten till the end of schooling. The knowledge teachers need in order to guide learning should include a considerable understanding of the nature of written language and of the developmental phases in learning to control the written code which, we have argued, mark children's progress up the years of schooling from early childhood to late adolescence. Too often, in fact, there is a general perception, even in the teaching profession, and certainly in the wider community, that writing and reading are learned in the first three or four years of the primary school, when some 'basic skills' are established, after which these get endlessly recycled as children grow older in some reasonably unproblematic way. The truth is that there are developmental phases in mastering the written mode, and though these are not to be understood as functioning in some 'lock step' fashion, they do apply, having consequences for the kinds of writing children should produce at different stages of their lives. In our discussions we have chosen to examine a range of children's texts, and we have used these to construct an account of the ontogenesis of writing ability. Moreover, our observations are supported by examination of the many other texts held in our total corpus – those judged good, and others judged rather poor. Not all children move easily and well through the various developmental phases in order to become successfully independent writers. Hence, we argue that if teachers were better informed about the developmental phases in learning to write, they could the better monitor their students' progress, anticipate the challenges ahead, identify sources of difficulty and teach many writing skills that otherwise tend to remain implicit or tacit, left to be 'picked up' along the way. The difficulty in the latter cases, where things remain tacit, and left to be 'picked up', is that such a step advantages the already advantaged – those children who, because of family background and opportunity, can successfully intuit many skills needed in writing. In fact, all children – advantaged and disadvantaged – benefit from active teaching about writing. However, the disadvantaged are in particular badly served by school policies that fail to deliver good writing programmes, leaving much knowledge about how to write to be 'caught', rather than deliberately taught. These matters are discussed by Schleppegrell (2004: 147), who writes of 'the challenges of schooling in linguistic terms', arguing the values of a functional grammar in developing pedagogies for teaching writing and reading.

Some contemporary policies on literacy and writing

In the contemporary English-speaking world, literacy rates frequent mention in the daily press, and governments fund considerable research and/or inquiries into literacy and its teaching. The interest and the research are welcome, though it is unfortunate that 'literacy' has been often primarily understood as 'reading', while writing, though acknowledged, has received a rather diminished status in much official policy. A recent example of this tendency may be found in *Australia's National Literacy Inquiry* (2005), which produced a report, 'Teaching Reading', whose primary thrust was with reading. The latter is a document remarkable both for its failure to look closely at writing rather than reading capacity (though some perfunctory reference is made to writing), and for its lack of interest in engaging with the forms of written language children must master on the developmental journey from age 6 to about 17 or 18. Some international evidence for the tendency to foreground reading over writing in consideration of literacy is apparent in the work of the OECD with its regular *Programme for International Student Assessment* (PISA) surveys of reading, mathematical and scientific literacy, conducted among 15 year olds in several languages and – at the time of the last survey in 2006 – in some 57 countries throughout the world. The PISA tests, though sophisticated, measure reading ability and 'problem solving', and this is justified in terms of an interest in assessing 'how far students near the end of compulsory education have acquired some of the knowledge and skills that are essential for full participation in society' (OECD (PISA) 2007: 1). Yet writing as well as reading ability is surely an important measure of an individual's preparedness for 'full participation in society'.

In fact, concern about writing performance as well as reading has begun to attract more official interest, evident in Australia in state testing regimes devoted to literacy and numeracy, to be nationally coordinated and conducted from 2009 (*National Assessment Program: Literacy and Numeracy* 2008) and which include a writing component. In England, national testing programs at 'Key Stages', devoted to writing and reading (as well as other things) have been conducted for some years, currently at the direction of the *National Assessment Agency*, an arm of the *Qualifications and Curriculum Authority* (ND). In the USA, the various states conduct writing tests, providing statements of 'Grade level content expectations' (or some comparable term) for use in guiding teaching and assessment in all areas of English, including writing (e.g. Michigan Department of Education, ND), while the efforts of the National Commission on Writing (2006) or of the Carnegie Corporation (e.g. Graham and Perin 2007) reveal a concern to improve research into the teaching of writing, since, so Graham and Perin (2007: 22) write, it is acknowledged in the USA 'that writing difficulties are occurring across the nation'.

Many curriculum and assessment initiatives that are intended to improve writing and its teaching tend to offer their advice in rather general terms, so that what constitutes successful performance is not always easy to see. For example, the *English Syllabus for New South Wales for School Years 7–10* (New South Wales Board of Studies 2003b) sets out 'Objectives' for 'Stages 4' and '5' (covering ages 12–15 years). One such statement declares that 'through responding to and composing a wide range of texts in context', students will develop many skills and understandings, so that, at Level 4, among other things, a student 'responds to and composes texts for understanding, interpretation, critical analysis and pleasure', while at Level 5 a student 'responds to and composes increasingly sophisticated and sustained texts for understanding, interpretation, critical analysis and pleasure' (*New South Wales Board of Studies English Syllabus 7–10*, 2003b: 13). Such statements are very general, and little precise or practical advice is given about how students' performances are realized linguistically.

Moving to an entirely different jurisdiction and a different level of schooling, we find that in the American state of Michigan, a set of 'Course/Credit Content Expectations' has been drawn up for the advice of students preparing for high school graduation. A *Writing Score Guide* provides 'characteristics' of argumentative essays that 'take a stand' with respect to four headings: 'Position', 'Complexity', 'Organization' and 'Language'. A student at the highest level writes an essay that 'takes a position on the issue' and that, among other things, 'maintains focus across the response', while in terms of 'Complexity', the essay 'may demonstrate insight and complexity by evaluating various implications' and/or 'responding to arguments that differ from the writer's position'. As for 'Organization' this is 'well controlled, with a logical sequence of reasons and strong transitions and relationships among reasons' while as for Language, the essay 'shows a good command of varied, precise language that supports meaning' (Michigan Department of Education ND). Such advice is again rather general.

Recent developments in England provide evidence for provision of more specific advice to teachers of writing in that country. Under the terms of a *Government Green Paper* (2001), a two year pilot study was conducted (2003–05), intended to improve children's school performance at Key Stage 3, when children are aged 11–14 years, and in their first years of secondary education. This particular Key Stage had been chosen as part of the *National Secondary Strategy*, designed to improve the quality of education in the secondary years. The study involved work in 100 schools in 20 local school authorities, and it led to a programme called *Assessing Pupils' Progress* (APP), which provides advice to teachers about assessment in reading and writing through Key Stage 3. A Handbook outlines the aims and procedures for APP and sets of materials are provided. A particular strength of the materials is that actual examples of children's writing are set out , while commentary is provided in the light of 'Assessment Foci'. Several kinds of representative writing tasks are used, including writing stories, but also responses to literary texts (Department for Education and Skills and Qualifications and Curriculum Authority 2006a).

This is potentially a good model for development of policies for the teaching and assessment of writing, since it seeks to exemplify the principles of assessment involved by use of actual scripts. However, our reservation about the programme is that the language advice involved draws on largely traditional, rather than functional linguistic theory, and much of what is provided is in any case rather meagre. Features of cohesion, for example, rate some attention, as in references to 'subordinating connectives', or 'common connectives', while such things as 'adverbials used to introduce elaboration of (a) point' are sometimes identified. Reasonably enough, tense, punctuation and spelling matters all are referred to as well. Sometimes comments are made on style, such as one drawing attention to an 'attempt to build tension to sustain reader's interest', and elsewhere comment is made on vocabulary that is 'appropriate'. (Department for Education and Skills and Qualifications and Curriculum Authority: Standards Site, 2006a) Such matters, though not trivial, are rather limited in their scope and significance, nor are more informative observations made about the language choices in which meanings are realized, nor about the genres involved. As a model for teacher development and for curriculum design and assessment, the APP has much to commend it. However, we would nonetheless argue that the model would be more powerful if it were informed by a coherent and properly theorized account of student progress in writing.

An overview of the developmental trajectory in control of written language in English, history and science

We commence this account by summarizing the major linguistic changes in written language across the four phases we have identified in previous chapters. These phases provide a useful framework for planning writing programs in all subjects across the years of schooling.

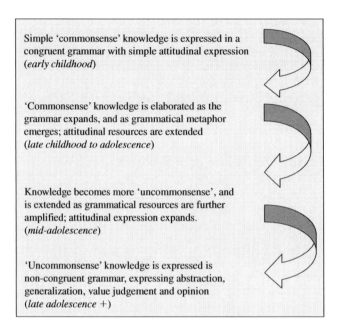

Simple 'commonsense' knowledge is expressed in a
congruent grammar with simple attitudinal expression
(*early childhood*)

'Commonsense' knowledge is elaborated as the
grammar expands, and as grammatical metaphor
emerges; attitudinal resources are extended
(*late childhood to adolescence*)

Knowledge becomes more 'uncommonsense', and
is extended as grammatical resources are further
amplified; attitudinal expression expands.
(*mid-adolescence*)

'Uncommonsense' knowledge is expressed is
non-congruent grammar, expressing abstraction,
generalization, value judgement and opinion
(*late adolescence* +)

FIGURE 8.1 Developmental phases in learning to write: the broad picture

Figure 8.1 provides an overview of the developmental phases, where we have invoked Bernstein's notions of 'commonsense' and 'uncommonsense' knowledge. 'Commonsense' knowledge is 'everyday community knowledge, of the pupil, his family and his peer group', while 'uncommonsense knowledge (is) freed from the particular, the local, through the various languages of the sciences or forms of reflexiveness of the arts which make possible either the creation or the discovery of new realities'. (Bernstein 1975: 99) Such a movement in knowledge parallels, and is made possible by, the movement in the grammar, from the congruent to the increasingly non-congruent.

Table 8.1 provides a summary of the general grammatical tendencies in each of the four phases. Then, Tables 8.2, 8.3 and 8.4 set out corresponding summaries for the three subjects involved, so that similarities and differences emerge across the phases.

Table 8.1 A summary of the major linguistic changes in control of written language in children's writing from early childhood to late adolescence

Early childhood: 6–8 years	Late childhood-early adolescence: 9–12 years	Mid-adolescence: 13–15 years	Late adolescence: 16–18 years +
Experiential resources: Processes are realized in simple verbal groups. Participants are realized in simple nominal groups (may include embedded clauses). Circumstantial information is realized in prepositional phrases, primarily of time and place.	**Experiential resources:** Processes are more varied, expressed in expanding verbal group structures. Participants are realized in much expanded nominal groups, involving both pre- and pos-modification of Headword. Circumstantial information is realized in a growing range of prepositional phrases and some adverbs.	**Experiential resources:** The full range of Process types appears, and they are realized in a developing variety of lexical verbs, as lexis generally expands. Participants are realized in dense nominal groups involving increasing abstractions and/or technicality. Circumstances are often abstract, realizing a growing range of meanings.	**Experiential resources:** A full range of Process types is present, including often abstract material Processes, causative Processes and identifying Processes, used to interpret texts and/or human behaviour in English, historical events or movements in history, and phenomena of the natural world in science. Participants are realized in dense nominal groups, creating abstractions of many kinds, and sometimes involving nominal groups in apposition. Circumstantial information is expressed in a full range of prepositional phrases, often containing extended nominal group structures, and in adverbs, which are varied.

(*Continued*)

Table 8.1—Cont'd

Early childhood: 6–8 years	Late childhood-early adolescence: 9–12 years	Mid-adolescence: 13–15 years	Late adolescence: 16–18 years +
Clause types and logical relations: Sentences may consist of single clauses or combine clauses of equal status. The commonest unequal or dependent clauses present are of time. Occasional uses of dependent non-finite clauses of purpose.	**Clause types and logical relations:** Equal clauses remain, but an expanding range of dependent clauses appears – reason, purpose, condition, concession, manner. Non-finite instances appear a little more often. Also some clauses of projection. An overall growing capacity for grammatical intricacy in using and linking different clause types.	**Clause types and logical relations:** Considerable range of clauses, singular, equal and unequal in different combinations. Some loss of otherwise independent clauses because grammatical metaphor compresses them. Non-finite clauses are now quite frequent. Clause types and interdependencies differ, depending on field and genre.	**Clause types and logical relations:** A full range of clause types is available, and clauses are deployed in strategic ways, sometimes using singular clauses for their effect, and sometimes using several interdependent clauses, displaying grammatical intricacy. However, texts at this stage are often not grammatically very intricate, as their complexity is created by dense lexis and grammatical metaphor, whose effect is to bury otherwise independent clauses and their relations. Overall, clause types are deployed in strategically skilled ways.
	Grammatical metaphor emerges as nominalization.	Lexical and grammatical metaphors are more common. Grammatical metaphor is used purposefully.	There are frequent uses of grammatical and lexical metaphor.

Interpersonal resources:
Tendency to use first person. Attitudinal expression (when present) mainly simple Affect, expressed in adjectives, occasionally with adverbs of intensity, and sometimes simple Processes of affect. Limited awareness of audience.

Textual resources:
Simple repetitive topical Themes, which are often realized in first person pronoun. Sometimes uncertain use of Reference to build internal links.

Interpersonal resources:
Tendency to greater use of third person. Occasional use of modal verbs. Attitudinal expression in adverbs, as well as adjectives and a greater range of adverbs of intensity. Attitudinal expression is more evident than in earlier years, though not in science. In English and history, a more marked awareness of audience and some recognition of personal voice and engaging with others.

Textual resources:
Developing use of Given and New Information to create topical Theme choices; marked Themes are expressed in Circumstances or dependent clauses, some of which are enclosed dependent clauses. Better control of Reference.

Interpersonal resources:
A more regular use of third person; first person is retained for some fields and genres. Modal adverbs and verbs are used selectively, depending on field and genre. An extensive range of lexis to express attitude is also available, also used selectively, as attitude has no great role in science. In history and English, a greater engagement with audience and some awareness of differing perspectives.

Textual resources:
Good control of Given and New Information to create topical Theme choices; greater use of dependent clauses in marked Theme position, some enclosed; growing capacity to create macroThemes and hyperThemes to direct overall organization of texts as they become longer.

Interpersonal resources:
There is a confident use of first or third person (depending on field and genre); a broad range of lexis is potentially available to express attitude. Modality is used judiciously, depending on field. Attitudinal and experiential values are often 'fused' in English and history. Science is attitudinally restrained. Dialogic engagement with a wider discourse community is evident, especially in English and history.

Textual resources:
Good control of thematic development; frequent use of marked Theme choices to signal new phases in texts; good capacity in developing and sustaining overall textual organization, using macroThemes and hyperThemes.

Table 8.2 Exemplifying major linguistic features in writing in English from early childhood to late adolescence

Early childhood: 6–8 years	Late childhood–early adolescence: 9–12 years	Mid-adolescence: 13–15 years	Late adolescence: 16–18 years +
Experientially: Processes are material to realize actions (*we got off the bus*); sometimes existential to initiate a tale (*there was a minotaur*); sometimes relational to identify or describe (*we were in the bird section.*)	**Experientially:** In stories the range of verbs expands, creating material Processes to realize actions (*this offering had happened every 20 years.*), or relational attributive to describe (*every man was agitated and excited*), and occasionally relational identifying to define (*[[the only way I could survive]] was [[to dive under the water]] or mental to reveal thoughts (*I noticed that the only way..*). In response genres relational attributive Processes to describe (*he was merry*).	**Experientially:** A full range of Processes potentially in stories, revealing an expanding vocabulary (*while parading around his castle, he trudged ..; we trudged our way to Richmond station ..*). In response genres material Processes build actions of characters (*Sally Milroy lived with her family*) and frequent use of relational Processes to describe ('*Who Framed Roger Rabbit' is a combination of cartoon backdrops and real backdrops and characters*). Grammatical metaphor creates causative Processes (*our newly extended lives are causing our population to rise like never before*).	**Experientially:** In stories, Processes include abstract material, realized in varied lexical verbs (*the sun dipped with surprising haste into narrow gaps .. ; the ever present, ever constant percussion surrounds me*). In response genres, Processes are often realized in verbs creating lexical metaphors (*the play seems to centre around Antonio; Ed acted as a barrier .. ; studying the concept of imaginative journeys has expanded my understanding of myself ..)* Relational identifying Processes reveal what is understood in texts, contributing to interpretation (*Melvyn Bragg's (work) shows how individual can influence others; these relationships demonstrated ....*. aspects of the characters' worlds..*)

Participants are often realized in pronouns, though sometimes in nominal groups with clause embeddings (*a minotaur [[that was very nice and kind // and lived in a cave]]*).	Participants in stories and response genres often realized in denser nominal groups (*the waves [[crashing on the shore of the Aqualand]]*), some with nominal groups in apposition (*the griffin, a dog-like creature with wings*).	Participants are often realized in nominal groups compressing information, some in apposition (*the fairies) held a meeting, a meeting [[that none of the other clans or even the Queen knew existed]]*; others involve grammatical metaphor (*award-winning Robert Zemeckis),* and others lexical metaphor (*a ringing silence*).	Participants are often abstract in stories (*the lazy swaying of leafy trees and merry frolicking of laughing children*) and in response genres often involve grammatical metaphor (*studying the concept of imaginative journeys has expanded...; people's perceptions of the world are often hindered.*)
Circumstances of time (*in the ancient times*) or place (*to the museum*).	Circumstances are more varied in stories and response genres, realized in prepositional phrases (*he disappeared under the foam*), and also adverbs (*we could swim away from the rocks quickly; the author can't express her ideas clearly*). Some have grammatical metaphor (*in a heavily decorated carriage*).	Circumstances are realized in the full range of prepositional phrases (*this movie is suitable for both children and adults*) and a developing range of adverbs (*nimbly I asked where we could sit; cartoons didn't have to be drawn repetitively.*)	Circumstances are varied in stories (*The sun dipped with surprising haste.*) and often abstract in response genres (*in the context of individual journeys Melvyn Bragg's depiction of science....*). Some are realized in adverbs (*he teaches them wisely and well*).

(*Continued*)

Table 8.2—Cont'd

Early childhood: 6–8 years	Late childhood–early adolescence: 9–12 years	Mid-adolescence: 13–15 years	Late adolescence: 16–18 years +
Clause types and logical relations: Clauses are mainly equal (*then we went to see the animals // and we saw lambs sheep ducks . . .*).	**Clause types and logical relations:** Clauses are arranged more intricately, extending clause interdependencies. Dependent clauses of enhancement are mainly of time and reason, though conditional can occur as in a response genre (*if I were to recommend this book // I would recommend it to people..*); some non-finite dependent clauses occur, and some of projection (*once we had finished // my sister and I jumped into the water // thinking // that we could swim away from the rocks quickly // because the water was flat // and (because) we were good swimmers; while getting his armour on // to test it a month ago // a wave came crashing down on him// // and then he was sucked away . . .*)	**Clause types and logical relations:** A range of clause types in various interdependencies, building intricacy (*It was still raining // the seats were wet // and piled up along the barriers were a loud group of drunken Pies supporters // who << even though the game had not yet started >> were yelling insults out to the umpires and team staff.*) In response genres clauses are often singular, used to reconstruct details of stories reviewed, (*Sally lived with her family in a small suburban house*), while clause complexes provide series of events and/or observations, linked with additive conjunctions in equal relationship (*the plot is very easy to understand // and the characters are very child friendly*). Dependent clauses elaborate on information (*This story is written in an interesting way // which helps us to understand the challenges [[faced by Sally and her family]].*)	**Clause types and logical relations:** Clauses are various. Frequent use of dependent non-finite clauses (*emerging from the side avenue. . . they directed their steps; no longer guided by my own mind and thoughts alone I feel this dark world. . . .*) Often singular clauses appear in stories at strategic points, while simple sequences of equal clauses are also found. In response genres clause complexes may be intricate, using non-finite clauses among others (*In Frankenstein strong emotions form a large part of the story // in allowing us to engage in the book // by reading of the intense emotions between characters*). Sometimes grammatically simple clauses build complexity through their lexical density (*The journey, especially in the imaginative sense, is a process [[by which the traveller encounters a series of challenges, tangents and serendipitous discoveries // to arrive finally at a destination and/or transformation]].*).

Interpersonally: First or third person, depending on field and genre. Attitudinally simple Affect is expressed in verbs realizing mental Processes (*I liked the beds*) and occasional expressions of Judgement are realized in adjectives (*he was nice and kind*).	**Interpersonally:** First or third person, depending on field and genre. Attitude is expressed mainly in adjectives and adverbs, sometimes with intensity, creating Affect (*I was really excited*). Appreciation (*the water seemed calm; we tried desperately to swim away..*), and occasional Judgement (*we were good swimmers; the author can't express her ideas clearly*); and some Engagement with others (*this book is a good book for eight, nine year olds but not for ten, eleven years..*).	**Interpersonally:** First person for personal recounts, otherwise third person. Attitude involves Appreciation (*Cody had a kind heart but no money and nothing [[to eat]] but a stale ice of bread*. ; *The tram was approaching more slowly than usual. . .*) or Affect (*then to our disappointment the rain came*) or Judgement (*but if you try to become something you're not, nothing works..*) Response genres express evaluation. Frequent intrusion of personal opinion (*in my opinion this is an excellent movie*). A wide range of resources builds Affect (*I enjoyed this book*), though Appreciation of qualities of books or films is common (*its revolutionary animation; its remarkably realistic effect; a rich, zesty, moving story*), as is Judgement of these qualities (*the people [[who were involved in this movie]] quite obviously have an amazing talent for [[what they do]]*).	**Interpersonally:** First person is selected for personal recounts, third person for other stories. Both types of story use attitudinally rich language, so that experiential and attitudinal values are often 'fused' as in Appreciation (*voices. . . . . . provide colour in my lost and blackened environment; the new landscape [[I have journey towards]] is unlike my former residence*). Response genres are also attitudinally rich, offering Appreciation of text qualities (*dramatic tension plays a part. . . . enthralling the audience and enticing us to hang on to every word..*) Mental Processes of cognition express opinion, often contributing to Appraisal of texts, as do many adverbs. (*these elements I believe have been used effectively*). Others contribute to interpretation, sometimes combined with modality (*we can see examples of strong emotions..*)

(*Continued*)

Table 8.2—Cont'd

Early childhood: 6–8 years	Late childhood–early adolescence: 9–12 years	Mid-adolescence: 13–15 years	Late adolescence: 16–18 years +
Textually: simple unmarked topical <u>Themes</u> and marked Themes are realized in dependent clauses of time (*when we got off the bus* // *we went in the mansion*).	**Textually:** <u>Theme</u> choices are often marked in stories and response genres, to signal a new stage (*once we had finished our lunch* // *my sister and I jumped into the water*) or to achieve effect (*into his scabbard it went*; *while he is on holiday* // *he meets the griffin*..) Given and New Information are used to create thematic progression (*Last summer holidays my family went to South West Rocks*. . . . *In South West Rocks the surf isn't too rough.*.)	**Textually:** good <u>thematic progression</u> in stories and response genres, and both become longer. Marked Themes are realized in Circumstances and dependent clauses, some of them enclosed (*The Fairy Realm lived in peace for many years. But << as time went on>> the separate clans began to fight.* . . . .) Developing control of macroThemes and hyperThemes emerges.	**Textually:** topical <u>Themes</u> sometimes involve enclosed clauses (*the warm summer air << so easily associated by many with the chirruping of swallows, lazy swaying of leafy trees and merry frolicking of laughing children >> had only in the last few minutes . . . .*). Sometimes they are marked, pacing stages in the story (*on the sidewalks and amongst the hectic whirl of traffic people were to be observed* . . .). In other cases, thematic progression is achieved with series of unmarked Themes, using reference and lexical cohesion (*Only <u>the voices</u> return me to consciousness, <u>they</u> provide colour in my lost and blackened environment. <u>Voices</u> break into a thousand colours.*.) . Response genres make successful use of marked and unmarked topical Themes, the latter often introducing new stages of the discussion. MacroThemes and hyperThemes direct development of texts.

Table 8.3 Exemplifying major linguistic features in writing in history from early childhood to late adolescence

Early childhood: 6–8 year	Late childhood-early adolescence: 9–12 years	Mid-adolescence: 13–15 years	Late adolescence: 16–18 years +
Experientially: Processes are material to realize actions (*we went to the museum*) sometimes mental (*I saw a canoe*), sometimes relational attributive to describe (*we were in the bird section.*)	**Experientially:** a growing range of Process types include: relational identifying to specify (*the reason [[why I am studying Galileo]] is [[because I have been interested in his life . . . .]]*), material to create activities (*Galileo graduated from the University of Pisa*), an occasional causative Process (*there was no jetty // causing us a big inconvenience..*), and mental Processes to reveal what historical figures 'found' (*he discovered that <<even though the cannonballs were different weights>> they made contact with the ground at the same time.*)	**Experientially:** material Processes become abstract in historical accounts (*the Japanese Empire expanded down through Burma, Thailand . . . ; the French abandoned their colonial empire*) but more concrete in site and period studies (*often the walls were covered with wall hangings...; these gods guarded the state or country*), some mental Processes to build interpretation (*we can assume..*) Relational attributive Processes occur in site and period studies to describe (*a commoner's house was usually two or three storeys high; the Roman religion was a savage one*).	**Experientially:** Processes are abstract material (*women's lives and roles in Australian society were irreversibly changed and impacted upon by WWII*), and often causative, creating lexical metaphors and compressing causal connections between events in nominal groups (*the Wall Street Crash sparked the Great Depression; three vital factors [[determining the victory of the Greeks]]..*). Verbal and mental Processes are used to report what historians have argued or stated (*N. Marionatos states that all Theran frescoes feature..; we can assume they had an understanding.. she believes they were a religious society*).

(Continued)

Table 8.3—Cont'd

Early childhood: 6–8 year	Late childhood-early adolescence: 9–12 years	Mid adolescence: 13–15 years	Late adolescence: 16–18+ years
Participants in historical recounts are realized simple nominal groups and pronouns (*we saw the old chemist*)	Participants are realized in denser nominal groups (*it was a fine flour and timber mill with a brewery and piggery*); some Participants realize abstractions, involving grammatical metaphor (*Galileo made this discovery*).	Participants in historical accounts are used to generalize (*many European countries established colonies...*) while others are abstract (*their tactics were unable to match the guerilla tactics*); in site and period studies they are sometimes abstract (*much of ancient Egyptian life occurred in their house..*) Some grammatical metaphor occurs, producing abstract nominalizations (*the importance of the Vietnam war in history is that it ...*)	Many Participants involve grammatical metaphor (*an estimation of the town's population; the newly formulated national constitution: the effect of the German people attaining power; the reliability of Gilbert's argument*) and various types of abstraction (*This bias and attitude towards appeasement; There has been much debate*) Abstractions are often used with a summarizing function.
Circumstances are of time and place (*yesterday we went to the museum*)	Circumstances are frequently of time, sometimes precise (*in 1588*) sometimes more general (*in those days there was no jetty..*); also of place (*we were glad to set foot on land*); sometimes of manner (*. a Dutch lens maker experimented with some lenses*).	Circumstances in historical accounts are often abstract (*towards the end of the war when the Japanese were thinking of surrendering..*) though in site and period studies they are not abstract (*the family often slept on the top of the house*), and an occasional one of angle appears (*from the burial rites we can assume..*)	Circumstances are also abstract, often involving grammatical metaphor (*the policy came into prominence with the appeasement of Adolf Hitler prior to the outbreak of the Second World War; The victory of the Greeks . . . came about due to many factors.*)

Clause types and logical relations: clauses are sometimes singular (*we saw antique bikes and insects, mummy cases and a skeleton*), mainly equal, though dependent clauses of time sometimes appear: (*when we were in the bird section // we could press a button..*)

Clause types and logical relations: More intricate clause interdependencies start to occur (*as you know // we came out on the Earl of Durham 1839- a tiring voyage, // and we were glad to set foot on land.*). Dependent clauses of concession appear (*he stood up for what he believed in // even when his thoughts were rejected by the people*) and of condition (*he found out that if the lenses were arranged in a certain order // they would magnify // and make things seem nearer*). Both clause types create enhanced flexibility in deploying information, as do clauses of projection (*he discovered. . . . he found out . . .*)

Clause types and logical relations: clauses are varied. In historical accounts, dependent clauses of time occur (*while the French were leaving // the Americans came in..*) and there are some of purpose (*not to claim territory // but to help the south Vietnamese . . .*) others are of reason (*the French tried to fight the Vietnamese // but failed . . . // because they were using the wrong tactics for the wrong place*). In site and period studies clauses are sometimes singular (*a commoner's house was usually two or three storeys high*) others are equal and linked by additive or consequential conjunctions (*the Romans would go up to the temple // and sacrifice an animal such as an ox*), though there are dependent clauses of reason ((*their houses were made of mud*) *// because wood was in short supply in the desert.*)

Clause types and logical relations: Clause interdependencies are often intricate to build interpretation (*He also thinks // the policy was reasonable // in that the Government was cautious after World War I // had no allies // and could only fight a war // if their dominions supported it.*). However, clauses can be grammatically reasonably simple as various connections are built through abstractions within clauses, where grammatical metaphor is involved (*the naval strength of Greece led to the Greek defeat of the Persians; the first debate [[that can be examined in terms of these issues]] is that of the origins of appeasement.*)

(*Continued*)

Table 8.3—Cont'd

Early childhood: 6–8 year	Late childhood-early adolescence: 9–12 years	Mid-adolescence: 13–15 years	Late adolescence: 16–18 years+
Interpersonally: First or third person, depending on field and genre. Attitudinally simple Appreciation is expressed in adjectives (*the funniest part was the magic mirrors*), evaluating aspects of personal experience. Little or no consideration of other views or possibilities.	**Interpersonally:** First person for empathetic biographies building the imagined experience of others and third person for biographical recounts, building the experience of past figures. Empathetic biographies use a range of lexical resources to express Appreciation of events or entities (*it was a glorious sight*) and some Affect (*I was extremely glad to see the Presbyterian church...*) Biographical recounts express Appreciation of events or phenomena ((Galileo made) *ingenious inventions*) and some Judgement of historical figures ((Galileo) *was bold enough to say that Aristotle was wrong. . . .*)	**Interpersonally:** Texts are written largely in the third person. Attitudinally rather dispassionate, especially in site and period studies. In historical accounts some Appreciation is found in evaluating movements or whole periods of history (*the importance of the Vietnam war in history is [[that it turned Vietnam from a foreign controlled country into an independent communist country]].*) Occasional appeals to the reader's emotions through the use of high levels of Graduation (*the hygiene conditions were abominable and corpses lay rotting in no-mans-land*). Early evidence of Engagement with other points of view (*Darlington explains how women's independence was taken away . . .*). Some use of modality for intrusion of interpretation (*possibly the greatest factor in women's fight for equality . . .*)	**Interpersonally:** Historical explanations, arguments and discussions are written in the third person. Attitude is used to enable interpretation, showing Appreciation of events and movements in history (*the policy was introduced based on a number of factors including it being a pragmatic, conciliatory, reasonable approach*) or Judgement of people's behaviour (*They misjudged Hitler*). Considered use of Graduation to emphasize key points (*it is essential [[to identify the historiographical issues [[that influenced their writing]]]]*). Engagement resources are deployed to acknowledge diverse perspectives (*His views differ to Kennedy's as he believes that . . .*). Modality is drawn on to temper Judgements (*perhaps the most important man [[in leading the Greeks to victory]]*).

Textually: Theme choices are simple nominal groups, sometimes pronouns, often used repetitively. Marked Themes expressed in dependent clauses of time (*when we got to the Aboriginal part // I saw a canoe.*)

Textually: Theme choices are often marked, frequently realizing time (e.g. *Today Jamberoo is a hustling and thriving village*) but also manner (*with the telescope he was able to look up to the stars . . . .*) Developing ability to 'pick up' and thematize matters expressed in complete prior clauses (*Today Jamberoo is a hustling and thriving village. The main changes //I have noticed11 in my time here is* . . . Also developing control of Given and New Information.

Textually: there are patterns of unmarked topical Themes in site and period studies, with some marked Themes to introduce new stages in description (*on very special occasions the Romans would go up to the temple . . .*) In historical accounts marked Themes often signal shifts in time and help stage the unfolding of events (*when the Viet Minh had beaten the Japanese with the aid of the United States // the Vietnamese took pride and realized that they..*)

Textually: In historical argument and explanation thematic progression is achieved through a strong sense of macroTheme and associated hyperThemes, used to sustain often long interpretive texts.

Table 8.4 Exemplifying major linguistic features in writing in science from early childhood to late adolescence

Early childhood: 6–8 years	Late childhood-early adolescence: 9–12 years	Mid-adolescence: 13–15 years	Late adolescence: 16–18 years +
Experientially: Processes are material, used to realize actions in procedural recounts (*we soaked beans*) and in explanations, reports and field studies telling how things occur (*people pick the fruit in cherry pickers*) while relational attributive Processes are common to describe (*Venus is very old and rocky*).	**Experientially:** Relational attributive Processes are used to describe in reports and explanations (*almost all life in Antarctica is in the sea*) or are relational identifying to specify (*the secondary consumers consist of whales* (*preferably the blue whale*) *seals, larger fishes and penguins; an eclipse is* [[*when the earth or Moon blocks out the light of the Sun.*]]); existential Processes introduce (*first off, there is plankton, phyto plankton.; there are two different eclipses..*); material Processes build actions in explanations (*it is tipped into a big bin..*)	**Experientially:** In procedural recounts, Processes are mainly material to realize actions (*we were aiming to prevent boiling; it started to rise and bubble.*). In explanations, frequent use of relational identifying Processes to specify (*the reproductive female part of a flower consists of a stigma; the first step in fertilization is pollination*) and some attributive Processes to describe (*cross pollinated plants are usually healthier than self pollinated ones.*)	**Experientially:** Processes are often material, to do with steps taken or observed (*move the magnet*) but relational attributive Processes describe (*the movement* [[*produced in the plate*]] *was minimal*) or relational identifying to define. The only definite way [[to diagnose Down Syndrome]] is [[to perform an amniocentesis]] verbal Processes are used to reveal what is found (*this showed me // why algae was one of the first life forms . . .*

Participants are realized in pronouns in procedural recounts, otherwise in simple nominal groups sometimes with embedded phrases (*the seeds [in the bottle [with the cap off]*). Technical lexis emerges early (*Venus, planet, mammals*)	Participants are often realized in simple nominal groups (*a lunar eclipse*) though some show expansion of the nominal group structure (*the outer atmosphere of the sun*). There is frequent use of technical lexis (*krill; primary consumers; Umbra*)	Participants can be realized in dense nominal groups involving grammatical metaphor (*the reproductive female part of a flower; many times of repeating this process; the lemon scented tea tree oil*) Much technical lexis (*condensor tube, pollen sacs, anthers.*)	Participants are also realized in dense nominal groups often involving grammatical metaphor *non-destructive testing; one of the hardiest and most widespread living organisms on this planet; a chromosomal disorder [[that affects the genetic make up of a human being]; some level of learning disabilities.* They often involve technical lexis (*Down Syndrome; AC generator; eddy current; chromosome.*)

(*Continued*)

Table 8.4—Cont'd

Early childhood: 6–8 years	Late childhood-early adolescence: 9–12 years	Mid-adolescence: 13–15 years	Late adolescence: 16–18 years +
Circumstances are realized in prepositional phrases of place (*we shook the water over the beans*; *a bat can hear from a Kilometre away*), occasional examples of manner (*we filled both bottles with the soaked beans*)	Circumstances are still realized in prepositional phrases and can be of extent (*The blue whale can weigh up to one hundred and seventy four tones*; *scientists discovered a long time ago*), and also place (*the earth's shadow falls on the moon.*) Circumstances realized in adverbs are rare (*the moon doesn't disappear completely*)	Circumstances are typically of place (*it started to drip out of the end of the condensor tube*; *it goes through the ovule.*), though can be of reason (*many plants do not self pollinate because of this*). Circumstances realized in adverbs are not common.	Circumstances of place are common (*most life cannot survive in this environment*), though other types are found, including manner (*the eddy current [[produced]] must have been produced in such a way [[as to oppose the motion of the magnet]].*) or extent (*cared for, for the rest of their lives*) Some Circumstances involve grammatical metaphor (*I would test these factors in an effort [[to understand // why our spa does not have blackspot algae / and the pool does // even when the chlorine level in both is the same]]*) Circumstances realized in adverbs are still rare and where they appear, are typically of manner (*the soil would suffer dreadfully; small bends and riffles rated fairly.*)

Clauses types and logical relations: <u>clauses</u> are mainly equal. Dependent clauses of time may occur in explanations (*After they have been labeled* // *they are taken to the supermarket.*) and clauses of reason can occur in field studies (*The tissue is gone because they fall apart easily*)

Clause types and logical relations: in reports <u>clauses</u> are mainly equal, linked with additive conjunctions. (*these creatures feed on the smaller primary consumers* // *and are fed to the secondary consumers*). In explanations clause complexes are more intricate, to do with building events and their relations (*A solar eclipse occurs* // *when the moon moves in front of the Earth* // *and blocks the Sun,* // *but the Sun is not completely blocked* // *because the outer atmosphere of the sun flashes* // *and (because it) can still be seen* // *and that is called the Corona*).

Clause types and logical relations: equal and dependent <u>clauses</u> are both involved in building intricate clause complexes (*When the plant fertilization is finished* // *nearly all the lower parts* (of the flower) *die* // *and fall off* // *because their work is done.;* *We were aiming to prevent boiling so* << *as soon as bubbles appeared* >> *the Bunsen would be moved away, and so on.*)

Clause types and logical relations: <u>Clause complexes</u> are often intricate (*During a fieldtrip on Thursday 2*nd *June, tests were carried out* // *in order to describe current conditions at Mullet Creek* // *and identify the impacts of human activities* // *so that management could be formulated and recommended; My hypothesis may be biased* // *as I already know the effectiveness of the pool products from past use in the pool* // *so they would appear to be the most efficient*). Clauses of projection often appear when recording what is concluded (*it* <u>*proves*</u> *to me* // *that* <u>*algae will survive*</u> . . ..)

(*Continued*)

Table 8.4—Cont'd

Early childhood: 6–8 years	Late childhood–early adolescence: 9–12 years	Mid-adolescence: 13–15 years	Late adolescence: 16–18 years +
Interpersonally: use of the first person in procedural recounts and field studies. Occasional use of passive voice to remove human agency (*the fruit gets put into a big bin*) Occasional use of modal adverbs (*Maybe the garbage men will take it.*) Attitudinally neutral.	**Interpersonally:** typically in the third person in procedural recounts, explanations and field studies. Passive voice removes human agency. An occasional modal verb appears in field studies (*people shouldn't leave the autumn leaves*). Texts are normally attitudinally neutral.	**Interpersonally:** First person is sometimes used in procedural recounts, but third person in explanations. Some modal adverbs (*cross pollinated plants are usually healthier than self pollinated ones*). Both genres are generally attitudinally neutral, as are research articles.	**Interpersonally:** senior science texts use mainly third person, though first person is used sometimes in field studies, and occasionally in research articles. Passive voice is often used to remove human agency (*care was taken to reduce this risk*). Modality may appear, (*this may cause injury; ultra sounds can pick up abnormalities..*) Research articles and demonstration genres use third person and are attitudinally neutral. Field studies may express attitudes, and discussions do so (***In my opinion*** *. . . . there is no reason to stress and worry about it.*) In discussion genres, Engagement with the opinions of others is evident (*some believe that mobile phones can cause illness while others believe..*)

Textually: topical Themes are unmarked in procedural recounts and reports, often realized in the same item used repetitively. In explanations, marked topical Themes are quite frequent (*At the cannery the fruit is washed and checked*) Use of headings to order information in procedural recounts and field studies. Pictures or images sometimes accompany text.

Textually: Theme choices are mainly unmarked, but unmarked Themes can occur (*With powerful teeth, they are the top of the food chain..*) Reference is generally good. Texts are often accompanied by pictures or images.

Textually: marked topical Themes of time are important to signal steps in either an experiment (*after heating the contents of the flask // it started to rise and bubble*) or in an explanation sequence (*once the pollen reaches the stigma of the same species of flower // it begins to grow . . . when it arrives // it pierces the ovary wall . . .*) Procedural recounts normally have images, and explanations commonly have them. Procedural recounts and research articles use headings and sub heading to order the texts and explanations may use them. Emergent control of macroThemes and hyperThemes

Textually: Topical Themes are often marked (*as shown in the field sketch/ / there is a huge man-made rock..; due to the learning and behavioral disorders]]caused by Down Syndrome] people]]who have it]] usually need special care..*) . All senior science genres (apart from discussions) use headings and sub -headings to display their information, and they make frequent use of images, diagrams and graphs. Texts become longer in the senior years and macroTheme and hyperThemes are important, supported by headings and sub headings.

Lexical density

We have relied on texts discussed throughout the earlier chapters to build the summaries in the above tables, and since we provided data on lexical density in each of those chapters, it will be appropriate to conclude by displaying over-all lexical density counts.

Figure 8.2 provides an account of the lexical density counts of the texts we discussed in our previous six chapters. For each of the subjects we have aver-aged the densities in the different texts at each age, achieving one value for each. Had we used different texts, there might have been some variations in the averages, since we are dealing with tendencies, not absolute measures. Across the three subjects, one general trend emerges. It is that as children gain confidence in control of the written language, the lexical density in their texts increases. Thus, after about the ages of 7 or 8, the average density is more than 3, while densities beyond 4 become more common after the ages of 11 or 12, reaching as high 6 or 7 in the latter years. Halliday (1985: 80), cited earlier, argued that the figure for written English 'settles down somewhere between 3 and 6, depending on the level of formality in the writing'. Increasing lexical density is not in itself a sufficient measure of development in writing. However, it is of some interest to this study that the overall trend in all three subjects demonstrates a steady growth in lexical density as children move through childhood and into the years of adolescence, mastering the relatively dense nature of written language.

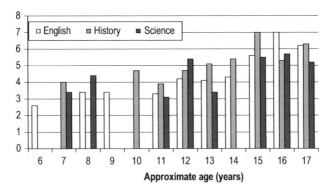

FIGURE 8.2   Average lexical densities in English, history and science, age 6 to 17 years

Writing development and the curriculum

The developmental phases we have proposed provide a useful framework for planning writing programmes in all subjects across the years of schooling. In using the phases to guide educational policy, several overriding principles should apply:

- Learning to write should be understood in developmental terms across all the years of schooling.
- While responsibility for teaching much knowledge about language rests with the English programme, teachers of other subjects should be encouraged to use selected knowledge of language as well.
- Teaching of writing should focus on genres to be written, selected for their relevance to areas of knowledge to be covered, building a strong sense of the language resources in which these are realized, and hence also building a repertoire of knowledge and skills for subsequent work.
- A metalanguage for talking about, interpreting, playing with and critiquing written language should emerge from the first years and be pursued in later years; use of a metalanguage is essential in terms of building a consciousness about language, and teachers must constantly make decisions about when to introduce it most productively.
- The metalanguage involved should slowly build across the years, using selected traditional and functional terms.
- Teachers should use their own understanding of the various developmental phases to monitor children's progress, challenging them to move in new directions and supporting them where adequate progress does not seem to be made.

In what follows we shall say more of the developments in each phase.

Phase 1

The oral language is the primary meaning-making system available to young children, and they rely heavily on their knowledge of this in learning the 'second – order symbolic system' that is written language. So effortful is the process of learning and internalizing the written mode – its spelling and writing systems and its grammar – that children's language regresses, and their written language is simpler than that they speak. Halliday suggests children 'typically regress in semiotic age by anything up to three years' (Halliday 1993: 110) in the first years of learning to read and write. Strategies to promote writing development should include:

- generating a teaching/learning context which encourages shared goals for writing and an understanding of the knowledge or field to be written about;
- extensive guided talk about the genre, supported by relevant resources;
- teacher reading of model patterns of written language, establishing familiarity with these patterns;

- joint reading of texts and discussion of their features;
- joint writing of texts from class activity, naming their genre types and their steps;
- guided talk about the texts, exploring the 'commonsense' meanings involved;
- guided independent writing of texts by children;
- teaching a metalanguage, including the conventional terms to do with spelling and writing, and introducing such functional terms as 'process' and 'participant' to inform interpretation of texts; Williams (1998: 31–8) has demonstrated how teaching these to six-year-olds can enhance their understanding of texts; Feez (2007), using Montessori's principles, has also demonstrated the values of teaching grammar in developing a consciousness about language even in very young children;
- teacher monitoring of these matters, at least: (i) the emergence of clauses, equal and dependent, intervening to assist children to master sequencing of these; (ii) some developing sense of thematic progression (iii) developing control of reference; and (iv) emergent capacity to talk about texts (both read and written), interpreting and discussing their meanings.

Phase 2

Much received wisdom in the matter has focused on the importance of the first years of schooling (Phase 1 in fact) and while we agree this period is important, the evidence suggests that it is the second phase which is in many ways critical, for it marks an important transitional passage away from forms of language like those of speech, towards forms closer to mature writing, and the grammatical organization of children's texts must change if children are to succeed. Among other matters, texts develop a greater range of clause types and clause interdependencies, as children must master 'the information-packed clause structure characteristic of academic registers' (Schleppegrell 2004: 78–9).

Phase 2 straddles the transition from the primary to the secondary school, when the curriculum changes, showing greater subject specialization. This makes changing demands on children's language capacities, at a time moreover, when children advance into puberty, undergoing various physiological changes, including changes to the brain. Brain development continues throughout adolescence (Society for Neuroscience 2005: 10–21). It is in this phase that many students begin to fall behind, a phenomenon recognized for some time. In the 1970s, the then national *Curriculum Development Centre* coordinated an Australia-wide initiative addressing language learning needs in the 'interface' between primary and secondary school, specifically school years 5–8 (Curriculum Development Centre 1979; Maling-Keepes and Keepes 1979), when, it was said, many children dropped behind and literacy performance was identified as a major source of the problem. Significant amounts of government funds have been devoted since the 1970s to similar initiatives to improve language education in the 'middle years', revealing that the problems have not easily been resolved.

These problems have sometimes been spoken of in terms of the 'literacy gap' (e.g. Strickland and Alvermann 2004), though the decline in performance is often attributed to decline in reading, rather than writing. The Carnegie Corporation (2007) for example, is presently promoting in the USA a major programme of research studies into *Advancing Literacy*, noting that while a great deal has been achieved in developing appropriate reading programmes for children up to the third grade, more needs to be done to establish 'the knowledge base for how to teach reading for grades beyond this point', and the problem is said to grow progressively worse as students proceed into high schools (*Carnegie Corporation News*, 2007: 1). The preoccupation with reading mentioned earlier is evident here, though poor literacy performance is as much a matter of writing as of reading. At least one other study from the USA addressed writing, referring to it as the 'neglected "R" ' (*National Commission on Writing*, 2003) while Snow and Biancarosa (2003) and Biancarosa and Snow (2004) have brought writing to greater prominence. It is significant too, that the *National Secondary Strategy* in England, alluded to earlier, is specifically devoted to improving educational attainment in reading and writing in the junior secondary years, when children are aged 11–14 years.

Strategies to promote writing development, to be phased in over several years, should include:

- Modelling of target genres in all subjects, focusing on the meanings constructed in their various stages, and exploring purposes in writing them. Polias and Dare 2006 report a genre based programme developed with the functional grammar, which extended into the middle years. Love et al. 2006 and 2008 provides DVD programmes outlining different genres across the school subjects, and extending into the secondary years. Rose (2008) has created a professional development package for teachers of reading and writing, relevant for teaching in late childhood to adolescence;
- Joint and/or independent construction of the genres, where joint practices are maintained longer for weak students;
- Teaching a metalanguage for discussing the grammatical organization of texts, including both class labels (e.g. nouns, verbs, adjectives, prepositional phrase etc.) and selected functional labels (e.g. process, participant, theme, circumstance) (see Derewianka 1999; Christie and Soosai, 2000, 2001; Droga and Humphrey 2003 for strategies);
- Observing and naming different patterns of clauses types, discussing the ways various clauses contribute to meaning making, and playing with them to achieve different effects;

- Practising the sequencing of clauses in different genres;
- Demonstrating ways to create enlarged nominal groups (with pre- and post-modifiers);
- Teaching ways to compress independent clauses by creating enlarged nominal groups through the resources of grammatical metaphor (though the latter term need necessarily not be used);
- Identifying processes characteristic of genres, discussing how these are realized in different verbal groups;
- Exploring different patterns of thematic progression, as students learn to create and play with marked themes and their relevance in different types of genres.
- Exploring language resources to express attitude, considering ways writers persuade, move or interest their readers;
- Teacher monitoring of these matters, at least: (i) control of relevant genres; (ii) growing sense of thematic progression in different genres; (iii) a developing sense of different clauses and clause interdependencies, depending on genre; (iv) emergent control of modality and resources for attitudinal expression; (v) a shifting from 'everyday' to more technical/specialist language; (vi) expansion of evaluative language for expression of value and judgement; (vii) capacity to engage in talk about texts (read and written), interpreting and critiquing them where necessary.

Phase 3

The third phase falls in the mid-secondary years, when a great deal of the overall control of the grammar of written language is achieved by successful students, though those not managing in the earlier years can continue to struggle. Childhood has been left behind and successful students come to terms with secondary education, with all its challenges in addressing growing bodies of 'uncommonsense' knowledge. The challenges involve dealing with abstraction in all school subjects, though this is expressed rather differently in science from the humanities like history and English. The hierarchical knowledge structures of science produce a technical lexis, representing scientific abstractions. Some are to do with classification, as in the case of scientific taxonomies identifying living creatures as part of the Animal Kingdom. Others are to do with generalizations about phenomena, leading to scientific principles or laws, as in the case of Lenz's law. History and English lack a technical language, though they build abstractions of a different order, and they are not hierarchically organized, nor do they create 'laws'. The abstractions of English offer reflections on human experience in stories, or interpretations of works of art in response genres. Such abstractions, often created using grammatical metaphor, offer judgement or ethical positioning of some kind. The abstractions of history are typically built up by constructing causal accounts of events, interpretations of events and/or arguments about the relevance of historical events and artefacts, often also involving grammatical metaphor. Finally, one of the several challenges of these mid-secondary years lies in writing what become gradually longer texts in many subjects, requiring good control of schematic structure and thematic progression.

Where needed, some of the strategies of the earlier years should be maintained, while others should be introduced to extend and challenge students:

- Modelling of target genres in all subjects (where necessary), focusing on the meanings constructed in their various stages, and exploring purposes in writing them;
- Joint and/or independent construction of the genres, where joint practices are maintained longer for weak students;
- Active discussion and exploration of the organization of texts read and written, bringing to consciousness a great deal of the ways they are crafted;
- Examination of attitudinal expression in different kinds of texts, reviewing the impact of such expression;
- Use of the metalanguage to examine different texts, examining, for example, identifying processes and their role in building argumentative and interpretative texts, or the role of dense nominal groups in compressing meaning, or the role of dense prepositional phrases building circumstances;
- Work on thematic progression, including introducing marked themes as well as macroThemes and hyperThemes, and the value of these for developing the longer texts students much write. Marshall 2006, reports success in using notions of Theme and nominalizatiom in teaching the writing of response genres in secondary school;
- Teacher monitoring of these matters, at least: (i) control of relevant genres; (ii) possession of a metalanguage for talk about texts: (iii) an understanding of thematic progression, including use of macroThemes and hyperThemes; (iv) an awareness of different clause interdependencies and their role in creating meaning; (iv) control of resources for attitudinal expression; (v) capacity to engage in talk about texts (both read and written), interpreting, evaluating and critiquing them where necessary.

Phase 4

The last phase marks the completion of schooling and the entry to adult life, though in principle the phase lasts throughout life, depending on the ways in which students go on to write beyond their school days. In the last years of schooling, when students are aged about 16 to 17 or 18, the evidence available to us is that the texts they must read and write are generally very abstract and dense. Students must typically complete their schooling, undergo assessment, often by public examination, and move on to further study or entry to the workplace. In these years they need to consolidate the gains they have made in control of written language, achieving the capacity to function with increasing independence of teachers or other mentors.

Strategies of the earlier years should be maintained, and much work should be done to consolidate learning include:

- active discussion and exploration of the organization of texts read and written, bringing to consciousness a great deal of the ways they are crafted;
- use of the metalanguage to examine grammatical organization of texts;
- further work on thematic progression, examining the value of thematic choices in developing the longer texts students must write; Walsh (2006: 174–5) reports successful use of nominalization and of theme in teaching senior students of English writing literary response genres; Hewings and North (2006) report the value of studying thematic progression in examining undergraduate essays in geography and history of science;
- Teacher monitoring of these matters, at least: (i) control of relevant genres; (ii) possession of a meta-language for talk about texts: (iii) an understanding of thematic progression, including use of macrothemes and hyperthemes to sustain long texts; (iv) skill in deploying aspects of the grammar in strategically different ways to create meanings; (v) capacity to engage in talk about texts, interpreting, evaluating, and critiquing them; (vi) control of attitudinal expression, revealing a consciousness of the impact of various attitudinal resources.

Conclusion

The ability to write is prized in English-speaking cultures, bringing considerable advantage to those who can do it well in many sites, personal, occupational, political and communal. Many children do not succeed in their writing, for it is in fact quite difficult to learn to write well. All children deserve the opportunity to learn to write. We argue that where teachers are possessed of appropriate knowledge of the ontogenesis of writing ability, of a kind the functional grammar provides, they can the more effectively guide their students as they learn to write.

References

Agnew, V. (2007), 'History's affective turn: historical reenactment and its work in the present', *Rethinking History*, 11 (3): 299–312.

Aidman, M. (1999), 'Biliteracy development through early and mid primary years'. Unpub. PhD thesis, Melbourne: University of Melbourne.

Applebee, A.N. (2000), 'Alternative models of writing development', in R. Indrisano, and J.R. Squire (eds), *Perspectives on Writing*, Newark, DE: International Reading Association, pp. 90–110.

Arnold, M. (1869), *Culture and Anarchy. An Essay in Political and Social Criticism.* London, Edinburgh and New York: Thomas Nelson and Sons.

Australian Government Department of Education, Science and Training (2007), *Guide to the Teaching of Australian History in Years 9 and 10* (http://www.dest.gov.au/schools/australianhistory accessed 10 December 2007).

Bazerman, C. (1988), *Shaping Written Knowledge. The Genre and Activity of the Experimental Article in Science.* London and Madison, WI: University of Wisconsin Press.

Beard, C. (1934), 'Written history as an act of faith', *The American Historical Review*, 39 (2): 219–31.

Bernstein, B. (1975), *Class, Codes and Control Vol. 3. Towards a Theory of Educational Transmissions.* London and Boston, MA: Routledge and Kegan Paul.

Bernstein, B. (1990), *The Structuring of Pedagogic Discourse. Class, Codes and Control, Vol. IV.* London and New York: Routledge.

Bernstein, B. (1999) 'Vertical and horizontal discourse: an essay', *British Journal of Sociology of Education*, 20 (2): 157–73.

Bernstein, B. (2000), *Pedagogy, Symbolic Control and Identity. Theory, Research, Critique* (revised edn). Lanham, MD, Boulder, CO, New York and Oxford: Rowman and Littlefield.

Biancarosa, G. and C.E. Snow (2004), *Reading Next: A Vision for Action and Research in Middle and High School Literacy: A Report from Carnegie Corporation of New York.* Washington, DC: Alliance for Excellent Education.

Bissex, G. (1980), *GNYS AT WRK: A Child Learns to Write and Read.* Cambridge, MA: Harvard University Press.

Britton, J.N., T. Burgess, N. Martin, A. McLeod, and H. Rosen (1975), *The Development of Writing Abilities (11–18)*. Urbana, IL: National Council of Teachers of English.

Bruning, R. and C. Horn (2000), 'Developing motivation to write', *Educational Psychologist*, 35 (1): 25–37.

Carnegie Corporation of New York (2007), *Advancing Literacy* (http://www.carnegie.org/literacy/index.html accessed 5 December 2007).

Christie, F. (1998), 'Learning the literacies of primary and secondary schooling', in F. Christie and R. Misson (eds), *Literacy and Schooling*, London and New York: Routledge, pp. 47–73.

Christie, F. (2002), 'The development of abstraction in adolescence in subject English', in M.J. Schleppegrell and M.C. Colombi (eds), *Developing Advanced Literacy in First and Second Languages*, Mahwah, NJ and London: Erlbaum, pp. 45–66.

Christie, F. (2004a), 'Authority and its role in the pedagogic relationship of schooling', in L. Young and C. Harrison (eds), *Systemic Functional Linguistics and Critical Discourse Analysis. Studies in Social Change*, London and New York: Continuum, pp. 173–201.

Christie, F. (2004b), 'Revisiting some old themes: the role of grammar in the teaching of English', in J.A. Foley (ed.), *Language, Education and Discourse. Functional Approaches*. London and New York: Continuum, pp. 145–73.

Christie, F. and S. Dreyfus (2007), 'Letting the secret out: Mentoring successful writing in secondary English studies', in *Australian Journal of Language and Literacy*, 30 (3): 235–47.

Christie, F. and S. Humphrey (2008), 'Senior secondary English and its goals: making sense of "The Journey" ', in L. Unsworth (ed.) *Multimodal Semiotics and Multiliteracies Education: Transdisciplinary Approaches to Research and Professional Practice*, London and New York: Continuum, pp. 215–37.

Christie, F. and M. Macken-Horarik (2007), 'Building verticality in subject English', in F. Christie and J.R. Martin (eds), *Language, Knowledge and Pedagogy. Functional Linguistic and Sociological Perspectives*, London and New York: Continuum, pp. 156–83.

Christie, F. and J.R. Martin (eds) (1997), *Genre and Institutions. Social Processes in the Workplace and School*. London and New York: Continuum.

Christie, F. and J.R. Martin (eds) (2007), *Language, Knowledge and Pedagogy. Functional Linguistic and Sociological Perspectives*. London and New York: Continuum.

Christie, F. and A. Soosai (2000), *Language and Meaning 1*. Melbourne: Macmillan Education.

Christie, F. and A. Soosai (2001), *Language and Meaning 2*. Melbourne: Macmillan Education.

Clay, M. (1975), *What Did I Write?* Auckland, New Zealand: Heinemann.

Clendinnen, I. (2006), 'The history question: who owns the past?' *Quarterly Essay*, 23: 1–72. Melbourne: Black Inc.

Coffin, C. (1996), *Exploring Literacy in School History*. Sydney: Disadvantaged Schools Program, Metropolitan East Region.

Coffin, C. (1997), 'Constructing and giving value to the past: an investigation into secondary school history', in F. Christie and J.R. Martin (eds), *Genre and Institutions. Social Processes in the Workplace and School*. London and New York: Continuum, pp. 196–230.

Coffin, C. (2004), 'Learning to write history: the role of causality', *Written Communication*, 21 (3): 261–89.

Coffin, C. (2006a), *Historical Discourse*. London: Continuum.

Coffin, C. (2006b), 'Reconstruing "personal time" as "collective time" ': learning the discourse of history', in R. Whittaker, M. O'Donnell and A. McCabe (eds), *Language and Literacy: Functional Approaches*, London and New York: Continuum, pp. 207–32.

Coffin, C. and Derewianka, B. (2008a), 'Visual representations of time in history textbooks', in L. Unsworth (ed.), *Multimodal Semiotics*, London and New York: Continuum.

Coffin, C. and Derewianka, B. (2008b), 'Reader pathways in secondary history textbooks', in G. Thompson and G. Forey (eds), *Text Type and Texture*, London: Equinox.

Coulmas, F. (1989), *The Writing Systems of the World*. Oxford: Blackwell.

Curriculum Development Centre (1979), *The Language Development Project Discussion Paper No. 1*. Canberra: Curriculum Development Centre.

Curthoys, A. and J. Docker (2006), *Is History Fiction?* Sydney: UNSW Press.

Czerniewska, P. (1992), *Learning about Writing*. Oxford: Blackwell.

Deacon, T. (1997), *The Symbolic Species*. London, New York and Melbourne: Penguin Books.

DeFrancis, J. (1989), *Visible Speech: The Diverse Oneness of Writing Systems*. Honolulu, HI: University of Hawaii Press.

Department for Education and Skills and Qualifications and Curriculum Authority (2006a), *A Condensed Key Stage 3: Designing a Flexible Curriculum* (http://www.standards.dfes.gov.uk/secondary/keystage3/all/respub/ks3flexcurricupd025906 accessed 8 February 2008).

Department for Education and Skills and Qualifications and Curriculum Authority (2006b) *Handbook on Assessing Pupils' Progress in English* (http://www.standards.dfes.gov.uk/secondary/keystage3/all/respub/en_asspup accessed 8 February 2008).

Derewianka, B. (1996), 'Language in later childhood', in C. Reynolds (ed.), *Teaching about Language: Learning about Language*, Melbourne: AATE/NPDP, pp. 62–85.

Derewianka, B. (1999), *A Grammar Companion for Primary Teachers*. Sydney: Primary English Teaching Association.

Derewianka, B. (2003), 'Grammatical metaphor in the transition to adolescence', in A.M. Simon-Vandenbergen et al. (eds), *Grammatical Metaphor. (Amsterdam Studies in the Theory and History of Linguistic Science. Series IV: Current Issues in Linguistic Theory*. General Ed. E.F. Konrad Koerner). Amsterdam and Philadelphia, PA: Benjamins, pp. 185–219.

Derewianka, B. (2007), 'Using appraisal theory to track interpersonal development in adolescent academic writing', in A. McCabe, M. O'Donnell and R. Whittaker (eds), *Advances in Language and Education*, London and New York: Continuum, pp. 142–65.

Droga, L. and Humphrey, S. (2003), *Grammar and Meaning. An Introduction for Primary Teachers*. Berry, NSW: Target Texts.

Dyson, A.H. and S.W. Freedman (1991), 'Writing', in J. Flood, J.M. Jensen, D. Lapp, J.R. Squire (eds), *Handbook of Research on Teaching English Language Arts*, New York: Macmillan Publishing Co., pp. 754–74.

Edelman, G. (1992), *Bright Air, Brilliant Fire: On the Matter of the Mind*. London: Penguin Books.

Edelman, G. and G. Tononi (2000), *A Universe of Consciousness. How Matter Becomes Imagination*. New York: Basic Books.

Edelsky, C. (1986), *Writing in a Bilingual Program: Haba una vez*. Norwood, NJ: Ablex.

Educational Assessment Australia (2008) *International Competitions and Assessment Tests* (http://www.eaa.unsw.edu.au/about_icas/writing accessed 22 February 2008).

Edwards, L. (2003), 'Writing instruction in kindergarten: examining an emerging area of research for children with writing and reading difficulties', *Journal of Learning Disabilities*, 36 (2): 136–48.

Ehri, L.C. (2000), 'Learning to read and learning to spell: two sides of a coin', *Topics in Language Disorders*, 20 (3): 19–36.

Ethington, P.J. (2007), 'Placing the past: "Groundwork" for a spatial theory of history', *Rethinking History*, 11 (4): 465–93.

Feez, S. (2007), 'Montessori's mediation of meaning: a social semiotic perspective'. Unpub. PhD thesis, Sydney: University of Sydney.

Ferreiro, E. and A. Teberosky (1982), *Literacy before Schooling*. Exeter, NH: Heinemann.

Francis, G. (1994), 'Labelling discourse: an aspect of nominal-group lexical cohesion', in M. Coulthard (ed.), *Advances in Written Text Analysis*, London: Routledge, pp. 83–101.

Gilderhus, M. (2003), *History and Historians: A Historiographical Introduction*. Upper Saddle River, NJ: Prentice-Hall.

Graham, S. and D. Perin (2007), *Writing Next: Effective Strategies to Improve Writing of Adolescents in Middle and High School. A Report to the Carnegie Corporation of NY*. Washington, DC: Carnegie.

Graham, S. and K.R. Harris (2000), 'The role of self-regulation and transcription skills in writing and writing development', *Educational Psychologist*, 35 (1): 3–12.

Graves, D. H. (1983), *Writing: Teachers and Children at Work*. Portsmouth, NH and London: Heinemann Educational.

Green, B. (1988), 'Subject-specific literacy and school learning: a focus on writing', *Australian Journal of Education*, 37 (2): 119–41.

Halliday, M.A.K. (1975), *Learning How to Mean. Explorations in the Development of Language*. (Series Editors P. Doughty and G. Thornton, *Explorations in Language Study*). London: Arnold.

Halliday, M.A.K. (1985), *Spoken and Written Language*. Geelong, Victoria: Deakin University Press.

Halliday, M.A.K. (1993), 'Towards a language-based theory of learning', *Linguistics and Education*, 5 (2): 93–116.

Halliday, M.A.K. (2004a), 'On the language of physical science', in *The Language of Science, Collected Works of M.A.K. Halliday, Vol. 5*. (ed. J. Webster), London and New York: Continuum, pp. 140–58. (Also published in M.A.K. Halliday and J.R. Martin (1993), *Writing Science. Literacy and Discursive Power* (*Critical Perspectives on Literacy and Education*. Series Editor A. Luke). London and Washington, DC: Falmer Press. pp. 54–68.)

Halliday, M.A.K. (2004b), 'On grammar as the driving force from primary to higher-order consciousness', in G. Williams and A. Lukin (eds), *The Development of*

Language. Functional Perspectives on Species and Individuals, London and New York: Continuum, pp. 15–44.

Halliday, M.A.K. and J.R. Martin (1993), *Writing Science. Literacy and Discursive Power* (*Critical Perspectives on Literacy and Education.* Series Editor A. Luke). London and Washington, DC: Falmer Press.

Halliday, M.A.K and C.M.I.M. Matthiessen (1999), *Construing Experience Through Meaning. A Language-Based Approach to Cognition.* London and New York: Cassell.

Halliday, M.A.K and C.M.I.M. Matthiessen (2004), *An Introduction to Functional Grammar* (3rd edn). London: Arnold.

Harpin, W. (1976), *The Second 'R'. Writing Development in the Junior School.* London: Allen and Unwin.

Hasan, R. (2005), *Language, Society and Consciousness. The Collected Works of Ruqaiya Hasan* (ed. Jonathan Webster), Equinox: London and Oakville.

Hasan, R., Matthiessen, C. and Webster, J. (eds.) (2005), *Continuing Discourse on Language. A Functional Perspective, Vol. 1.* Equinox: London and Oakville.

Hewings, A. and S. North (2006), 'Emergent disciplinarity: a comparative study of theme in undergraduate essay in geography and history of science', in R. Whittaker, M. O'Donnell and A. McCabe (eds), *Language and Literacy. Functional Approaches.* London and New York: Continuum, pp. 266–84.

Hunt, K. (1965), *Grammatical Structures written at Three Grade Levels: Research Report No.3* Urbana, IL: National Council of Teachers of English.

Hunt, K.W. (1977), 'Early blooming and late blooming syntactic structures', in C.R. Cooper and L. Odell (eds), *Evaluating Writing: Describing, Measuring, Judging,* Buffalo, NY: National Council of Teachers of English, pp. 91–106.

Hyland, K. (2002), *Teaching and Researching Writing,* Essex, UK: Pearson Education.

Johnson, D.J. (1993), 'Relationships between oral and written language', *School Psychology Review,* 22 (4): 595–609.

Kelly, G.J. (2008), 'Learning science: discursive practices', in M. Martin-Jones, A.M. De Meja and N.H. Hornberger (eds), *Encyclopedia of Language and Education. Vol. 3: Discourse and Education,* New York: Springer, pp. 329–40.

King, M. and Rentel, V. (1982), *Transition to Writing* (Technical Report NIE-G-79-0137; NIE-G-79-0039), Columbus, Ohio: The Ohio State University Research Foundation.

Korner, H., D. McInnes and D. Rose (2007), *Science Literacy.* (NSW Department of Education and Training, Adult Migrant Services, Quality Language and Literacy Services, Series Editor H. de Silva). Sydney: NSW Adult Migrant Education Service.

Kress, G. (1994), *Learning to Write.* London: Routledge.

Kress, G., C. Jewitt, J. Bourne, A. Franks, J. Hardcastle, K. Jones and E. Reid (2005), *English in Urban Classrooms. A Multimodal Perspective on Teaching and Learning Language.* London and New York: Routledge/Falmer.

Labbo, L.D. and W.H. Teale (1997), 'An emergent-literacy perspective on reading instruction in kindergarten', in S.A. Stahl and D.A. Hayes (eds), *Instructional Models in Reading,* Mahwah, NJ: Erlbaum, pp. 249–81.

Labov, W. and W. Waletsky (1967), 'Narrative analysis: oral versions of personal experience', in J. Helm (ed.), *Essays in the Verbal and Visual Arts (American Ethnological*

Society: Proceedings of Spring Meeting, 1966,. Washington, DC: University of Washington Press, pp. 12–44.

Lemke, J.L. (1990), *Talking Science: Language, Learning and Values*. Norwood, NJ: Ablex Publishing.

Lemke, J.L. (2002), 'Multimedia semiotics: genres for science education and science literacy', in M.J. Schleppegrell and M.C. Colombi (eds), *Developing Advanced Literacy in First and Second Languages. Meaning with Power*, Mahwah, NJ: Erlbaum, pp. 21–44.

Loban, W. (1976), *Language Development: Kindergarten through Grade Twelve. No. 18 in a Series of Reports sponsored by the NCTE Committee on Research*. Urbana, IL: National Council of Teachers of English.

Locke, T. (2007), 'Constructing English in New Zealand: a report on a decade of reform', *Educational Studies in Language and Literature*, 7 (2): 5–33.

Love, K., K. Pigdon and G. Baker (2006), *Building Understandings in Literacy and Teaching* (3rd edn), Melbourne: The University of Melbourne Publishing.

Love, K., G. Baker and M. Quinn (2008), *Literacy across the School Subjects*. Melbourne: The University of Melbourne Publishing.

Macintyre, S. and A. Clark (2003), *The History Wars*. Melbourne: Melbourne University Press.

Macken-Horarik, M. (2002), ' "Something to shoot for": a systemic functional approach to teaching genre in secondary school', in A.M. Johns (ed.), *Genre in the Classroom: Multiple Perspectives*, Mahwah, NJ: Erlbaum, pp. 17–42.

Macken-Horarik, M. (2006), 'Knowledge through "know how": systemic functional grammatics and the symbolic reading', *English Teaching: Practice and Critique*, 5 (1): 102–21.

MacLean, M. and L.J. Chapman (1989), 'The processing of cohesion in fiction and non-fiction by good and poor readers', *Journal of Research in Reading* 12 (1): 13–28.

Maling-Keepes, J. and B.D. Keepes (1979), *Language in Education. The Language Development Project, Phase 1*. Canberra: Curriculum Development Centre.

Marshall, S. (2006), 'Guiding senior secondary students towards writing academically-valued responses to poetry', in R. Whittaker, M. O'Donnell and A. McCabe (eds), *Language and Literacy. Functional Approaches*, London and New York: Continuum, pp. 251–65.

Martin, J. R. (1992), *English Text. System and Structure*. Philadelphia, PA and Amsterdam: Benjamins.

Martin, J.R (1997), 'Analysing genre: functional parameters', in F. Christie and J.R. Martin (eds), *Genre and Institutions. Social Processes in the Workplace and School*, London and New York: Continuum, pp. 3–39.

Martin, J.R. (2002), 'Writing history: construing time and value in discourses of the past', in M. Schleppegrell and C. Colombi (eds), *Developing Advanced Literacy in First and Second Languages*, Mahwah, NJ: Lawrence Erlbaum Associates, pp. 87–118.

Martin, J.R. (2003), 'Making history: grammar for explanation', in J.R. Martin and R. Wodak (eds), *Re/reading the Past. Critical and Functional Perspectives on Time and Value*, Amsterdam and Philadelphia, PA: Benjamins, pp. 19–57.

Martin, J.R. (2007), 'Construing knowledge: a functional linguistic perspective', in F. Christie, F. and J.R. Martin (eds), *Language, Knowledge and Pedagogy. Functional Linguistic and Sociological Perspectives*, London and New York: Continuum, pp. 34–64.

Martin, J.R. and G.A. Plum (1997), 'Construing experience: some story genres', in *Journal of Narrative and Life History*, 7 (1–4): 299–308.

Martin, J.R. and D. Rose (2003), *Working with Discourse. Meaning beyond the Clause.* London and New York: Continuum.

Martin, J.R. and D. Rose (2008), *Genre Relations: Mapping Culture.* London: Equinox.

Martin, J.R. and J. Rothery (1986), *Writing Project: Report* (Working Papers in Linguistics 4). Sydney: Department of Linguistics, University of Sydney.

Martin, J.R. and R. Veel (eds) (1998), *Reading Science: Critical and Functional Perspectives on Discourses of Science.* London: Routledge.

Martin, J.R. and P.R.R. White (2005), *The Language of Evaluation. Appraisal in English.* Basingstoke, UK and New York: Palgrave Macmillan.

Martin, J.R. and R. Wodak (eds) (2003), *Re/reading the Past. Critical and Functional Perspectives on Time and Value.* Amsterdam and Philadelphia, PA: Benjamins.

Maton, K. (2006), 'Invisible tribunals. Canons, knower structures and democratic access in the arts and humanities'. A paper presented at the *Fourth Basil Bernstein Symposium*, Rutgers University, Newark, 6–9 July.

Maton, K. (2007), 'Segmentalism: The problem of knowledge-building in education, work and life'. A paper presented at the *Conference on Explorations in Knowledge, Society and Education*, July, Cambridge University.

Matthiessen, C.M.I.M. (1995), 'THEME as an enabling resource in ideational "knowledge" ', in M. Ghadessy (ed.) *Thematic Development in English Texts.* London and New York: Pinter, pp. 20–54.

Matthiessen, C.M.I.M. (2004), 'The evolution of language: a systemic functional exploration of phylogenetic phases', in G. Williams and A. Lukin (eds), *The Development of Language. Functional Perspectives on Species and Individuals*, London and New York: Continuum, pp. 45–90.

Michaels, S. (1986), 'Narrative presentations: an oral preparation for literacy with first graders', in J. Cook-Gumperz (ed.), *The Social Construction of Literacy*, Cambridge, MA: University Press, pp. 94–116.

Michigan Department of Education (ND) *English Language Arts. Grade Level Content Expectation.* (http://www.michigan.gov/documents/mde/Final_ELA_Assessable_Content_Document_Gr._2-7_178042_7.pdf accessed 6 February 2008.

Michigan Department of Education (ND), *Michigan Merit Curriculum – English Language Arts: Michigan Merit Exam Persuasive Writing Score Task II: Taking a Stand* (http://www.michigan.gov/documents/mde/ELA-MME_Persuasive_Writing_Analytic8-15_173099_7.pdf accessed 6 February 2008).

Moats, L. C. (1995), *Spelling: Development, Disability, and Instruction.* Baltimore, MD: York Press.

Moore, R., M. Arnot, J. Beck and H. Daniels (eds) (2006), *Knowledge, Power and Educational Reform: Applying the Sociology of Basil Bernstein.* London: Routledge/Falmer.

Muller, J. (2000), *Reclaiming Knowledge. Social Theory, Curriculum and Education Policy (Knowledge Identity and School Life Series,* Series Eds P. Wexler and I. Goodson). London and New York: Routledge/Falmer.

Myhill, D. (2005), 'Good sentences or sentenced to death?: the development of the sentence in secondary age writers', paper presented at British Educational Research Association Annual Conference, Pontypridd, Wales, 15–17 September 2005.

Myhill, D. (2008a), 'Towards a linguistic model of sentence development', in *Language and Education.* <details to follow>

Myhill, D. (2008b), 'Becoming a designer: trajectories of linguistic development', in R. Beard, D. Myhill, M. Nystrand and J. Riley (eds), *The SAGE Handbook of Writing Development.* London: SAGE.

National Assessment Agency (2008), *Statutory National Curriculum Tasks and Tests* (http://www.qca.org.uk/qca_14666.aspx accessed 21 January 2008).

National Assessment Program for Australia: Literacy and Numeracy (2008), (http://www.curriculumsupport.education.nsw.gov.au/policies/nap/index.htm accessed 21 January 2008).

National Commission on Writing (2003), *The Neglected 'R'. The Need for a Writing Revolution* (http://www.writingcommission.org/prod_downloads/writingcom/writing-school-reform-natl-comm-writing.pdf accessed 22 January 2008).

National Commission on Writing (2006), *Writing and School Reform.* College Board (http://www.writingcommission.org/ accessed 5 February 2008).

National English Curriculum for England and Wales (2007), *Key Stage 3 Qualifications and Curriculum Authority* (http://curriculum.qca.org.uk/subjects/english/keystage3/index.aspx?return=http%3A//curriculum.qca.org.uk/subjects/index.aspx accessed 14 November 2007).

National Literacy Inquiry: Teaching Reading (December 2005), (http://www.dest.gov.au/nitl/report.htm accessed 3 December 2007).

Newcomer, P.L. and E.M. Barenbaum (1991), 'The written composing ability of children with learning disabilities: a review of the literature from 1980 to 1990', *Journal of Learning Disabilities,* 24: 578–93.

New South Wales Board of Studies (1991), *Science and Technology Syllabus K-6* (http://k6.boardofstudies.nsw.edu.au/go/science-and-technology accessed 20 September 2007).

New South Wales Board of Studies (1999), *HSC History Extension Stage 6 Syllabus* (http://www.boardofstudies.nsw.edu.au/syllabus_hsc/syllabus2000_listh.html accessed 14 October 2007).

New South Wales Board of Studies (2003a), *History Years 7–10 Syllabus* (http://www.boardofstudies.nsw.edu.au/syllabus_sc/#hebrew accessed 15 December 2007).

New South Wales Board of Studies (2003b), *English Syllabus for School Years 7–10* (http://www.boardofstudies.nsw.edu.au/syllabus_hsc/syllabus2000 accessed 30 August 2007).

New South Wales Board of Studies (2003c), *Science Syllabus Years 7–10* (http://www.boardofstudies.nsw.edu.au/syllabus_sc/pdf_doc/science_710_syl.pdf accessed 1 November 2007).

New South Wales Board of Studies (2006), *English Stage 6. Higher School Certificate 2005–2006. Prescriptions: Area of Study Electives and Texts.* Sydney: Board of Studies (www.boardofstudies.nsw.edu.au: accessed 20 October 2006).

New South Wales Board of Studies (2007), *Higher School Certificate English Syllabus* (http://www.boardofstudies.nsw.edu.au/syllabus_hsc/syllabus2000 accessed 30 August 2007).

New South Wales Department of School Education, Metropolitan East Region (1994), *Exploring Literacy in School Literacy. The 'Write it Right Project'.* Sydney: Department of School Education and the Disadvantaged Schools Program.

O'Donnell, R.C., W.J. Griffin and R.C. Norris (1967), *Syntax of Kindergarten and Elementary School Children: A Transformational Analysis.* Champaign, IL: NCTE.

O'Halloran, K. (2007), 'Mathematical and scientific forms of knowledge: a systemic functional multimodal grammatical approach', in F. Christie and J.R. Martin (eds), *Language, Knowledge and Pedagogy. Functional Linguistic and Sociological Perspectives,* London and New York: Continuum, pp. 205–38.

Oldenburg, J. (1986). 'The transitional stage of a second child: 18 months to 2 years', *Australian Review of Applied Linguistics,* 9 (12): 123–35.

Oppenheimer, S. (2003), *Out of Eden. The Peopling of the World.* London: Robinson.

Organization for Economic Co-operation and Development (OECD) (2000, 2003, 2007) *PISA Surveys* (http://www.oecd.org/pages/0,3417,en_32252351_32235918_1_1_1_1_1,00.html accessed 21 January 2008).

Painter, C. (1999), *Learning through Language in Early Childhood.* London and New York: Cassell.

Peel, R., A. Patterson and J. Gerlach (2000), *Questions of English. Ethics, Aesthetics, Rhetoric, and the Formation of the Subject in England, Australia and the United States.* London and New York: Routledge/Falmer.

Perera, K. (1984), *Children's Writing and Reading. Analysing Classroom Language.* Oxford and New York: Blackwell.

Perera, K. (1985), 'Grammatical differentiation between speech and writing in children aged 8 to 12', paper presented at the *Annual Meeting of the International Writing Convention,* Norwich, 1985. ED263 593.

Perera, K. (1990), 'Grammatical differentiation between speech and writing in children aged 8–12', in R. Carter (ed.) *Knowledge about language and the curriculum,* London: Hodder & Stoughton, pp. 216–33.

Plum, G.A. (1988), 'Text and contextual conditioning in spoken English: a genre-based approach'. Unpub. PhD thesis, Sydney: University of Sydney.

Polias, J. and B. Dare (2006), 'Towards a pedagogical grammar', in R. Whittaker, M. O'Donnell and A. McCabe (eds), *Language and Literacy. Functional Approaches,* London and New York: Continuum, pp. 123–42.

Qualifications and Curriculum Authority (QCA), UK, (1997–2008), *History at Key Stage 3* (Unit 1: Introductory unit: What's it all about?) (http://www.standards.dfes.gov.uk/schemes2/secondary_history accessed 20 October 2007).

Quirk, R, S. Greenbaum, G. Leech and J. Svartvik (1972), *A Grammar of Contemporary English.* London: Longman.

Rentel, V. and M. King (1983), 'A longitudinal study of coherence in children's written narratives', *Journal of Teacher Education,* 25 (4): 323–9.

Ridley, M. (2003), *Nature via Nurture. Genes, Experience and What Makes us Human*. London and New York: Fourth Estate.

Romaine, S. (1984), *The Language of Children and Adolescents: The Acquisition of Communicative Competence*, Oxford: Basil Blackwell.

Rose, D. (2008), *Reading to Learn: Accelerating Learning and Closing the Gap*. Professional Development Course. Sydney: Rose Publication.

Rothery, J. (1991), ' "Story" writing in primary school: assessing narrative type genres'. Unpub. PhD thesis, Sydney: University of Sydney.

Rothery, J. and M. Stenglin (2000), 'Interpreting literature: the role of "APPRAISAL" ', in L. Unsworth (ed.), *Researching Language in Schools and Communities: Functional Linguistic Perspectives*, London: Cassell, pp. 222–44.

Sandiford, C. (1997), 'Teaching explanations to primary school children: the how and the why'. Unpub. MEd thesis, Melbourne: University of Melbourne.

Schleppegrell, M.J. (2004), *The Language of Schooling. A Functional Linguistic Perspective*. Mahwah, NJ: Erlbaum.

Schleppegrell, M.J., M. Achugar and T. Oteýza (2004), 'The grammar of history: enhancing content-based instruction through a functional focus on language', *TESOL Quarterly*. 38 (1): 67–93.

Schmandt-Besserat, D. (1996), *How Writing Came About*. Austin, TX: University of Texas Press.

Science Teachers' Association of New South Wales (2007), *Young Scientist of the Year Award* (http://www.stansw.asn.au/ys/ysmain.htm accessed 12 December 2007).

Simon-Vandenbergen, A.M., Taverniers, M and Ravelli, L. J. (eds.) (2003), *Metaphor: Systemic and Functional Perspectives*. Amsterdam: Benjamins.

Simpson, A. (2003), 'Book raps as online multimodal communication. Towards a model of interactive pedagogy', *International Journal of Learning*, 10: 2705–14.

Snow, C. and Biancarosa, G. (2003), *Adolescent Literacy and the Achievement Gap: What Do We Know and Where Do We Go from Here?* New York: Carnegie Corporation.

Society for Neuroscience (2005), *Brain Facts. A Primer on the Brain and Nervous System*. Washington: Society for Neuroscience.

Street, B. (1984), *Literacy in Theory and Practice*. Cambridge: Cambridge University Press.

Strickland, D.S. and D.E. Alvermann (eds), (2004), *Bridging the Literacy Achievement Gap, Grades 4–12*. New York and London: Teachers College Press.

Sulzby, E. (1996), 'Roles of oral and written language as children approach conventional literacy', in C. Pontecorvo, M. Orsolini, B. Burge and L. Resnick (eds), *Children's Early Text Construction*, Mahwah, NJ: Lawrence Erlbaum Associates.

Sutherland, G. (ed.) (1973), *Arnold on Education*. London and Melbourne: Penguin Education.

Tomasello, M. (1999), *The Cultural Origins of Human Cognition*. Cambridge, MA and London, UK: Harvard University Press.

Torr, J. and A. Simpson (2003), 'The emergence of grammatical metaphor: literacy-oriented expressions in the everyday speech of young children', in A.M. Simon-Vandenbergen et al. (eds), *Grammatical Metaphor. (Amsterdam Studies in the Theory and History of Linguistic Science. Series IV: Current Issues in Linguistic Theory*. General Ed. E.F. Konrad Koerner). Amsterdam and Philadelphia, PA: Benjamins, pp. 169–84.

Tronick, E. (2007), *The Neurobehavioral and Social-Emotional Development of Infants and Children*. New York and London: W.W. Norton and Company.

Unsworth, L. (2000), 'Investigating subject-specific literacies in school learning', in L. Unsworth (ed.), *Researching Language in Schools and Communities. Functional Linguistic Perspectives*. London and Washington, DC: Cassell, pp. 245–74.

Unsworth, L. (2001), *Teaching Multiliteracies across the Curriculum. Changing Contexts of Text and Image in Classroom Practice*. Buckingham and Philadelphia, PA: Open University Press.

Veel, R. (1997), 'Learning how to mean – scientifically speaking: apprenticeship into scientific discourse in the secondary school', in F. Christie and J.R. Martin (eds) *Genre and Institutions. Social Processes in the Workplace and School*, London and New York: Continuum, pp. 161–95.

Veel, R. and C. Coffin (1996), 'Learning to think like an historian: the language of secondary school History', in R. Hasan and G. Williams (eds), *Literacy in Society*, London: Longmans, pp. 191–231.

Walsh, P. (2006), 'The impact of genre theory and pedagogy and systemic functional linguistics on National Literacy Strategies in the UK', in R. Whittaker, M. O'Donnell and A. McCabe (eds), *Language and Literacy. Functional Approaches*, London and New York: Continuum, pp. 159–76.

Watson, J.D. and F.H.C Crick (1953), 'A structure for deoxyribose nucleic acid', *Nature*, 3 (171): 737–8.

Wells, G. (1986), *The Meaning Makers: Children Learning Language and Using Language to Learn*. Portsmouth, NH: Heinemann.

Wignell, P. (2007a), *On the Discourse of Social Science*. Darwin: Charles Darwin University.

Wignell, P. (2007b), 'Vertical and horizontal discourse and the social sciences', in F. Christie and J.R Martin (eds) (2007), *Language, Knowledge and Pedagogy. Functional Linguistic and Sociological Perspectives*. London and New York: Continuum, pp. 184–204.

Wilkinson, A., G. Barnsley, P. Hanna and M. Swan (1980), *Assessing Language Development*. London: OUP.

Williams, G. (1998), 'Children entering literate worlds: perspectives from the study of textual practices', in F. Christie and R. Misson (eds) *Literacy and Schooling*, London and New York: Routledge, pp. 18–46.

Wray, D. and J. Medwell (2006), *Progression in Writing and the Northern Ireland Levels for Writing: A Research Review Undertaken for CCEA*. Warwick: University of Warwick.

Zimmerman, B.J. and R. Risemberg (1997), 'Becoming a self-regulated writer: A social cognitive perspective', *Contemporary Educational Psychology*, 22 (1): 73–101.

Index

Printed in Great Britain
by Amazon